The Life of the Author: William Shakespeare

The Life of the Author: William Shakespeare

Anna Beer

WILEY Blackwell

Registered Office(s)
John Wiley & Sons, Inc., 111 River Street, Hoboken, NJ 07030, USA
John Wiley & Sons Ltd, The Atrium, Southern Gate, Chichester, West Sussex, PO19 8SQ, UK

Editorial Office
The Atrium, Southern Gate, Chichester, West Sussex, PO19 8SQ, UK

For details of our global editorial offices, customer services, and more information about Wiley products visit us at www.wiley.com.

Wiley also publishes its books in a variety of electronic formats and by print-on-demand. Some content that appears in standard print versions of this book may not be available in other formats.

Library of Congress Cataloging-in-Publication Data
Names: Beer, Anna R., 1964- author.
Title: Shakespeare / Anna Beer.
Description: Hoboken, NJ: John Wiley & Sons, 2021. | Series: The life of the author | Includes bibliographical references and index.
Identifiers: LCCN 2020043060 (print) | LCCN 2020043061 (ebook) | ISBN 9781119605218 (paperback) | ISBN 9781119605270 (pdf) | ISBN 9781119605317 (epub)
Subjects: LCSH: Shakespeare, William, 1564-1616. | Dramatists, English—Early modern, 1500-1700—Biography.
Classification: LCC PR2894.B38 2021 (print) | LCC PR2894 (ebook) | DDC 822.3/3 [B]—dc23
LC record available at https://lccn.loc.gov/2020043060
LC ebook record available at https://lccn.loc.gov/2020043061

Cover image: © Heritage Images/Contributor/Hulton Archive/Getty Images
Cover design by Wiley

Set in 9.5/12.5pt STIX Two Text by Integra Software Services, Pondicherry, India
Printed and bound by CPI Group (UK) Ltd, Croydon, CR0 4YY

C099290_060421

Contents

Acknowledgments

Much virtue in if

As You Like It (5.4.101)

I began work on this book long before any of us knew of Covid-19. As I write these words, the theaters in my own country remain closed, in an eerie echo of Shakespeare's working life. The vast majority of people who work in the arts have had their creative lives disrupted at best, completely destroyed at worst. And those of us who took for granted a ready stream of live performances are thirsty for culture in ways we could not have imagined a year ago. Knowing that Shakespeare wrote his remarkable plays during similar times has, however, been strangely comforting, above and beyond the enduring comfort offered by his words. I, like millions of others, am now even more grateful for his legacy.

More prosaically, thank you to Richard Bradford who asked me to write a life of Shakespeare, and who has been wise and supportive throughout. It's been an interesting ride, but one I would not have wanted to miss. Thank you also to the anonymous readers whose comments have made this, I hope, a better book.

I am grateful to Thomas Evans, who helped get the first draft into some sort of order, and to Louise Spencely who has been a patient, assiduous, and perceptive copyeditor. Any and all remaining errors are my own.

My friends and family have, as ever, kept me (relatively) sane. It is, however, Becca, Elise, and Hugh who have done the heavy lifting, and with grace. Most importantly, they learned quickly not to ask whether the world really needed another biography of Shakespeare. Thank you.

Last but most definitely not least, I would like to dedicate this book to every one of my students over the years. I have learned so much from all of you. I am particularly lucky to have worked with adult students at the Department for Continuing Education in Oxford. Your questions about, and insights into, Shakespeare's work inform every page that follows.

The Life of the Author: William Shakespeare, First Edition. Anna Beer.
© 2021 John Wiley & Sons, Ltd. Published 2021 by John Wiley & Sons, Ltd.

It is invidious to single out one former student, but I would like to dedicate this book to my dear friend Karen Elliott, a woman who knows that there may be days when one has to milk one's ewes (*The Winter's Tale* 4.4.455), but that there is still plenty of time to "queen it" (4.4.454).

All references to Shakespeare's plays are taken from the Arden Third Series, unless stated otherwise.

Prologue

The impossibility of writing Shakespeare's biography has not prevented a great many people (including yours truly) from trying.

(Richard Dutton 2010, p. 122)

Before conjuring up an April 1564 christening in Holy Trinity Parish Church, Stratford-upon-Avon, the traditional starting point for a biography, a few words about my own ambivalence about writing Shakespeare's life. By all means, move straight to the baptismal register in Chapter One, or if it is the plays, and only the plays, that interest you, then head to Chapter Two when William Shakespeare begins his career as a dramatist.[1] But, if the biographical project itself interests you – and it fascinates me almost but not quite as much as the plays themselves – then stay with this Prologue in which, inspired and provoked by Dutton's wry comment, I explore what happens when we, when I, attempt the impossible.

Putting aside for a moment the validity of any biographical project, why might it be specifically impossible to write a biography of *Shakespeare*? One common answer is the perceived paucity of the kinds of archival documents that are the traditional raw materials for the writing of a literary life. Not a single letter written by Shakespeare or written to him survives, except one which was not sent. We have no information, beyond their names, about his relationship with his parents, wife, children, or grandchildren. Shakespeare almost never writes *about* his creations as a playwright and poet, and only a handful of people in his own time bothered to comment on his work.

Therefore, although there are plenty of things we want to know about Shakespeare (his political views, his religious beliefs, whom he loved, what he did with his time when he wasn't writing or acting, and so on) these things cannot be known. This list is based on that of James Shapiro (2015, p. 12) who argues that, once the people who knew Shakespeare died, it became impossible to write "that sort of biography."

The Life of the Author: William Shakespeare, First Edition. Anna Beer.
© 2021 John Wiley & Sons, Ltd. Published 2021 by John Wiley & Sons, Ltd.

I will return to a couple of assumptions made here (about "that sort of biography" and concerning the need for evidence from people who "knew" Shakespeare), but first I need to pick up the gauntlet thrown down by Shapiro's next sentence: "Modern biographers who nonetheless speculate on such matters, or in the absence of archival evidence read the plays and poems as transparently autobiographical, inevitably end up revealing more about themselves than they do about Shakespeare." This is harsh and not very fair, the more so since it comes in the Prologue to his own literary biographical account of *1606: William Shakespeare and the Year of Lear*. Most literary biographers shy away from reading the plays and poems as "transparently autobiographical." All those who engage with Shakespeare's life and works are, on one level, speculating. It is just that some do it more openly than others. There are plenty of critics who make their assumptions discreetly, hiding behind the screen of, say, a discussion of Shakespeare's literary influences. Did Shakespeare know the work of his fellow writer, Thomas Nashe? Shakespeare would "probably have read" Nashe's *Unfortunate Traveller*; "some believe" that Moth, a character in *Love's Labour's Lost* written "around" 1594, is based on Nashe; Nashe might even have been involved with *Tamburlaine* in 1587 (Hadfield 2004, p. 2). Or, what prompted Shakespeare to write the moment in *A Midsummer Night's Dream* when Oberon asks Puck if he remembers when he, Oberon, sat "upon a promontory / And heard a mermaid on a dolphin's back"? Could this be an echo of a production at Kenilworth in 1575? Kenilworth is in Warwickshire: we are in the right county, and William is 11 years old, so he could have been there. The evidence is unstable (one eyewitness noted the dolphin, another remembers a mermaid, but neither record seeing a mermaid on a dolphin's back), but is nevertheless used to imagine scenarios rooted in Shakespeare's lived experience. "Did Shakespeare's memory play tricks on him over the years, or did he embroider the event for his own artistic purposes? Or, more prosaically, did Shakespeare simply read about these famous events in one or both printed accounts, and adapt them to his needs?" (Dutton 2018, pp. 25–27).

This kind of thing is not a million miles away from the assumptions made by previous generations that the playwright could not have created characters of such depth unless he had experienced at least something similar to those characters. Thomas Carlyle, for one, saw a bit of Macbeth, Hamlet, and Coriolanus in William Shakespeare, the man. This might be too simplistic for us now, but we still perceive that Shakespeare is concerned with, or preoccupied by, some aspect of life, and slide into the assumption that the concern is rooted in lived experience. His "particular sensitivity to ravaged landscapes of continental battlefields" for example, leads a critic to wonder whether Shakespeare went to be a soldier in France (Brennan 2004, p. 58).

Others, including the hugely popular Stephen Greenblatt (2004, p. 151), openly ask us to use our imaginations because what matters is "not the degree of evidence but rather the imaginative life that the incident has." This comes very close to saying what matters is not the true story, but a good story, a stance complicated by the moments when Greenblatt does assert (his own) truths about Shakespeare. But it is at least honest, recognizing that each of our Shakespeares will be different, dependent on our imaginations.

The challenge remains, to read a consistent "Shakespeare" from his deeply inconsistent drama. Reading from the plays to the life, some argue that Shakespeare was aware of his own aging from, say, 1599, and is exploring this new awareness in *As You Like It*. But which experience of aging is William's? Consider Jaques and Touchstone, both additions to Shakespeare's source material. Jaques "constructs an existential stage-play world in which 'All the world's a stage, / And all the men and women merely players'" with life viewed as "a series of declining stages to an old age 'sans teeth, sans eyes, sans taste, sans everything'" (2.7.139–166) (Smith 2012, p. 17). But "Touchstone has a parallel speech on the seven degrees of quarrelling: more expansive, more verbally witty, and ultimately more optimistic" (ibid.). Is Shakespeare Jaques or Touchstone, both or neither?

These kinds of micro-biographical turns abound, but often remain unexplored asides to more conventional literary critical analyses. The enduring consensus in the academy, to return to Shapiro's words, is that a particular "sort of biography" should be avoided, not least because it is "impossible" to write. And perhaps unnecessary to write. The editor of one edition of *Hamlet* (Edwards 2003) refuses to engage with any discussion of Shakespeare the human being. The man who wrote the play is irrelevant. Instead, the focus is on deciphering the genealogy of the surviving texts and deciding which is "best" for performance.

In the face of this kind of thing, cautious biographers turn – tentatively – to the plays and – much less tentatively – to what we do know (or think we know) about the world *around* Shakespeare. James Shapiro has demonstrated, triumphantly, the powerful results of this approach in his two best-selling studies of the years 1599 and 1606. He argues that Shakespeare's age, friendships, family relationships, location, and finances at any one time must have impacted in some way upon his writing: a new patron, a new king, a new playhouse, a new rival could – and did – change his drama and poetry. By focusing on both Shakespeare's times in a general sense, and on a specific time in his life, we can get "a slice of a writer's life." Shakespeare's emotional life in 1606, the "year of Lear," may be lost to us but "by looking at what he wrote in dialogue with these times we can begin to recover what he was thinking about and wrestling with" (2015, pp. 15–16).

Shapiro clusters plays together, challenging simple generic clusterings, teases out their themes and preoccupations, and then maps those onto (the little we know about) Shakespeare's lived experience or (the considerable amount we know about) the world in which he worked. Grouping plays chronologically rather than generically allows us to see the connections between *Henry V* and

> plays like *Julius Caesar* or *As You Like It*, written at much the same time, and with which it shares a different set of preoccupations. Shakespeare himself seems to have taken for granted that 'the purpose of playing' was to show, as Hamlet put it, "the very age and body of the time his form and pressure" (3.2.20–24). To see how Shakespeare's plays managed to do so depends upon knowing when each one was written.
>
> *(Shapiro 2005b, p. 10)*

And that's both the virtue of and the faultline in Shapiro's approach. We simply do not know "when each one was written." Was 1606 even "the year of Lear"? In the vast majority of cases, it remains unclear when, precisely, Shakespeare wrote individual plays or when a play was first performed. And the challenges don't end there. It may be hard to date the plays with any precision, but what precisely are we dating? What do we mean by, say, *Hamlet?*[2] Some editors will prioritize the date of a first performance of a play. Others will seek to work out when Shakespeare actually put pen to paper. In fact, there are at least three separate significant dates for any Shakespeare play. The moment when he completed the manuscript (although the idea of completion is misleading, since playbooks were constantly adapted); the play's first performance (again, performance can and did take many forms); and the first printing. With *Hamlet*, as Thompson and Taylor (2006, p. 44) point out, we are dealing with not one printed text but three, each of which might have had different performance histories then, and certainly have different performance histories now. There's more: "behind the printed text there may be more than one 'completed' manuscript." And still more: "it is generally held that there was an earlier Hamlet play, the so-called Ur-Hamlet, either by Shakespeare or by someone else, with its own necessarily different set of dates, and this hypothetical lost play continues to complicate the issue of the date of Shakespeare's play and indeed the issue of its sources." And that's all before we even start factoring in collaboration with other playwrights.

One way out of the textual dating mire is to ask more general questions. Why did this particular moment in our history produce a Shakespeare? How did the commercial theater produce plays of such extraordinary linguistic and emotional complexity? These are the questions asked, and answered brilliantly, by Bart van Es (2013). Shakespeare is special, in part, because of the unparalleled working conditions that he enjoyed, because he worked so well "in company," and because that "company" was exceptional. Shakespeare is born into the right time, and the right place, for his particular talents to flourish. Other answers to similar questions appeal to the "richness of contemporary language" in Shakespeare's time, or "the rhetorical treatises of the grammar school curriculum," both of which both contributed to Shakespeare's ability to capture "spoken cadences," his "semantic attentiveness" (Smith 2012, p. 239).

Right time, right place takes us, however, only so far. Why did this moment produce only one William Shakespeare? Maybe we just need to go straight for the notion of "genius." Jonathan Bate thinks so, thus his *The Genius of Shakespeare* (1997). For Stephen Greenblatt (writing in the same period) it is Shakespeare's genius itself that has created a problem for biographers: "[S]o absolute is Shakespeare's achievement that he has himself come to seem like great creating nature: the common bond of humankind, the principle of hope, the symbol of the imagination's power to transcend time-bound beliefs and assumptions, peculiar historical circumstances, and specific artistic conventions" (Greenblatt 2000, p. 1). His very ability means that he floats somewhere above material history, somehow ineffable. A less direct route to the same destination is taken by Dutton. "There is, moreover, nothing that we know, suspect or have made up about Shakespeare's early years that really helps us to explain the achievement of the plays and the poems" (Dutton 2016, p. 5). Once again, the biographical turn fails. It will not – perhaps cannot – explain "genius" and, more specifically, it cannot explain *this* genius: The Bard.

For some, this failure is a blessing in disguise. As Charles Dickens put it, the "life of Shakespeare is a fine mystery and I tremble every day lest something should turn up" (quoted in Garber 2004, p. 21). What if something turned up and compromised our idea of genius, made the man ordinary, of his time, and not an empty vessel into which we can pour our own vision of the great artist?

There are other reasons not to delve too deeply. What happens if the man we find is not merely ordinary, but unpleasant, even hateful? For many years, a convenient biographical syllogism (here unpacked by Emma Smith with exemplary brevity) kept this kind of thing at bay. "1. Prospero is a good guy. 2. Shakespeare is a good guy. 3. Therefore Prospero is Shakespeare." But the same syllogism is far more problematic if Prospero is viewed as "irascible, tyrannical, subjecting Caliban to slavery," or "a distinctly unlikeable, manipulative control freak." As Smith puts it: "if this Prospero is Shakespeare, we wouldn't much like Shakespeare" (2019, pp. 312–317). When it comes to his portrayal of women, the novelist Gayl Jones (2000, p. 103) has her character

Joan say what a lot of us are thinking: Shakespeare "knows what a man wants, and what a man thinks a woman wants, even the best of women. He's good at portraying bitches, but even they're a man's idea of a bitch. You know, even Shakespeare's sweet bitches are still a man's idea of a sweet bitch."

The reluctance, even now, to countenance an unlikeable Shakespeare informs or suppresses the debate over (Christian, white, male) Shakespeare's representation of Jewish people, of people of color, of women. Far better to duck a discussion of the writer's opinions entirely rather than to consider his potential anti-Semitism, racism, or misogyny. Even the superbly clear-sighted Marjorie Garber squirms away. Acknowledging that Shylock would have been portrayed as a "comic butt" (2004, p. 4), that the actors would use the "standard signs of Jewishness on the Elizabethan stage" for laughs, she insists this tells us nothing about the man who created Shylock. For Garber, Shakespeare as a writer (and as a man?) is committed to balance and dialogue. Othello may have a "particularity as a black man and a Moor," but this is balanced against "a certain desire to see him as a figure of universal humanity" (Garber 2004, p. 6). That "certain desire" is presumably that of the playwright, a man who believes in balance, in a universal humanity – even for a black man and a Moor.

Garber (2004, p. 7) insists that because the plays work "contrapuntally" it is impossible to say "Shakespeare said …" or "Shakespeare believed …" These are, however, two different impossibilities. Yes, we cannot say "Shakespeare said" because we have no documents, no utterances from the man, other than his literary texts. What of "Shakespeare believed"? Surely Garber's Shakespeare, so wedded to "contrapuntal" drama, so careful to embed dialogue and balance into his plays, might just have believed in these qualities or virtues. Many of those who admire his work seem to accept this almost as a foundational fact. For many – not Garber – it is a short step to arguing that because William Shakespeare gave interiority to characters who were not fully human according to the *mores* of his own time – people of color; the Jew; servants; almost, but not quite, women – he must have understood and recognized those who were different to himself. It is a short step – and this time Garber makes it (2004, p. 6) – to seeing Shakespeare as every man, and every woman in his plays. "Shakespeare is Prospero, Caliban, Ariel and the wondering Miranda. He is Othello, Desdemona and Iago. Shylock, Portia and Antonio." No one voice is "definitively right," all are in dialogue with each other. All are Shakespeare.

This opens the door to more radical understandings of the plays. "Generations of readers and playgoers, many of them 'cultural others,' have experienced the powerful and pleasurable perception that in Shakespeare they are indeed represented. Witness Maya Angelou's famous declaration: 'I know that William Shakespeare was a black woman'" (Callaghan 2000, p. 6 drawing on Erickson

1992). It's a powerful, and liberating, way of sidestepping conventional biographical understandings of authorship.

But it also sidesteps the tough questions. Was Shakespeare racist? Is *Othello* the play racist? Are those two questions related? Or in the words of Marjorie Garber, again: "What is Shakespeare's own view of such political questions? The answer – which is not an answer – lies in his plays," in all their "brilliance and capaciousness" (Garber 2004, pp. 6–7). If you read to the end of this book, you will find that I too come back to the plays and poems. They are what we have, and I believe they do offer us answers (although not necessarily to traditional biographical questions). Even more importantly, they offer questions – which is one of the reasons they are so powerful.

What Garber cannot or will not say is whether the "brilliance" (another word for genius, perhaps?) of the plays, is also that of William Shakespeare, the human being. Nor can she or will she suggest where this "capaciousness" came from or how it found its way into his drama. Better to avoid the biographical turn entirely than end up with answers we do not want.

There are other, very good reasons, to be wary of reading the man from the plays. One is the literary practices of Shakespeare's own era. During his lifetime, writers were very unlikely to be driven by a desire for the confessional disclosure of the self, since the "primary impulse behind early modern dramaturgy – indeed, behind early modern writing more generally – is rhetorical rather than autobiographical" (Smith 2019, p. 312). This is absolutely true, but still leaves space for an author like Ben Jonson to write numerous prologues, epilogues, and essays about his own writing, and put his family and feelings into his poetry. It's possible to pick apart the rhetorical gestures at work in Jonson's sonnet on the death of his young son (even easier when considering his sonnet on the death of his daughter), but in the case of the former, the father's grief is palpable and intensely moving.

Then again, Ben grieves for his son in poetry, and therefore the absence of any direct reference to the death of William's son, Hamnet, in his plays may only be a reflection of a world in which "no playwright, including Shakespeare could make his own personal grief the centre of a play" (Potter 2012, p. 288). More generally, "no literature of this period has the elevation of the artist's own inner feelings as its legible core, and drama even less so, where the animation of different voices and different people is more important than the single narrative consciousness of, say, the traditional novel or lyric poem" (Smith 2019, p. 313). Lyric poetry might, just, be starting to blur the boundaries, and Shakespeare's sonnets certainly play with those boundaries, but the playwright keeps well away.

It might be alien to the culture for an individual's personal grief to be expressed, but drama in Elizabethan and Jacobean England could be, and was, polemical. Not Shakespeare though, according to Potter (2019, p. 402), who, reflecting on her own biographical practice, sees a writer who likes "to work within parameters." Shakespeare "throughout his career, like me in my biography, was trying to fill specific requirements, as opposed to conveying a secret message about his views on sex, politics, or religion." This view is, to a degree, questioned by the work of Van Es (2013, p. 197) who argues that "to echo a theatrical fashion is not necessarily to endorse it: there is room for resistance alongside pragmatic imitation when Shakespeare responds to commercial trends." Simply because Shakespeare was writing to order does not mean that he did not, at times, question the order of things.

Of course, a strongly anti-Catholic play might not reflect the strongly anti-Catholic views of its creator, merely a writer keen to pander to his audience's prejudice, but Shakespeare – according to many – never writes a drama from which the audience can take a single, straightforward political message. Instead, not only does he refuse to be overtly autobiographical (standard practice for his time), but he pursues a "model of authorial near-anonymity," a model that was evidently "congenial to his purposes" (Bevington 2010, p. 4). Those purposes may have included survival in an era when a political or religious word out of place could have the most drastic consequences.

Bearing this in mind, the strangely lacking archive deserves another look. Could the lack of documentation be strategic – a sign of Shakespeare's caution in a dangerous era? Or is it precisely what we might expect from an individual of his class and profession? Either way, the archive only appears to be thin because we are so interested in Shakespeare: "what we know falls a long way short of what we would like to know" (Dutton 1989, p. 1).

Yet the problem with the archival evidence may not be its scarcity. Indeed, some would argue there is no dearth in the first place. It is simply that biographers have given "a special weight to what we might call documented fact: those details of Shakespeare's life that can be supported by footnoted reference to archival materials" (Stewart 2016, p. 57). Schoenbaum's *William Shakespeare: A Documentary Life* from 1975 is the perfect example, keeping strictly to the "facts." But this "documentary life" "obscures an earlier biographical tradition, which fails to meet Schoenbaum's insistence on documentation – one that may be exploited by biographers for anecdotal colour, but which is routinely dismissed as apocryphal." This earlier tradition, stretching through the seventeenth century and beyond, is in fact "remarkably coherent, and serves to conjure a notably different Shakespeare from the one attested to by 'documents'" (Stewart 2016, pp. 57–58).

This notably different Shakespeare is conjured from a tradition of life-writing rooted in homosocial cultures of the seventeenth century. That tradition excludes the domestic. It should be no surprise therefore that early modern sources for Shakespearean biography ignore the presence of his wife and children. Stratford appears, but "until Rowe cites the still unnamed daughter of Hathaway, this is Shakespeare without a wife: a woman who is mentioned only once in the seventeenth century, and then only to be banned from the posterity of his grave." Hamnet is not mentioned. Instead, there are hints of an illegitimate son, Davenant, "a poet-playwright son conceived adulterously in a tavern on the road from London to Stratford" (Stewart 2016, pp. 72–73).

Stewart offers a powerful corrective to our placing of familial relationships at the heart of biography and, even more importantly, reveals the mechanics of this particular biographical turn. The recorded events in early lives "routinely take place at various 'merry' meetings of men – in chambers at Eton, at a baptism, at a tavern." But there is a twist. These venues would, in real life, be open to women but when turned into biographical anecdote, almost all female presence is written out of the story. More than that, Shakespeare's network, his dynasty even, is not his family, but the theater.

> He is consistently presented in rivalries with fellow players (Burbage) and playwrights (Jonson); anecdotes attesting to his worth come down through theatre luminaries (Jonson, Davenant, Shadwell); in the first full life, even the archival research is carried out by a Hamlet, Thomas Betterton, and written up by another playwright, Nicholas Rowe. The seventeenth-century Shakespeare is thus insistently embodied as a man of the theatre – but a theatre that takes place in the largely homosocial conviviality of the tavern; is judged in the homosocial conviviality of its critics in Eton; and talked about in the homosocial conviviality of its target audience in Middle Temple chambers.
>
> *(Stewart 2016, p. 72)*

In some ways, contemporary approaches to life-writing (including my own) return Shakespeare to this biographical tradition. I admire hugely, and have drawn unashamedly upon, the work of scholars such as Van Es, Potter, and Dutton, all of whom offer profound insights into Shakespeare the working playwright, the man of the theater.

Samuel Schoenbaum (1991, p. 5), who should know, argues that the records "nevertheless possess a pattern and significance of their own." The problem is that the pattern and significance is not always to our taste:

> Perhaps the reason we so desperately want the plays to speak to us, is that the story the legal documents tell us is not always the story we want to hear. Many biographers have been troubled by Shakespeare's lack of civic or institutional philanthropy (given his affluence) in his

will or by the evidence of Shakespeare hoarding grain in 1599, at a time when a series of bad harvests meant that many of Stratford's poor were starving, especially as he writes about exactly this scenario at the beginning of *Coriolanus*. Or by the fact that in a Stratford protest against proposed land enclosures by William Combe in 1614–15, Shakespeare hired a lawyer to protect his own land and appears to have supported Combe.

(Maguire and Smith 2012, p. 109)

Whatever the reasons for the lack of traditional "documentary" biographical materials, it has had an effect on our understanding of Shakespeare's life. Since nature abhors a vacuum, "later ages have filled the picture with guesswork, legend and sentiment," writes Dutton (2016, p. 2), who is tolerant of guesswork, but critical of legend and sentiment. And harnessed "Shakespeare" to their cause.

Emma Smith (2012, p. 223) offers a scathing critique of this kind of thing: claims that "he retained the old religion of Roman Catholicism, or that he was gay, or that he was politically conservative, or whatever, tend to reveal more about the priorities of the speaker than the subject." Smith's list is a little slippery. "Gay" is a modern term: if we call Shakespeare gay we are very obviously co-opting modern terminology to understand a man 400 years dead. But keeping the "old religion" and "politically conservative" are less straightforward. Both concepts meant something very different then than they do now. Shapiro (2005b, pp. 9–10) is excellent on this:

Even the meaning of such concepts as individuality was different. Writers, including Shakespeare, were only beginning to speak of "individual" in the modern sense of "distinctive" or "special", the exact opposite of what it had long meant, "inseparable". This was also an age of faith, or at the least one in which church attendance was mandatory; religion, too played a greater role in shaping how life, death and the afterlife were imagined. All this suggests that, as much as we might want Shakespeare to have been like us, he wasn't. We call this period early modern or pre-modern for good reason.

Let's go back to April 1564, the documentary record, and conventional life-writing. "*Gulielmus filius Johannes Shakspere*" is baptised in Holy Trinity Parish Church, Stratford-upon-Avon, Warwickshire. He is named William by his parents John and Mary perhaps in honor of their friends and business associates, William Smith the haberdasher and William Tyler the butcher. Baby William, one of eight children to be born to the Shakespeares, but one of only five who would survive into adulthood, will become the most famous British playwright, perhaps the most famous writer in English, ever known.

That Latin quotation means William, son of John Shakespeare. The archive begins with a statement of patriarchal lineage because this is what "family" means in Tudor England. The patriarchal archive was then elaborated with anecdote. In 1657, the first story about Shakespeare's family would be recorded: he "was a glover's son – Sir John Mennes saw once his old Father in his shop – a merry cheeked old man – that said – Will was a good Honest Fellow – but he darest have cracked a jest with him at any Time" (Plume MS 25, fo. 161^r; transcription in Tromly 2010, p. 278). No matter that Mennes was only two years old when the elder Shakespeare died in 1601, this story informed and still informs the kinds of the Lives we write. Stewart (2016, p. 66) points to Stephen Greenblatt's (2004) understanding of "merry-cheeked" as an allusion to John Shakespeare's heavy drinking, which leads him to surmise an alcoholic legacy that Will sought to evade. Duncan-Jones (2001) offers a more niche interpretation: John is a prototype for the husband of Juliet's Nurse.

There is not an *absence* of archival evidence as such (and what we do know grows each year). Instead, the evidence which survives skews the telling of Shakespeare's life in particular directions. Those two examples above, for example, are rooted in patriarchal understandings of what is significant to a man's life. But there are new questions that can be asked of what has been known for centuries, and familiar anecdotes can be viewed in different ways. Shakespeare's life, and his Lives, start looking a little different when those questions are asked.

Smith offers a powerful reminder of what's at stake. "Shakespeare's stock is so high that to recruit him to your ideological team is a real coup" (Smith 2012, p. 223). Suddenly having the *man* on our team, not just his writing, becomes important. We feel the need to recruit the author himself, not just his works. This may be why biographies should still be attempted. Yes, any and all biographies are fictions, but the lives they tell were not. Our picture of Shakespeare the man is, in the end, created by the questions we ask of the archive we have, by the value we place on different kinds of documentation: those questions and values have, for centuries, been predominantly driven and informed by elite, white men. We need different eyes looking at Shakespeare. His plays matter to us, but what we write about the man matters too.

Chapter One

William was not the first-born of John and Mary Shakespeare, for two baby daughters had died back in 1558 and 1563, but he was the first to survive infancy. Our post-Romantic, post-Freudian idea that the child maketh the man is anachronistic to a Tudor boyhood, but there were aspects of William's early years which necessarily shaped the adult and writer he would become.[1] Class was one of them. What the Elizabethans called "degree" mattered in Shakespeare's time. Baby William and his four surviving siblings grew up in a substantial house in a busy market town, Stratford-upon-Avon. His father John, making good money, was able to buy the house next door as well, and at some point linked the two to make "a single, imposing, close-timbered building" (Schoenbaum 1991, p. 7) Mary, William's mother, who brought land to the marriage, came from a nearby village, her family being prosperous, well-established farmers, the Ardens.

The "intimacy of daily life" (Edmondson and Wells 2015a, p. 329) in the Shakespeare household in Henley Street can be hard to imagine: the manicured buildings in Stratford-upon-Avon today now give very little sense of the dirt and chaos of a sixteenth-century house and thoroughfare. It's a valuable corrective to read that "the first reference to the father of the National Poet occurs in April 1552, when he was fined a shilling for making a dungheap (*sterquinarium*) before his house" (Schoenbaum 1991, p. 7). The dung-heap maker, John, made his money in various ways: glove making, tanning, dealing in wool and corn, and some moneylending. The last two were the most lucrative for him, despite or because of his lack of a dealer's licence and his tendency to charge in excess of the legal rate of interest (Fallow 2015). John was, suggests Potter (2012, pp. 42–43), adept at illegal wool-brogging, "buying wool outside the town, smuggling it in so as to avoid paying duty on it, and undercutting the official market, known as the Staple of Wool, by selling it more cheaply." The wealth he accrued, never mind how, came with responsibilities.

The Life of the Author: William Shakespeare, First Edition. Anna Beer.
© 2021 John Wiley & Sons, Ltd. Published 2021 by John Wiley & Sons, Ltd.

Men of John Shakespeare's financial standing were expected to involve themselves actively in the civic life of the town. This John did, being elected chief burgess three years before William's birth and then High Bailiff (the name for the Stratford-upon-Avon mayor) in the year his son turned four. So, we can place young William in a fairly prosperous, comfortable, and locally influential household as a child. What is more, John Shakespeare's status gave him the right to have his sons educated without charge at the King's New School in Stratford.

Records don't survive from the period, but most assume that William went there, "because otherwise how could he have learned about Ovid and Plautus?" (Garber 2004, p. 163). Marjorie Garber's question reveals that education didn't mean quite the same in the 1570s as it does in our own time. Lessons focused primarily on classical texts, Ovid and Plautus amongst others, and the curriculum was demanding. Garber (ibid.), for one, is amused that William, who would later be mocked for his "small Latin and less Greek" still learned "far more Latin and Greek than is commanded by most college graduates today." The "intense concentration on language" meant that "boys from the age of eight onwards spent around nine hours a day, six days a week, in all but seven weeks a year on literary exercises such as learning by rote, writing according to formulae, reproducing *sententiae*, imitating classical authors, and constructing arguments for and against set propositions" (Van Es 2013, p. 4). A boy could not fail to become good at the construction of arguments and have an armory of literary tropes and figures to draw upon when instructed to create compositions of their own. This emphasis on eloquence and rhetorical skills would stand many other playwrights in good stead. George Chapman, Thomas Kyd, John Webster, Michael Drayton, and Ben Jonson all relied on their "schoolboy training" and no wonder.

William's education was strikingly different to that of his parents. Neither John nor Mary could write, although both clearly functioned successfully in daily life and business, whether in the home or workshop. And yet, William's parentage was not unusual for a professional playwright, indeed it was "entirely typical" (Van Es 2013, p. 2). The list of Shakespeare's contemporaries' fathers' occupations provides a roster of artisan trades: Christopher Marlowe (shoemaker); Anthony Munday (stationer); John Webster (cartwright); Henry Chettle (dyer); Thomas Kyd (scrivener); Robert Greene (cordwainer or saddlemaker).

His schooling may have exposed a young Shakespeare to classical literature, but everyday Stratford town life exposed him to popular drama. Robust traditions of playing in provincial England ranged from the acting companies who performed under the protection of a member of the nobility, and took his name, through to informal local groups of actors, neighbors, or guilds gathering to make theater in domestic or communal spaces.[2] Much of this playing went on under the radar since the 1572 Act for the Punishment of Vagabonds (and an even more draconian measure passed in 1598) stipulated that all traveling players had to be attached to a "baron of the realm or any other honourable person of greater degree."[3] The Queen's Men, formed as the result of a Privy Council directive designed to take back control of the anarchic world of playing, were expected to entertain their patron, the queen, of course, but also spent much of the year touring. It was a relentless life on the road, with limited runs in each town: only three shows for the Queen's Men, even less for other companies.[4] But stars were born and occasionally fortunes made: the renowned comedian dancer Richard Tarlton left the magnificent sum of £700 at his death and had Sir Philip Sidney as godfather to his son. And when the players did come to town, civic leaders would get the best seats in the house, good news if you were the High Bailiff's son, as William was.

Until the late 1570s that is, when John Shakespeare stopped attending council meetings. William was in his early teens and would have lost his privileged entrance to the Guild Hall, although he, like everyone else, could still have joined the paying customers for the players' shows in the town. John's fortunes determined William's and those fortunes were becoming dangerously troubled according to some. The crisis was precipitated for a whole range of reasons depending on which biographer you consult: "rash business practices, a general economic downturn in the Midlands, changes in the licensing and practice of wool merchants, an obdurate commitment to Catholicism that led to fines and harassment, and perhaps a drinking problem for good measure" (Tromly 2010, p. 246).

However, the family's financial crisis has been downgraded recently. Examining the year 1586, when John was expelled as alderman, Potter notes that most men did not really *want* to serve their community because corporation business was "expensive and time-consuming," pointing out that none of John's sons would contribute to local government (Potter 2012, pp. 46–47). Moreover, 1586 was not a good year for anyone, with "dearth" in Stratford and beyond bringing to an end a 20-year period of relative prosperity and, more problematically for John Shakespeare, the calling in of debts. John mortgaged his wife Mary's inheritance to meet the short-term financial challenge, but this was standard practice in a volatile, debt-heavy system. It may well be that John Shakespeare's financial problems have been exaggerated by posterity and, in the first instance, by the man himself in order to avoid his debtors (Fallow 2015).

It is a biographical stretch, therefore, to argue that young William was motivated by the desire to reverse his father's and his family's decline, but it is certain that John, as father, would have determined the course of his son's life as a teenager. More than that, "in Elizabethan families the eldest son stands in a special relationship to the father as the primary inheritor of property and as the transmitter of patrilineal values," the father's "legal successor and metaphysical continuation" (Tromly 2010, p. 248). Simply by virtue of the patriarchal control invested in him by church and state, John had almost total sway over his son's future (Fallow 2015, p. 38). And that future did not include university.

Biographer Jonathan Bate (2008, p. 75) views this as significant, contrasting Shakespeare with his almost exact contemporary Christopher Marlowe. As a student at Cambridge University, Marlowe was drawn into a dangerous intellectual world of philosophy, Machiavellian thinking, even atheism and, for Bate, this was a natural route to the edgy life of poet and playwright. Bart van Es (2013, p. 14) sees things differently. "A playwright's literary accomplishment was in practice little affected by attendance at university: Oxford and Cambridge specialized in the teaching of theology, philosophy, history, and similar branches of exact learning, and not in literature of a kind that a poet might readily apply."

So, no university for William – but how *did* he spend his youth? Some suggest he was informally apprenticed to the family business. Both John and Mary "were capable and tough-minded business people" (Edmondson and Wells 2015a, p. 330), unlikely to employ other people when there was a healthy eldest son to be trained up: there's a "logical possibility" therefore that William was apprenticed to "the unregulated family business" (Fallow 2015, p. 38). This apprenticeship would not necessarily preclude an engagement with the acting world, whether in Stratford, its surroundings, or even in faraway London, the business capital. Indeed, as Bart van Es (2013, pp. 9–10) points out, we don't need to make a choice between William the apprentice and William the actor, because so many actors had their "roots in practical professions," the theater industry itself having its foundations in medieval guilds and corporations.

The truth is, we just don't know whether Shakespeare was apprenticed to the family business. Nor do we know much about his or his family's religious practices, let alone beliefs, but there is nevertheless a noisy debate as to whether the Shakespeares were closet Catholics in a Protestant England.[5] Hard evidence is elusive, although one can argue that it would be. The religious changes over the course of John Shakespeare's life did not help the quest of future generations seeking insight into any individual's belief. The Reformation made it easier to be labeled a heretic, as there was no longer a unified church to guide the faithful, and, especially in countries such as England, the authorities who determined religious policy changed at an alarming rate.

Those with Catholic sympathies were wise to conform outwardly in an era where opposition to the established Protestant Church of England was punishable by, at best, fines, and at worst – at least for those who actively supported the pope's command to overthrow Queen Elizabeth I in the name of the Catholic religion - torture and execution. In the 15 years or so prior to William's birth, England had gone from a country in the grip of a zealous Protestant Reformation under the young king Edward VI to an equally zealous return to Roman Catholicism under his sister Mary, only to be returned to Protestantism with the accession of Queen Elizabeth I in 1558. Put another way, it became ever more important to think about individual salvation but equally dangerous to declare one's confessional allegiance (Hadfield 2019, p. 18). In an era of traumatic religious change, caution was wise.

We do know that when William was 19, two Catholic members of his mother's Arden family, Mary and Edward, were arrested for conspiring to kill the queen. Mary was pardoned. Edward was executed, his head displayed on London Bridge as was the custom of the time. There are, furthermore, two pieces of evidence to suggest that William's father, John, was Catholic. A "Testament of Faith" with his name written on it was found hidden in the rafters of the Henley Street house in 1757. Crypto-Catholics kept these documents, a profession of their faith, close by them to be used if they faced death and there was no priest available for the last rites. The second piece of evidence shows that, in 1592, by which time William was approaching 30, his father got in trouble twice for recusancy, that is, failing to attend church. Did Shakespeare's – possible – Catholic heritage, beliefs, or merely "sympathies" result in a body of works which lack an "overt polemical edge," result in a writer's life of caution, as Dutton (1989, p. 10) argues?

The evidence for John's beliefs is not entirely reliable. The "Testament" was found some 150 years after Shakespeare senior lived in Henley Street, and was then promptly lost. Those recusancy records of 1592 ascribe his avoidance of church to fearful pragmatism, rather than religious nonconformity. John Shakespeare owed money; it was far too easy to be found at church; he thus kept away "for fear of process for debt."

Moreover, it is all too easy to impose reductive labels on what was a fluid belief system. As James Shapiro (2005a, p. 167) writes, "to argue that the Shakespeares were secretly Catholic or alternatively, mainstream Protestants misses the point that except for a small minority at one doctrinal extreme or other, those labels failed to capture the layered nature of what Elizabethans, from the queen on down, actually believed." The Elizabethan Church Settlement was, in part, designed to accommodate this, tolerating "a wide range of spiritual and religious beliefs among those who were happy outwardly to conform" (Edmondson and Wells 2015b, p. 9).

Old beliefs and habits died hard, much harder than historians in the past believed.

Yet, despite the tenuous evidence, we remain fascinated by Shakespeare's possible Catholicism. Maguire and Smith (2012) argue that the fascination stems at least in part from the glimpse it offers of a

> Shakespeare who is not simply accumulating wealth and property but who apparently suffers inner conflict, a struggle with his conscience, and whose writing is shaped by the mechanisms he has developed for his own psychological and physical self-protection. In this model, Catholicism registers as much as an act of individual assertion and defiance – the poet at an angle to establishment values – as it does as a specific doctrinal allegiance. While the question of whether Shakespeare was a Catholic is unlikely to be definitively answered, we can certainly affirm that we want him to have been.

Whether we want him to be an apprentice is another matter. Some have seen 18-year-old William's activities in the summer of 1582 as evidence that he would do anything to avoid joining the family business. An apprentice was not allowed to marry. To escape apprenticeship, therefore, William has sex with Anne Hathaway, perhaps six years his senior and, almost as soon as she finds she is pregnant, marries her, welcoming the marriage and pregnancy "as ways to break free of an enforced apprenticeship" (Orlin 2016, p. 39).[6]

John Shakespeare gave his consent to the marriage of William and Anne in November 1582, that consent necessary because his son, at 18, was still a minor. The Hathaway family appeared content with the marriage, providing the "bondsmen" to safeguard the wife's interests, as was conventional (Schoenbaum 1991, p. 12). Anne received 10 marks on her wedding day, the equivalent to £6 13s 4d, probably a bit more than a playwright in the next decade received for a completed play (Potter 2012, p. 56). And she duly gave birth to a baby girl the following spring. Susanna Shakespeare was baptized on 26 May 1583, in Holy Trinity Church, as her father had been just over 19 years earlier. Around a year later, Anne was pregnant again. The Shakespeare twins, Hamnet and Judith, were christened on 2 February 1585, probably named for close friends of their parents, the baker Hamnet Sadler and his wife Judith. Richard Barton, a new minister in Stratford, a man unreservedly praised by the more vocal Protestants of the town, baptised the twins. This might offer a glimpse of Shakespeare's religious position: "either a good Church of England Protestant or doing his best to look like one" (Potter 2012, p. 59). His "distinctive anonymity" (Dutton 2010, p. 11) is the one thing that is certain, although whether this was a reaction against his parent's alleged crypto-Catholicism, a product of having been brought up in a household which was not fervidly religious or simply all that emerges from a sparse archive, is a matter for debate.

Married at 18, and to an older woman. A father of three children before he was 21. We might think these are crucial events in the formation of William Shakespeare, the man. Yet Alan Stewart (2016, p. 38) has demonstrated how thoroughly the "marriage was effaced by Shakespeare's seventeenth century 'biographers' who constructed for him not a familial but a theatrical dynasty" (Traub 2016, p. 38). These earliest accounts of Shakespeare's life are almost completely silent about family – and more specifically, silent about women. "Aubrey gives us a father, but only as the representation of a trade that Shakespeare rejects; and there are no women, except an unnamed sister" (Stewart 2016, p. 68). This is normal for seventeenth-century life-writing, so it should not be surprising that only in 1693 is Shakespeare represented as married. Twentieth-century literary critics are, ironically, equally unwilling to consider Shakespeare the married man, not because of a lack of interest in these trivial, domestic (feminine) matters but because of a distrust of the biographical turn. Marjorie Garber (2004, p. 20), for example, is typical in her pronouncement that there has been much "speculation" about William's marriage to Anne. She does not mention the matter again.

Dismissing talk of marriage at least avoids the at times unedifying biographical feeding frenzy that surrounds William and Anne Shakespeare's marriage when it *is* considered. Part of the problem is that the biographers are feeding on nothing. There is no direct evidence to show how William felt about Anne, or vice versa. And nature and biographers abhor a vacuum.

That there were no more children born to Anne and William after the twins prompts the normally cautious Lois Potter (2012, p. 59) to wild speculation, an "if" leading to a "might": "If Shakespeare did indeed have Catholic sympathies, he might have been unable to envisage any way except separation to avoid having more children." Potter is determined to discredit an alternative interpretation – that William was repelled by sex with women and the resultant babies. We will return to Shakespeare's sex life later.

For others, the vacuum itself is viewed as telling. The "supremely eloquent" Shakespeare does not write anything to or about Anne, no "signs of shared joy or grief, no words of advice," not even any financial transactions (Greenblatt 2004, p. 125). This proves that William "could not find what he craved, emotionally or sexually, within his marriage." Assuming the Shakespeare family's Catholicism, and that William's earliest sexual experiences would have been with other boys at school, Greenblatt goes on to try to work out why Will would have found Anne attractive. She is different: Protestant to his Catholic, straight to his queer. Anne (Greenblatt 2004, p. 119) represents an antidote, "a reassuringly conventional resolution to his sexual ambivalence and perplexity." And because the great writer is so complicated, tortured, and bisexual it can't possibly last. In this scenario, William becomes a "reluctant, perhaps highly reluctant" bridegroom (Greenblatt 2004, p. 123), trapped in a marriage that he cannot escape.

It's an old, old story, as Lena Cowen Orlin (2016, p. 42) points out in her reassessment of the evidence. "By the early nineteenth century, the narrative of Shakespeare's relationship with Anne Hathaway was fixed: the eighteen-year-old William was trapped by the pregnancy of a twenty-six-year-old into a marriage that he fled as soon as possible, years later confirming his disaffection for his enforced wife in the derisory dying bequest of a second-best bed."

The marriage is, however, a blessing in disguise, because these nuptial disappointments prompted Shakespeare's migration to London. Shakespeare, in other words, needed to cast off an unfortunate marriage in order to realize his destiny.

Archeological evidence (Scheil 2015) discovered in William and Anne's marital home, New Place in Stratford, suggests a different picture. Anne Shakespeare ran a large and wealthy household. In the absence of any evidence of abandonment, let alone complaint from Anne regarding support, perhaps we should see her as the trusted partner in the marriage, the one keeping the home fires burning. Equally, that the Shakespeares had three children, then no more is not necessarily a sign that they were no longer sexually active. Miscarriages and stillbirths were distressingly common and most were unrecorded. What is more, Shakespeare remained involved in Stratford life as a family man and landowner during the years in which he achieved success on the London stage.

Even those biographers who do not see the marriage as an active evil nevertheless view Shakespeare escaping pleasant but provincial Stratford and seeking his fortune in dangerous but exciting London. This too may be based on a false premise, that somehow Stratford was a rural, pastoral idyll in comparison to the dirty, gritty capital. Nowhere was safe from the everyday catastrophes of life in late sixteenth-century England, whether political and religious regime change, fire, plague, and poor harvests, or infant (and maternal) mortality. Like all his contemporaries, Shakespeare was engaged with a complex web of loyalties grounded in the household or extended family, the sprawling social unit that characterized late Elizabethan life, but this did not mean that Warwickshire and London represented two entirely separate existences. Gilbert, William's closest brother in age, would act as his agent in Stratford during his frequent absences in London, whilst William would look out for his much younger brother Edmund in London (Richardson 2015).[7] Moreover, one's immediate family was important but not exclusively so. Other networks could be, and would be, just as important to William Shakespeare, not least those of the theater world.

For it is as an actor in London that William next appears in the archive, but only in 1592. After the christening of Hamnet and Judith, seven long years pass before their father's name appears again in any document. Most assume he had been in the city for some time before 1592. Park Honan has Shakespeare settled in London by 1589 or 1590 at the latest, living in Shoreditch, and remaining there during some of his apprentice days in the theater, close to his fellow playwright (and exact contemporary) Christopher Marlowe. Honan vividly evokes the streets of Shoreditch – until 1588 also Richard Tarlton's home turf – with its "jutting, far-overhanging storeys of shops" which "often broke off the sunlight so that, on a good day, the lanes were in shadow" (2005, p. 186).[8]

There's a gap to be filled between Shakespeare's christening in Holy Trinity Church, Stratford, and the seedy streets of Shoreditch, and biographers duly fill it. The goal is to get William to the big city and many and various are the routes by which he arrives.

One story goes that the return of the Queen's Men to Stratford-upon-Avon in 1589 changed the course of Shakespeare's life. The company were a man down after an unfortunate incident in Thame, Oxfordshire: their leading actor was killed in a street fight. Perhaps the 23-year-old William stepped in to fill the gap? It's a nice idea, but implausible, not least because he would have had to have been remarkably impressive to take over a leading role.

More plausible is seeing young Will as a strategic rather than reluctant bridegroom. "Let us suppose that Shakespeare did not want to spend his life – or any more months than he already had done – as a Stratford artificer. The wedding would have been a means of escaping the life that had been organized for him": Orlin (2016, p. 56) argues that this "new way to cluster the evidence" suggests that William's marriage "may have been not one from which Shakespeare had to break free but instead the means by which he was able to break free." The marriage remains a significant factor pushing him to London, his goal to support (not escape) his young family. Rather than a delusional act of self-destruction built on a fantasy from which Will had to escape as soon as possible, the marriage might have been a thoroughly sensible decision for an aspiring actor, intrinsic to his future success rather than an impediment to it.

Or perhaps William's marriage in fact allows him to be an actor. An apprenticeship (and university for that matter) could not be combined with marriage, an actor's life could. And that life could run parallel "with a very different life in Stratford" (Potter 2012, p. 55). Anne and the couple's three very young children could and did live in there with William's parents, while he – perhaps – toured the provinces with an acting troupe, moving in and out of the great houses of England, before ending up in London, his semi-permanent base, in 1588.[9]

William may disappear from the records for seven years, but it is quite possible he did not disappear from Stratford at all. According to David Fallow, despite his marriage precluding a formal apprenticeship, John Shakespeare was not going to let his eldest son do anything other than join the family business. This entailed visits to London, and therefore when William surfaces in the city it is "exactly where and when contacts in the wool trade would have been vital to the survival of the family business." Shakespeare therefore arrives in London as "a businessman rather than an impoverished poet" (Fallow 2015, p. 38).

In contrast, there are those who insist the pull of the theater for young William is heightened by the desire to leave Stratford: the "power of its language, the mystery of mimesis, the potential to travel away from provincial Warwickshire" all drew Shakespeare to the city (Dutton 2018, p. 28) – or to Lancashire. Those who view Shakespeare as a crypto-Catholic take William north in the later 1580s as schoolmaster (or possibly actor) in the household of Sir Thomas Hesketh, whose wife and at least one of his sons were active Catholics.[10] Some add the idea that William was sent to Lancashire to get him away from (religious) trouble in Warwickshire. When Hesketh died in 1588, the argument goes, Shakespeare passed into the household of the Earl of Derby, Hesketh's patron, and thence to the life of a touring actor and novice playwright with the Earl of Derby's son, Ferdinando, Lord Strange, the patron of one of the leading acting companies of the 1580s.[11] Shakespeare's experiences touring with Lord Strange's Men may even emerge in his plays: when he imagines a performance "it is not in a public playhouse but in the private space of a royal palace or a lord's house" (Potter 2012, p. 55).

And yet, for all the lure of London, Shakespeare is unlike his younger contemporary Ben Jonson, who refers to the city's streets and pubs and theaters in his plays. William "always retained something of a pre-urban sensibility, in which playing was closely attached to the service of a lord and to great private houses" (Dutton 2018, p. 38). Not just that, it is a Midlands' pre-urban sensibility, because Shakespeare's earliest plays are "dotted with names of places in the Midlands." Shakespeare's continued connection to his Warwickshire roots – understood variously as pre-urban, narrowly provincial, or idyllic pastoral, and existing in his imagination as much as his lived experience – is a powerful theme in many "Lives."

When and why Shakespeare began working in the theater in London (or elsewhere) remains murky. What is clearer is that to be an actor was to exist on the edge of convention. On the one hand, an actor was merely a household retainer, a lowly, liveried member within a deeply hierarchical unit, organized around the service of a lord and patron. At the same time, an actor was one step away from a vagabond, a byword for bad behavior, dissolute, "loitering" fellows, disrespectful of authority, "passing from country to country, from one gentleman's house to another, offering their service, which is a kind of beggary" (Van Es 2013, p. 8, quoting from Wickham, Berry, and Ingram 2020, pp. 157–171).[12] Hidden behind the invective was a horror of social mobility: "a common theme is the players' rapid rise from travelling minstrels to gaudy and wealthy men" (Van Es 2013, p. 8). Actors were indeed "entrepreneurs, seeking to make a living in a developing marketplace – though one contested by a number of different parties, notably the Crown (the Queen's government); Parliament; their own aristocratic patrons; and local authorities, often in the form of their mayors and councils" (Dutton 2018, p. 28). Acting could, and did, transform men's fortunes.

Particularly acting in London. The theater world in the city had been changing rapidly from the time of William's early childhood when performances (whether amateur or professional) were attached to a specific occasion, and at the invitation, and under the control, of the person commissioning the performance. By the time William entered his teens, playing companies were working through much of the year, performing to paying audiences, and even providing a selection of plays at each venue. And a few brave visionaries had started building theaters: in 1567, a stage and scaffolding in a farmhouse called the Red Lion about a mile from the city walls; 10 years on, The Curtain; 20, and the Rose is being built. The steady rate of building suggests that business was good. London was thriving in the years after 1588, temporarily free of the major epidemics which led to playhouse closures, and a population of 200,000 made it far and away the biggest city in England.

By 1590 there were "at least four substantial buildings attracting acting companies to London, with smaller venues existing besides. Playhouses proper, although partly open to the elements, could shelter thousands of spectators and were equipped with tiring houses for the purpose of costume changes and space for the storage of theatrical properties. Their occupation was changeable: individual troupes would come and go depending on touring routes and the seasons. Alternative entertainment, such as fencing contests or animal baiting, was also an option for the owners when no suitable players were in town" (Van Es 2013, p. 11).

It was a volatile world, involving extensive touring away from the capital, not always without trouble. The Queen's Men were in Dublin one month, invited to perform at the wedding of King James VI and Anne of Denmark in Edinburgh the next, with the more everyday mayor's plays filling in the gaps.[13] The death of a star performer in one company, the death of a patron of another, could change everything, as it did in 1588, the year in which Richard Tarlton (of the Queen's Men) died and in which Lord Strange formed a new company from the remnants of the Earl of Leicester's Men. Already disrupted when the earl had taken some of his playing troupe with him to war in the Low Countries, the company completely dissolved on Leicester's death.

The new players moved swiftly "into the highest league," not least because of the presence of Will Kemp, a comedian who was, almost, Tarlton's equal

(Dutton 2018, p. 61). Trouble came and was averted. The Lord Mayor, attempting to close the playhouses, instructed the two main London troupes (the Admiral's and Strange's Men) to stop playing. The former "dutifully obeyed, but the others in very contemptuous manner departing ... went to the Cross Keys [an inn] and played that afternoon" (Chambers 1923, Volume 4, p. 305). Some of Strange's players were imprisoned for their contempt, but most were protected by their patron.

Strange's Men prospered, being awarded six slots in the Revels Calendar of 1591–1592, and three the next year. And between 19 February and 22 June 1592 they performed the first fully recorded London season, playing continuously at the Rose. Prior to this, no company had attempted to set up more-or-less permanent residence in London. The new permanent theaters were changing drama. In this first season of 105 days, no fewer than 27 plays were staged.

This was very different from touring, when companies would take three or four plays out on the road, with perhaps two or three new plays in their repertoire because they could rely on a new audience in the next town or great house. In London, there was a pressing need to get the playgoers back for more. The new public theaters needed more plays, more playwrights: a perfect recipe for the young actor, and aspiring playwright, William Shakespeare. He was not alone, of course: "As the commercial theatre expanded, many young men, primed with a command of rhetoric thanks to their training in the new grammar schools, made their way to the capital. Under-employed and highly literate, they were soon called upon to produce copy for the players, who (with large venues and longer periods of residence) were turning over material at an unprecedented rate" (Van Es 2013, p. 1). It was an era of unprecedented opportunity for an actor-playwright. The new playhouses (when they were permitted to open) needed new material, far more than had been required when companies only went on the road: "itinerant acting companies could succeed by repeating in different places a small inventory of plays" (Bednarz 2018, p. 22). Those "with an established urban-based clientele were, instead, compelled to acquire larger and more differentiated repertoires – including diverse and innovative comedies – in order to satisfy the expectations of inveterate theatregoers who could choose among competing venues" (Bednarz 2018, p. 22).

In retrospect, we can see that William Shakespeare was in the right place, at the right time: London 1592. Whether his family, particularly his father, saw the situation in the same way is another question. Fred Tromly (2010, p. 251) speculates on John Shakespeare's response to his son's career choice, bearing in mind that no one knew just how lucrative the theater industry would be for his son. Believing that John saw William "rejecting the traditional forms of business in favour of an enterprise that, in addition to being morally questionable in the eyes of many, offered very little promise of stability and steady income," he sees an unbridgeable generation gap opening between father and son. For Jonathan Bate that rejection of artisan business in Stratford was less calculated but no less significant. Refusing to speculate about the Shakespeare family's Catholicism, Bate nevertheless asserts that "the balance of probability is that William Shakespeare's own instinct and inheritance were cautious, traditional, respectable, suspicious of change. We may as well say conservative" (2008, p. 66). This all changed when William "got the acting bug." For Bate, as with Tromly, John Shakespeare would not have been best pleased. Coming from a class where "idleness" was sin, he "would have subscribed to the common view that actors were little better than vagabonds [...] When John heard that his son had become employed in the theatre, he would have been flabbergasted. The dramatic profession was a completely unknown quantity" (2008, pp. 73–74).

What no one could have imagined was William Shakespeare's unlikely and swift rise from actor to jointsharer in a new acting company, The Lord Chamberlain's Men. But that is where he was headed.

Chapter Two

Shakespeare joined the theater world in London at a time of intense competition and serious challenges. Plague closed the theaters through the long, hot summer of 1592 and then again in 1593. Later in that year the playing companies were only permitted a brief Christmas season. Lord Strange's Men would play for only eight days in April 1593, then left the city, asking for and receiving (as they had done the year before) a special licence from the Privy Council to go on the road. Then, a year later, Lord Strange died, amidst rumors of poison. His brother took over the troupe, but actor after actor left, and the company lost their access to court.

Lord Strange's Men were in effect finished, but others flourished. The theater builder James Burbage was said at his death to have amassed goods and chattels "amounting to £1000," precisely the kind of success that angered theater's critics: the "evident token of a wicked time when players wax so rich that they can build such houses" (Bruster 1992, p. 2; Van Es 2013, p. 16). Burbage was no angel. He had traveled the country "at the head of Lord Leicester's players, a dangerous if rewarding pursuit," but his Theatre playhouse was perhaps his biggest gamble, and one which needed defending with "cunning and even violence over the years." An "aggressive investor" in tenement housing as well as the Theatre, he thrived in the "cut-throat conditions of playhouse management" (Van Es 2013, p. 16), as illustrated by a confrontation in May 1592. The widow of his business partner arrived with several men (including the alleged murderer of her husband) to demand payments. Burbage dismissed them with a beating and a curse: "hang her, whore." When the widow returned with reinforcements, Burbage was said to have told his sons to "provide charged pistols" and "shoot them in the legs."

Burbage's lucrative Theatre – an "entirely a local Tudor building: it was made from wood, and had sides of irregular length and a thatched roof" – was erected on a rented field in Halliwell, one of the suburbs or "liberties" of London, areas less subject to jurisdiction than the City of London itself (Stern

2004, p. 12). There, and in the other playhouses scattered on the margins of the city, audiences flocked to a "multisensory experience" (Bednarz 2018, p. 22), eating (fruit and nuts), drinking (beer), and surrounded by music before, during, and after the show, and both comedies and tragedies ending with the whole ensemble dancing a "jig."

On the comparatively bare stage, the actors – all male – played for two, perhaps more, hours.

> You shall hear
> Scenes, though below his art, may yet appear
> Worth two hours' travel. To his bones sweet sleep;
> Content to you. If this play do not keep
> A little dull time from us, we perceive
> Our losses fall so thick, we must needs leave.
> *(Two Noble Kinsmen, Prologue, ll. 27–32)*

That phrase, "two hours' travel" is richly evocative, suggesting the journey the audience take while seeing, or hearing, a play. Some editors emend travel to travail, adding the idea of labor, possibly even struggle, to the understanding of theater as a journey. Elsewhere in the literature of the time, there are references to running times of two or three hours. What seems certain is that plays were designed for one venue – and then cut or lengthened for another: constant adaptation was crucial to success.

For many years, scholars believed that this was a theater world dominated by two companies, a duopoly. Now, the active presence of other troupes is increasingly acknowledged, groups such as the Queen's Men, a "major, if perhaps old-fashioned, force – not just on the touring circuit but in the capital as well," Derby's Men, Sussex's Men, and Pembroke's Men (Syme 2012, p. 274). It may be frustrating to be unclear as to when exactly Shakespeare wrote one of his earliest plays, *Titus Andronicus*, to be unsure about the date of its first performance, and to have no less than five theater companies involved in its production, but this all points to the fluidity – and the precarious nature – of the theater world. The plague closures of 1592 and 1593 were, in particular, disastrous for the new industry: "All the major companies either went out of business or were reduced to shadows of their former selves, clearly not fit to perform at court" (Dutton 2018, p. 75). Did survivors of failed companies collaborate and perform *Titus*, or was the play passed from troupe to troupe, as each failed because of the desperate conditions? Similar kinds of questions surround another early play, *Richard III*, which is just as difficult both to date and to attach to a specific playing company. Is it from the winter season of 1592–1593 because of the verbal echoes of the *Henry VI* plays, in which case the players would have been either Pembroke's or Lord Strange's Men? Or was it written and performed later, after the reopening of the theaters in 1594 and therefore by the Lord Chamberlain's Men, a company only formed in that year? The truth is that the play could have been written at any time over a period of 10 years, between the second edition of Holinshed's *Chronicles* (1587) on which it draws and 20 October 1597 when a quarto edition of the play was entered in the Stationers' Register.[1]

Perhaps this is the moment to let go of attempts at precise dating of plays. Putting aside the difficulty, even impossibility, of the task in most cases, to work out when, say, *Richard III* was "completed" is somewhat reductive, since plays were modified throughout their creation, whether by authors, censors, actors, or others with a say in the performance and dissemination of the work.

In the midst of this volatile, exciting world, where do we put William Shakespeare, the man? Perhaps back home in Stratford, two days' ride away, managing his family's interests, seeing his parents, wife, and children from time to time; perhaps on the road with one acting troupe or another; perhaps based in London at one of the new permanent theaters; definitely writing as well as acting.

Most place Shakespeare at James Burbage's playhouse. "Good young authors" were writing for the Theatre, and "good young actors were performing in it" (Stern 2004, p. 12), including Burbage's son, Richard. And although we don't know when William Shakespeare, actor, first played there, we do know that William Shakespeare, dramatist, wrote his first plays for performance in the Theatre. Then again, the earliest reference to these first plays is to a successful run of "harey the vi," performed on 3 March 1592 at the Rose Theatre, and by Lord Strange's Men.[2] This is usually assumed to be Shakespeare's *Henry VI Part I*, part of his trilogy depicting the collapse of English power in France after the death of King Henry V, and England's subsequent descent into civil war, the Wars of the Roses. Patriotic history plays, indeed openly xenophobic plays, were popular in these years, perhaps because England remained threatened by the power of Catholic Spain, despite the Armada victory of 1588. As Thomas Nashe wrote at the time: "what a glorious thing it is to have *Henry* the fifth represented on the Stage, leading the French King prisoner, and forcing both him and the Dolphin to swear fealty." Calling up English victories of the past and creating foreign scapegoats were obvious ways to take the audience's mind off problems and divisions closer to home in these late Elizabethan years, but in the early 1590s Shakespeare instead chose to focus on England's internal divisions. His primary source, Edward Hall's history of the houses of Lancaster and York, shows this choice to have been equally patriotic, legitimizing the rule of the Tudors. Hall's history, written in 1548 and dedicated to Henry Tudor's son, Henry VIII, was, in effect, a defense of the Tudor regime, recounting the civil wars that ensued after the deposition of Richard II, the rise and fall of the murderous Richard III, the glorious ascendancy of Henry Tudor to the throne, and the marriage of the heirs of the two enemy houses, York and Lancaster.

Some have questioned this picture of a young(ish) Shakespeare as Tudor apologist, seeing him offering not only a nod to contemporary events (the June 1592 riots by the feltmakers' apprentices being echoed in Jack Cade's Rebellion in *Henry VI Part II*), but even a not-so-veiled critique of Henry Tudor's grand-daughter, Elizabeth I, in his representation of Joan of Arc, a monstrous man-woman. Joan was "associated" with the mystique of virginity and power surrounding England's queen, and her public rhetoric sounds like a "tinny echo" of the English Queen's tactics with Parliament at this time (Marcus 1988, p. 67). Conventional male anxiety about women in power aside, was newcomer Shakespeare risking a link between Joan and Elizabeth I? Or was he playing safe with the character of brave Talbot, English Talbot (whose stinking, flyblown corpse is mocked by the evil, French Joan)? Are these even the right questions, since the play is a collaboration?

It is impossible to know for sure which lines Shakespeare wrote. For, although the Talbot scenes are usually viewed as his, they are inserted into a play that is more Thomas Nashe than William Shakespeare. Therefore, to write about "Shakespeare's early plays" is misleading, because it glosses over the extent to which he collaborated with other playwrights during these years. Put cautiously: "Shakespeare's writing of the early 1590s, like that of his contempo-raries, is alive with the presence of other writers, both as co-authors and as a transformative influence" (Honan 2005, p. 205). Put so that it makes front page news:

THE SECOND PART OF HENRY THE SIXTH; OR, THE FIRST PART OF THE CONTENTION
WILLIAM SHAKESPEARE, CHRISTOPHER MARLOWE, AND OTHERS

Thus the *New Oxford Shakespeare* (Taylor et al. 2016) presented its *Modern Critical Edition* of *Henry VI Part II*. In the *Authorship Companion* to the *Critical Edition*, Taylor and Loughnane (2017) argue that Marlowe is the author of most of the Jack Cade material in act 4, with Shakespeare most "securely iden-tified" only as the author of four scenes in act 3, and Young Clifford's speech which begins "Shame and confusion, all is on the rout! / Fear frames disorder, and disorder wounds / Where it should guard" (from scene 24 in the *New Oxford* edition).

For the later *Henry VI Part I*, the *New Oxford* editors (Taylor et al. 2016) go even further. Marlowe, Nashe, and anonymous are the lead authors. Shakespeare is relegated to adaptor.

Some might argue that the reason we hear Marlowe's voice in the opening lines of *Henry VI Part I* (the "archaic imperatives, the outlandish and resplendent images, the recourse to cosmic forces in the light of an imperial superman" [Van Es 2013, pp. 21–22]) is because Shakespeare is drawing on *Tamburlaine* and other works by his more established rival. In a world in which every playwright was imitating his colleagues, if not downright stealing from their work, and in which Christopher Marlowe was preeminent, this would hardly be a surprising move on the part of Shakespeare. Indeed, some were upfront about their own work's relation to that of Marlowe: "Peele's *Battle of Alcazar* openly proclaims its task of bringing 'Tamburlaine into our Afric here' (1.2.35) and is likewise dominated by the language and visual icons of Marlowe's world." The overlaps are both visual and rhetorical. Alcazar literally borrows Tamburlaine's chariot, according to the accounts for the plays (Van Es 2013, p. 26).

Marlowe (and other more established playwrights) are crucial to the *Henry VI* plays, whether as lead authors, collaborators, or writerly models to be imitated. For me, whether Shakespeare is echoing Marlowe or working with him or challenging him, what is significant is not so much that he is an anxious newcomer nervously covering the tracks of his borrowing; not even that these years mark the beginning of a competition between two playwrights born in the same year – a competition which, for most critics, Shakespeare would win; but simply yet another insight into a playwriting world of collaboration and creative imitation.[3]

For *Titus Andronicus*, another of these "first" plays, Shakespeare worked with George Peele, whether in active collaboration, or revising Peele's work. Marlowe is, predictably, present (Aaron's opening speech is a "compendium of Marlovian rhetorical and metrical devices" [Van Es 2013, p. 33]), but so too are classical sources: direct allusions to Ovid's *Metamorphoses* and Titus himself quotes a Senecan tragedy. That Shakespeare frequently "showed off his literariness" (Bate 2008, p. 84) reflected the way in which he had learned Latin at school. This "shaped his subsequent life of writing as decisively as did the content of the books he went on to read in later years." For Bate (editing the work in 1995), *Titus* is something of a showpiece, a display of Shakespeare's ability to handle an intricate structure; to deploy theatrical resources in innovative ways; to ramp up the expressive language; and above all to display his ability to improvise in a complex and self-conscious way upon his classical sources.

Titus also shows Shakespeare (and Peele) following fashion by writing a revenge tragedy, responding to the phenomenal popularity of Thomas Kyd's 1588 *The Spanish Tragedy*, the bloody benchmark for the genre. The play echoes Kyd in various ways: there's a triumphant return from battle; a revenger descending into madness; a play-within-a-play to further the revenger's aim;

the utter destruction of a family; and a cloth dipped in blood, a device that Shakespeare himself had also used in *Henry VI Part III*.

The Taming of the Shrew offers yet more insight into the fluid, dialogic nature of playwriting in the early 1590s. An anonymous play, *The Taming of A Shrew* (whose frame, unlike Shakespeare's is complete, since the drunken tinker wakes up at the end of the play, and heads home to use what he has learned in his "dream" to tame his shrewish wife) was doing the rounds at the same time as Shakespeare's The *Shrew*. Is *A Shrew* a garbled and rewritten transmission of *The Shrew*? Or is *The Shrew* a version of *A Shrew* designed for a somewhat smaller company? In *The Shrew* the number of sisters is reduced from three to two; there's a stronger and more complex subplot; Christopher Sly disappears from the play leaving only the Induction; the setting is changed (England to Italy); and there's a much stronger sense of Shakespeare's literary source(s), the Italian poet, Ariosto, as translated by the English poet, George Gascoigne. In contrast, *A Shrew* nods to contemporary patriotic English theater rather than Italian poetry, specifically alluding to George Peele's blockbuster *The Battle of Alcazar* and its trademark visual: Muly Mahomet, a Moor, brandishing a sword with raw flesh on it.Whatever the relationship between the two *Shrew* plays, they reveal the ways in which playwrights responded to each other's work and to playing conditions, writing for specific forces, constantly adapting to theater fashions. In contrast to the pared-down *Taming of the Shrew*, Shakespeare and his collaborator(s) clearly had larger forces to work with in the case of the three early *Henry VI* plays, which make tough demands on a company: over 20 actors have speaking parts, and in the case of *Henry VI Part I*, there are over 25 needed.

Shakespeare is not only responding to the work of other dramatists. He is also writing with reference to his own earlier work. His *Henry VI* trilogy gave audiences a glimpse of an utterly familiar Richard of York (the man who would later become King Richard III) as "violent, ambitious, cunning and demonically isolated" (Siemon 2009, p. 44). Playgoers arriving to see the same playwright's *Richard III* were in for a surprise. Same character, same author, but now Richard is presented as a superb "performance artist," a man capable of "brazen religious hypocrisy, callous manipulation and bullying seduction" (ibid.). Even more startling, Richard is witty and compelling.

> Elizabethans thought they already knew about Richard. From the early sixteenth-century narratives of Polydore Vergil and Sir Thomas More, the malformed bogeyman, whose crimes – real, imputed, intended or imagined – included regicide, fratricide, infanticide,

uxoricide, incest and ecclesiastical corruption, had appeared not only in Shakespeare's immediate sources (Edward Hall's *Union*, Raphael Holinshed's *Chronicles* and *The Mirror for Magistrates*) but in sermons, ballads, plays, rhetorical exercises, satires, state propaganda and invective.

(Siemon 2009, p. 3)

Now they found they didn't.

Richard's acting skills are central to the play's effect, and for many this is further indication of Shakespeare's fascination with theater itself.[4] Richard himself has clearly thought about the business of acting:

> Come, cousin, canst thou quake and change thy colour,
> Murder thy breath in middle of a word,
> And then again begin, and stop again,
> As if thou were distraught and mad with terror?
>
> *(3.5.1–4)*

> Buckingham, intent on deception, insists he can
> Tut, I can counterfeit the deep tragedian,
> Speak, and look back, and pry on every side,
> Tremble and start at wagging of a straw,
> Intending deep suspicion. Ghastly looks
> Are at my service, like enforced smiles,
> And both are ready in their offices,
> At any time to grace my stratagems.
>
> *(3.5.6–11)*

On the face of it, this is a description of an actor's methods, but whether it is celebrating the skills of the "deep tragedian," mocking (other) actors for crass over-acting, or satirizing the naivety of an audience who lap this stuff up is a very Shakespearean conundrum. It works as all three, with a dose of political warning thrown in: our leaders can make us believe in, and follow, their stratagems through performance.

All Shakespeare's ambition and all his caution are present in *Richard III*. Indeed, the two are related: to get on he needed to stay on the right side of the authorities. He lived and wrote in a world in which "kings and princes sovereign" were not accountable to their subjects, including their Parliament. Monarchs owed "homage and service only unto the almighty god the king of all kings" and were therefore "not bound to yield account or render the reasons of their actions to any others but to God their only sovereign lord." This royal pronouncement referred specifically to the Crown's management of foreign policy, but sums up the concept of *arcana imperii*, matters of state that were properly secret.

Shakespeare's take on King Richard has a "more conservative political and moral purpose than its predecessors" (Potter 2012, p. 163), primarily by making Henry Tudor's accession to the throne as legitimate as possible and ensuring that all major characters recognize divine justice at work. Even when compared to his own Henry VI plays, *Richard III* is "ostentatiously Christian and moral." Shakespeare's ambition and obsequiousness may be evident (if, and it is a big if, the play was written while he was with Lord Strange's Men) in his development of Stanley's role in the play, and that of Old and Young Clifford: Ferdinando Lord Strange was the son of Margaret Clifford. Even minor characters could be used to flatter a patron.

There are glimpses of Shakespeare's working practice in *Richard III*. It seems likely not only that he went *back* to his Henry plays and revised them in order the better to set up his *Richard III*, but he would then go on to revise *Richard*, which survives in versions of different lengths. Again, Shakespeare's adaptability as a playwright, his ability to write for different audiences and venues, shines though. As does his caution. None of the surviving texts gives Richard a death speech. This is surprising since earlier in the Henry plays, almost all dying characters get some impressive last lines. Shakespeare was very good at them: everyone knew his Talbot death scene. Perhaps Richard's death speech was written and performed but removed from printed texts, out of political tact, or Crown intervention. In the charged political climate of the 1590s, it is likely that Shakespeare had one eye on the censor, or that the censor had an eye on him.

That political climate included attacks on theater itself. Nashe's commentary on *Henry VI Part I*, in which he piles on the praise for "Brave Talbot (the terror of the French)" who stands as the epitome of English manhood is, in part, a defense against these attacks. Nashe not only feels the need to defend playwriting itself as a "rare exercise of virtue," a way to reveal and give "immortality" to the brave acts of our "forefathers," but to insist that theater offers an antidote and a reproof to "these degenerate effeminate days of ours." To complicate matters, there is a moment in this defense of theater – and it needed defending in the early 1590s – which actually plays into the hands of drama's opponents. Nashe cites the audience response to Talbot's masculine heroism, pointing to "the tears of ten thousand spectators" when they behold Talbot "fresh bleeding." This is exactly the kind of womanish emotion the antitheater brigade abhorred.

Another work might have pleased them more. *The Taming of the Shrew*, probably written before 1592, probably sole-authored by William Shakespeare, has alpha-male Petruchio "taming" (and marrying) the feisty "shrew" Katherina. His methods include starving her, beating her, and making her believe she is mad.

James Joyce, for one, saw the play as autobiographical (revealing a "shrew-ridden Shakespeare"), yet another riff on the idea that William was escaping a loveless marriage to Anne. More recent critics may warn sternly against the biographical turn (the question of Shakespeare's own marriage "has little importance when it comes to interpreting the plays" [Garber 2004, p. 71]), but cannot quite get past the play's misogyny, explicating it, and implicitly forgiving its creator, by reassuring us that everyone was misogynist then. William, as an adult man, embodied patriarchal authority – although we have no idea how he experienced that authority, or its limits as son, brother, husband, and father. But in this early play, he depicts the impact of patriarchy, understood as a way of organizing life (whether political, religious, social, or personal) so that men have power over women, a way of life justified by the Bible. Still, in order to distract us from the patriarchy in action, and to prevent us mapping the play's misogyny onto its author, critics often reassure us that Shakespeare's real interest is not the tormenting and taming of Katherina but the transformational power of theater, now his new world.

The drunken tinker Sly, who appears at the beginning of the play and is convinced by actors that he is a lord (but then disappears from the play's end, at least in the text that survives) stands as a complex cipher for the playwright himself: "Sly's self-portrait is at once a proclamation of Shakespearean origins and an exemplification of the process through metamorphosis through role-playing that is the essence of theatre" (Bate 2008, p. 44).[5] Sly is preoccupied with old-style theater ("a comonty [comedy?] a Christmas gambold [gambol, lively merrymaking and leaping] or a tumbling trick"), and acts as an ironic preface to up-and-coming William Shakespeare's *new* way of writing. The country boy has come to the city and has something to say. That the something is an exercise in misogyny is disconcerting to some. Less contentiously, the prevalence of collaboration and multiple versions of similar plays serve to question any uncomplicated sense of these years as a moment of "authorial arrival" for Shakespeare.

In the midst of the confusion about what he wrote and when (not to mention for whom, and let alone what the words tell us about the man), one small piece of evidence appears: the first mention of William Shakespeare as a playwright. Fittingly, in this world of imitation and response, it comes in the form of a parody.[6] In his *Groatsworth of Wit* of 1592, Robert Greene parodies a line from *Henry VI Part III* ("O, tiger's heart wrapped in a woman's hide") reworking it as "Tiger's heart wrapped in a player's hide" as part of his attack on the "up-start Crow, beautified with our feathers, that with his Tiger's heart wrapped in a Player's hide, supposes he is as well able to bombast out a blank verse as the best of you: and being an absolute *Johannes fac totum* [Jack of all trades], is in his own conceit the only Shake-scene in a country."

Greene, referring to Aesop's fable of the crow which thought itself beautiful when it wore some peacock's feathers, attacks Shakespeare for stealing "our feathers" (which is a bit rich, since Greene – and pretty much every other writer – did exactly the same thing), and for his "bombast" both as a writer and as a man. It's a class-based attack as much as anything else, seeking to distinguish upstart Shakespeare from the university-educated playwrights. As Bart van Es (2013, p. 55) has argued, the comment is "designed, desperately, to resist" the narrowing of the gap between the two groups. In sharp contrast, Jonathan Bate has Shakespeare breaking the mould. Whilst his predecessors married for money or were bachelors, Shakespeare is the only major writer who married before "reaching his legal majority," making him "emphatically unlike the university-educated men, who lived from hand to mouth, got into trouble with the authorities, and died young" (Bate 2008, p. 171). One of the crowd or someone already standing apart from (maybe even above) his contemporaries?

In a crowded field of aspiring Marlowes, the "upstart crow" was making his presence known, but he needed to make some choices. His next step suggests he was actively exploring a new direction as a writer. *Venus and Adonis*, Shakespeare's first volume of poetry and the first work to carry his name, was registered for publication on 18 April 1593. The printer was Richard Field, from Stratford-upon-Avon, and he did a fine job. Both *Venus and Adonis* and the follow-up volume of poetry from Shakespeare, *The Rape of Lucrece*, are "well printed, elegant little books" designed, in both senses of the word, for well-educated readers familiar with both the Latin and English classics, "witty, inventive and stylish" as well as "daring, erotically explicit, even amoral" (Orgel 2007, p. 138). *Venus and Adonis* is in part yet another engagement with the work of Christopher Marlowe, specifically the latter's foray into the erotic epyllion, *Hero and Leander*, and reflects both writers' fascination with Ovid (the sexiest of writers) and with Virgil, whose controversial second eclogue explored the love of men for boys. The very physical format of *Venus and Adonis* mimicked recent editions of Ovid; a quotation from the Roman poet dismissed the "common herd" on the title page; and inside, Shakespeare offered his poem to a nobleman, Henry Wriothesley, Third Earl of Southampton.

For many years, it was asserted that Shakespeare only wrote poetry when he was prevented by plague from working in the theater. The quest for Southampton's patronage becomes a Plan B. The situation may have been precisely the opposite way round. Shakespeare's move into printed poetry carrying his name could have been, in part, a response to one of the problems of playwriting: like "many grammar school men who came into the theatrical profession," he had "little control over the dramatic fortunes" of his output (Van Es 2013, p. 54). He did not own his plays, he received no ongoing income from his plays, he was merely the employee of the acting company which controlled his work. And in 1593, Shakespeare was by no means established as a playwright. We have inflated the significance of Greene's attack, perhaps because we are so relieved to find even a shred of evidence of Shakespeare the playwright. By producing a polished work, in a carefully printed edition, dedicated to a well-placed patron, Shakespeare was keeping his options open, perhaps even looking for an escape from playwriting and a life in the literary service of a nobleman.

For aristocratic literary patronage in England was perhaps the most significant mechanism by which a writer could survive as a writer if he (or very occasionally she) did not belong to the leisured classes. The benefits to the author were many and various: money, obviously, but also bed and board in the noble's home, and, in some cases, access to valuable libraries or resources. Some patrons provided regular employment, as tutors for example. Almost all offered some form of protection. This was needed. Writers could and did get into trouble with the authorities, and a well-placed patron could save, quite literally, the writer's skin. Put simply, this is "the way ambitious Elizabethan poets got on in the world" (Van Es 2013, p. 138). *Venus and Adonis* reveals "Shakespeare's literary and social aspirations" at every turn.

He tapped into the favored Petrarchan discourse of the time, one ideally suited to explore the frustrations of the male courtier in a female monarchy, frustrations which mirrored those of the devoted Petrarchan lover pursuing an unattainable mistress. That frustration shaded into satire of the whole charade, subtle and not-so-subtle critiques of the chaste goddess queen on the English throne. Shakespeare was no courtier, although he may have aspired to be one, but his Queen of Love in *Venus and Adonis* is hardly venerated: "the love-sick queen began to sweat" is a typically anti-Petrarchan moment, Shakespeare running with the aspiring poets of his time.

In contrast to the fashionably daring content of the poem it precedes, Shakespeare's dedication to the Earl of Southampton is somewhat dull. He offers the earl a production of his "idle hours" (is Shakespeare representing himself as a member of the leisured classes?) and, significantly, a second work, a "graver labour," already touting for patronage for his next volume of poetry, *The Rape of Lucrece*. What is not mentioned is playwriting. Instead, *Venus and Adonis* is presented as "the first heir of my invention," thus erasing William Shakespeare's life as an actor and playwright.

By one measure, *Venus and Adonis* was phenomenally successful, with 14 editions before 1636, 10 of which appeared during Shakespeare's lifetime. The poem was widely quoted in manuscript commonplace books and printed anthologies, and the publication of Shakespeare's follow-up, *The Rape of Lucrece*, coincided with the second edition of *Venus* with good commercial reason. Registered for publication on 9 May 1594, *Lucrece* was calculated to "feed the Renaissance erotic, and sadistic, imagination" (Orgel 2007, p. 139). If there had been a trace of misogynistic satire of Elizabeth, queen of England, in Shakespeare's representation of the sweating, rejected Venus, Queen of Love, then *Lucrece* went further, touching on very real political concerns about the future of the English monarchy given the lack of an heir. Lucrece's suicide led directly to the exile of the Roman royal family and the creation of the Roman Republic. Nonconsensual sex is linked to the establishment of a tyrannical regime, with Emperor Tarquin's violation of his friend's wife not only damaging her but also revealing him unfit to govern the state.

Shakespeare's readers were fully conscious of the political implications of Lucrece's story. The names alone conjured inflammatory resemblances with the present day: if "the chaste Lucrece had come to stand as a byword for marital fidelity, Tarquin's name evoked the violent abuse of power" (Belsey 2007, p. 90). Anyone who read *Lucrece* in this context "would have taken the author for a political radical" (Potter 2012, p. 158). It was his edgiest work yet.

The publication of *Venus and Adonis* brought Shakespeare renown (and the opportunity to write the more politically provocative *Lucrece*), but did it gain him a lasting, or even a temporary, aristocratic patron? It seems not. The poem may be so "perfectly fitted" to its dedicatee that it seems its writer chose "the patron before the subject," but Shakespeare's choice of Southampton was at best surprising and at worst misguided (Potter 2012, p. 109). A more obvious choice would have been Ferdinando, Lord Strange, "both literary patron of the hour and likely patron of Shakespeare's playing company." Southampton was uncharted territory. Although the earl would go on to receive some 20 outright dedications, 8 dedicatory epistles, and 3 "presentations," prior to 1593 "only one book had been dedicated exclusively to him" (Nelson 2015, p. 279) and that one was Shakespeare's *Venus and Adonis*, the perfect poem to offer to beautiful, young Southampton, a man whose portrait was so androgynous that it was thought to be of a woman until 2002; who was rumored to prefer men to women; and who refused to marry Elizabeth de Vere. No wonder that Adonis, in the hands of Shakespeare, becomes a reluctant boy, completely (and comically) lacking all interest in the advances of Venus, the goddess of Love. This huge, and hugely comic, fail for heterosexual desire, coupled with the celebration of the young male body, was ideally pitched to Southampton as potential patron.

Whether he was more than that to Shakespeare is another question. That the rumors about Southampton's sex life came from an informer, who reported that the earl lay with a man in his tent where he would "coll [i.e. embrace] and hug him in his arms and play wantonly with him," is a reminder that male–male sexual relations were at best dangerous, at worst deadly, in a society which understood "sodomy" as both a sin and a capital crime. It may well be that socially unequal homosexual relationships were "understood, recognised and practiced" (Nelson 2015, pp. 286–287), but this fails to acknowledge the appalling punishments meted out to those who did not have the protection of rank, and even to some who did.

"Did Southampton 'play wantonly' with Shakespeare?" asks Nelson, and he does not quite answer no. Indeed, he becomes almost sentimental about a relationship that we are unsure ever existed: "the relationship would have been more balanced, and thus closer to a modern sense of a companionate partnership. Yes, Southampton was above the poet in social status, and considerably younger; but Shakespeare was a rock-star modern poet capable of setting young male hearts aflutter" (Nelson 2015, p. 287). It's a nice thought, if grounded on the assumption that Shakespeare was unable to find love and lust with his wife. In sharp contrast, there are those who are determined to keep both Southampton and Shakespeare firmly heterosexual, deeming as "unreliable" the informer witness to Southampton's homosexuality, and pointing to the earl's happy marriage, his fatherhood, and (the third badge of heterosexuality) his future achievements as a successful military leader (Potter 2012, p. 110).

Whatever the story these two poems tell us about Shakespeare and Southampton, there is one thing that is clear. Shakespeare chose not to pursue poetry. For a time, he had oscillated, as many did, "between the two great spheres of literary employment: print and court patronage on the one hand and the stage on the other. He could, as Ben Jonson would do after a short spell of employment as a hired actor, strive primarily for independence as a writer. This was the conventional course amongst his contemporaries, albeit one pursued with mixed success" (Van Es 2013, p. 17). But if through 1594 he was indeed engaged with drama *and* poetry (perhaps, as some argue, writing *Titus Andronicus* alongside *Lucrece*, both works drawing on Ovid's story of Philomela), there were to be no more exquisite volumes of verse after that year.[7]

This may well represent a disappointment for Shakespeare since he represents the patronage relationship as successful and ongoing in the dedication to *Lucrece*: "What I have done is yours, what I have to do is yours: being part in all I have, devoted yours." The word "love" is used, and Shakespeare writes of a "warrant" received from his patron, suggesting that *Venus and Adonis* had attracted both personal recognition and a substantial gratuity (Nelson 2015, p. 280). For Jonathan Bate (2008, p. 12), the

> association with Southampton had three key consequences. It transformed Shakespeare from jobbing playwright to courtly poet, marked him out as the crossover man who could appeal equally to penny-paying groundlings and powerful courtiers or even the queen herself. Politically, it brought

him into the orbit of the Earl of Essex, to whom young Southampton was devoted. This would have potentially dangerous consequences a few years later. And, intellectually, it introduced him to the work of the Anglo-Italian man of letters John Florio, Southampton's tutor, through whom he was exposed to Italianate culture, and, later, the essays of Michel de Montaigne, whose subtle, sympathetic mind was perfectly attuned to his own.

This is a remarkable and attractive list of benefits, although there is no evidence for any of them. Indeed, it is so seductive, that Lois Potter (2012, p. 123) spends a paragraph on the books Shakespeare might have read in the library of Southampton House. Samuel Schoenbaum (1991, p. 33) remains skeptical: "Had the poet been welcomed into the Southampton circle? A pleasant aristocratic thought."

Far from ongoing, *Lucrece* marked the end of the relationship. One reason was surely the inconvenient truth of the earl's financial situation when he came of age. Shakespeare may not have been looking ahead. It was common knowledge that when the earl turned 21 (in October 1594) he would be unable to escape paying a fine for his refusal to marry Elizabeth de Vere, and he would also be liable for the payments connected with coming of age. There was no money left over for supporting aspiring poets.

Nevertheless, a single failure whether of poem or patron didn't usually deter writers from trying again. Shakespeare did not do so, which may mean that he actively wanted to be a playwright, and a particular kind of playwright. Firstly, he would channel his poetry into drama: the plays of the mid-1590s are filled with verse. Secondly, he not only stepped off the path to writerly seclusion at a great house but he also chose not to follow his near-contemporary Ben Jonson who wrote masques and entertainments for the nobility and worked with the fashionable children's companies, established in the mid-1570s. Instead, William Shakespeare worked in and for the public playhouses. Others see Shakespeare stumbling into playwriting, a man torn between his "conservative heritage" and his ambition to "make his way as a new dramatist" (Bate 2008, p. 75). I see him choosing theater.

When Shakespeare wrote the dedication to *Lucrece* he was still able to declare "What I have done is yours, what I have to do is yours, being part in all I have, devoted yours" (Burrow 2002, Dedication, ll. 8–9). By the middle of that year the author was "part" of another body: the shared entity of the Lord Chamberlain's Men. Thereafter he would be the "devoted servant" of his fellow sharers, and their patron, the Lord Chamberlain. He would not present himself to the world in the conventional form of the dedications of *Venus* and *Lucrece* again. After 1594 Shakespeare's source of income would be quite different (and, it would soon prove, more reliable) than fees for play texts and the gifts of dedicatees (Van Es 2013, p. 76).

More reliable, first because in June 1594, the plague finally eased: "In the name of God, Amen. Beginning at Newington my Lord Admiral's Men & my Lord Chamberlain's Men. As followeth" wrote Philip Henslowe in his diary, with obvious relief (Henslow and Foakes 2002, p. 21). The players were back. In one heady week at the beginning of the month the two major London companies gave 10 performances, possibly even combining forces, at the Newington Butts playhouse, less successful than the Theatre "by reason of the tediousness of the way" (Chambers 1923, Volume 2, p. 405), since it was one long, muddy mile from London Bridge, but in the immediate aftermath of plague a welcome distance from the City. There were performances of the *Jew of Malta* (associated with Admiral's Men) and *Titus* (associated with the Chamberlain's), as well as *Hamlet* and *The Taming of a Shrew* (cousins to Shakespeare's plays with similar or identical titles.) By mid-June it was business as usual, with the Admiral's Men back in the Rose, and the Chamberlain's Men in the Theatre, ushering "a season of unprecedented stability" that ran until March 1595 (Rutter 1999, p. 84). If indeed Shakespeare did "stumble into his profession of full-time play-maker" he did so at an ideal moment (Bate 2008, p. 166).

More reliable because, in the year he turned 30, William Shakespeare became a sharer in the Lord Chamberlain's Men. It is unclear exactly what he had to do to gain this position – perhaps offer his existing plays and future rights, give up his future earnings as an actor, or provide a lump-sum investment. Whatever the financial arrangement, by the end of 1594 he was the inhouse playwright for a settled (or relatively settled) group of actors.[8] For Bart van Es (2013, p. 2), this, rather than his background, is what makes Shakespeare unusual: 23 years after the construction of the Theatre he would "come to own a portion of the very timbers that James Burbage had erected in 1576." For Jonathan Bate (2008, p. 172), this is what made Shakespeare wealthy: his "fortune was made not by literary innovation but by a business decision."

And business was good. In 1594, it has been estimated that the Lord Chamberlain's Men and the Lord Admiral's Men, its leading competitor, were visited approximately 15 000 times each week, during a period when London had 200 000 inhabitants. Competition nevertheless remained fierce and companies' personnel fluid. Shakespeare may have been experiencing unprecedented stability in his working life, but the theater world remained a precarious one. The Admiral's and Chamberlain's Men were to dominate the Christmas Revels at court of 1594, but they did not have a duopoly in the commercial world of the public theaters.[9] There, Pembroke's Men served as a healthy competition, staging a repertory that included plays both by the Chamberlain's Men's increasingly well-known playwright, Shakespeare, and by the already established Marlowe. Whether Shakespeare brought the performing rights of his early plays with him to the Chamberlain's Men is yet another subject of scholarly contention.

The theater world did not change overnight and Shakespeare's company did not only perform new plays by their sharer dramatist. Indeed, they did not only perform new plays. Shakespeare dusted down his own *Comedy of Errors*, written in the early 1590s, and revised it for the Christmas season of 1594. It was an old-fashioned play to choose, including passages of "fourteeners" (the 14-syllable lines which had once been the stuff of drama, before the arrival of iambic pentameter), and some jokes about the French wars which were well past their sell-by date. But the play requires far fewer actors than the histories he had been writing, and suggests the regular need for adaptable, portable plays which could be performed in multiple venues, not just the court or the public playhouses. The play was performed on 28 December 1594, the Feast of the Holy Innocents, in the hall of Gray's Inn in Holborn.[10] This evening of elite entertainment descended into chaos, in part because of overcrowding which led to scuffles. The chaos prompted someone to write about the players, a rare occurrence. There was "dancing and revelling with gentlewomen, and after such sports, a Comedy of Errors (like to Plautus his Menechmus) was played by the players. So that night was begun, and continued to the end, in nothing but confusion and errors, whereupon, it was ever after called, The Night of Errors" (quoted by Dutton 2018, p. 132). Despite all this, suggests Potter (2012, p. 155), there were "no hard feelings after the performance, since many of Shakespeare's other plays had connections with the Inns."

Old-fashioned in style it might have been, but the plotting in *The Comedy of Errors* is sophisticated, thanks in no small part to Shakespeare's turn to the classical playwright Plautus as a model. The play would encourage a response from up-and-coming dramatist, Ben Jonson, his own Plautus-based comedy *The Case Is Altered*. As usual, there is debate about authorship and dating, but the differences between the two dramatists is evident even in these early works. Jonson is far more satirical, formally far more structured. Shakespeare's formal control is far more loose, and his plots are much more romantic. With fewer characters, Shakespeare can explore (at least a bit) the emotional implications of his romantic plots. Jonson has his Rachel attract numerous suitors and yet only speaks 37 lines, leading Riggs (2015, pp. 186–187) to wonder what makes her so attractive. There is a one-word, and very Jonsonian answer: money.

Jonson would emerge as Shakespeare's new rival, replacing Christopher Marlowe, murdered on 30 May 1593, the year before the latter became a sharer in the Chamberlain's Men.[11] "Had Shakespeare died in 1593 along with Christopher Marlowe the two men would have looked much more alike as writers – their output split between dramatic writing, verse history, and epyllion; their compositional habits structurally in line with those of other professional dramatists" (Van Es 2013, p. 74). Both had worked with other writers, both had output owned by a diverse group of acting companies, both "in all likelihood wrote plays with the lead actor Edward Alleyn in mind" (ibid., p. 75). But, as Van Es concludes, neither Shakespeare nor Marlowe had appeared by name in any theatrical document. It rather begs the question: if William rather than Kit had been stabbed in that tavern in Deptford, would we even know the name of Shakespeare?

Now in 1594, alive and (occasionally) kicking, sharer Shakespeare had "long-term dramatic ownership of his drama. Not only did he now play a deter-mining role in first performance, his plays would take a permanent and central place in the company's repertory and would remain alive to him over the decades" (Van Es 2013, p. 110). Being able to write for the same theater and for the same group of players allowed Shakespeare to develop his particular brand of "relational drama" (Dutton 2018, p. 102; Van Es 2013, p. 76). As writer, reviser, and performer he was necessarily engaged with more than one work at any one time, and not always looking forward. The Chamberlain's Men's rep-ertory was "non-linear in its development" and "open to the introduction of older works" (as was likely the case with *A Comedy of Errors*) meaning that Shakespeare was "involved in a productive dialectical relationship with his own earlier efforts" (Syme 2012, p. 288). Recycling or reviving older works offered "both new opportunities and new challenges – in Shakespeare's case, the challenge of coming face to face with an earlier version of himself" (ibid.). No wonder his works bounce off each other.

His plays also continued to bounce off the work of his fellow dramatists, not least Ben Jonson. Six years' William's junior, Ben was similar to him in background: both sons of tradesmen, both with a good classical education, both married young, and both left their marital households for long periods. More than that, both men had made the move from acting to actor-playwright. But in 1594, Jonson was just starting out, and hardly known. Shakespeare on the other hand was established and, as far as it was possible in these volatile times, in control of his own output.

Chapter Three

Shoreditch, a cheap, disreputable neighborhood, conveniently situated for those dealing in working in the literary and sex industries: Shakespeare's headquarters as the inhouse playwright for the Chamberlain's Men. The company was based at the Theatre, the playhouse built nearly 20 years earlier by James Burbage, father of the Chamberlain's Men's leading actor, Richard. Shakespeare "was expected to keep turning out the box-office successes – the kind of plays that could be recycled time after time – for which he already had a track record" (Dutton 2018, p. 101). He may have been well-established as a playwright but still his name had only appeared in print as a poet, the author of *Venus and Adonis*, and, fleetingly, in the archive as an actor: William Shakespeare's name is in the cast list for Ben Jonson's *Every Man in His Humour*.

Shakespeare's output in the years immediately prior to his becoming a sharer in the Chamberlain's Men (following Wells and Taylor's datings of the plays) consisted of *Titus Andronicus, Richard III, Venus and Adonis, The Rape of Lucrece*, and *The Comedy of Errors*. Those who want to see a steady (or indeed mercurial) ascent to greatness, epitomized by the psychological and dramatic complexity of the plays he would write only a few years later, will be disappointed to see that, instead, Shakespeare appears drawn towards more erudite, contrived work. Technically virtuosic, with many, many nods to classical literature, the characterization – and the interplay between characters – remains unsubtle. The balance of power between speakers is "generally predictable" (Van Es 2013, p. 63), and characters can be disconcertingly interchangeable. It seems the best was yet to come, although equally obviously, whatever he was doing was good enough for the Chamberlain's Men to bring him in.

If Shakespeare the playwright/poet is erudite, artificial – and yet still exceptional - what of Shakespeare the man? He is, according to his most popular recent biographer, in London, enjoying a "separate and secluded private life," in which he found love, "intimacy and lust," "outside of the marriage bond," escaping a marriage of "bitterness, sourness and cynicism" (Greenblatt 2004,

The Life of the Author: William Shakespeare, First Edition. Anna Beer.

pp. 142–144). Perhaps. Putting aside the questionable notion of a "private life" in late Elizabethan England, it is easy to see how the nature of the archive encourages this kind of speculation. If we had just one letter from William to his wife of 10 years, Anne, such as that which survives from actor Edward Alleyn to his "good sweet mouse" (Henslowe and Foakes 2002, pp. 276–277). full of news of plague, of clothes, gardens, and affection, we would make some very different assumptions about the Shakespeares' marriage. But there is silence.

And so we turn to the plays. It may be significant that Shakespeare's early works feature over-mighty, transgressive wives who require disciplining by strong men. In *Henry VI Part II*, Gloucester moves from being dangerously in thrall to his wife, Eleanor, to asserting his proper masculine authority when he disowns her as a traitor. (Shakespeare changes his historical source to make Eleanor more treacherous.) I am sure it is significant that the question "Art thou a man?" is asked in all sorts of ways by Shakespeare's characters: these are plays preoccupied with anxiety about the answer. This particular formulation of the question comes from his early tragedy, *Romeo and Juliet* (1594–1595), in which Shakespeare makes his hero self-indulgently emotional, traumatized by his fear that he has killed his friend Tybalt. Romeo offers to stab himself. The Nurse snatches the dagger away, and then the young man is lectured by wise old Friar Lawrence:

> Hold thy desperate hand!
> Art thou a man? Thy form cries out thou art;
> Thy tears are womanish, thy wild acts denote
> The unreasonable fury of a beast.
> Unseemly woman in a seeming man,
> And ill-beseeming beast in seeming both,
> Thou has amazed me. By my holy order,
> I thought thy disposition better tempered.
>
> *(3.3.107–115)*

Here the Friar appeals to a familiar trope, wishing that Romeo's disposition be better "tempered." But the criticism that stings is that Romeo is being "womanish," an "unseemly woman in a seeming man." To be womanish is to be weak and Shakespeare will show again and again what happens when a man relinquishes his God-given dominance: the more-or-less monstrous masculine woman takes over.

The depiction of punished and tamed wives of the early plays is fascinatingly complicated by the character of Adriana in *A Comedy of Errors*. She is a deeply unhappy wife who articulates her despair at being confined to her house, waiting for a kind look from her husband, conscious all the time that she is aging. Her own sister sees her complaints as driven by jealousy, whilst

Adriana's husband calls her "shrewish" (3.1.2). The play as a whole seems to dismiss Adriana's anger and unhappiness. There is no condemnation offered when her husband, locked out of his own house through a misunderstanding, heads straight off to spend time with another woman, "the courtesan."

> I know a wench of excellent discourse,
> Pretty and witty; wild and yet, too, gentle;
> There will we dine. This woman that I mean,
> My wife (but I protest, without desert)
> Hath oftentimes upbraided me withal;
> To her will we to dinner.
> *(3.1.109–114)*

Luciana does challenge Antipholus's behavior, not on the grounds of infidelity (which is acceptable so long as it is "by stealth" [3.2.7]), but because he treats his wife unkindly when he is with her, by revealing in his "looks" that he is having sex elsewhere.

> 'Tis double wrong to truant with your bed,
> And let her read it in thy looks at board;
> Shame hath a bastard fame, well managed;
> Ill deeds is doubled with an evil word.
> Alas, poor women, make us but believe
> (Being compact of credit) that you love us;
> Though others have the arm, show us the sleeve;
> We in your motion turn, and you may move us.
> *(3.2.17–24)*

In a play full of men's banter about women's bodies ("No longer from head to foot than from hip to hip; she is spherical, like a globe; I could find out countries in her" [3.2.111–113]), banter which is often tinged with violence, Luciana does not ask that men are faithful, only that they sustain a fiction of respect in the marital home. It is a pretty low bar for a successful marriage but whether it tells us anything about William's relationship with Anne is impossible to say.

Back in Stratford, Anne and the couple's three children were still living with William's parents in Henley Street. He had not (yet) bought a house for his family, and in Stratford times were hard: first crop failures, and then a catastrophic fire which destroyed 200 houses in September 1594. In London, the news was better. The Chamberlain's Men had been chosen, after years of dominance by the Queen's Men and Strange's Men, to perform at court over the Christmas season. Shakespeare was making good money as a sharer, each court performance earning the sharers 10 pounds.

The next year brought another fire in Stratford, another bad harvest, and even bread and ale were in short supply. Given the nature and workings of family life in this era, it is unlikely that William Shakespeare remained detached from the problems besetting his home town, and which presumably threatened his family, although we don't know whether or how often he returned home. Jonathan Bate believes he did so, but in his literary imagination: the so-called Athenian wood in *A Midsummer Night's Dream* "is peopled by very English fairies and artisans," just as the French forest of Ardennes will be merged with the Warwickshire forest of Arden in *As You Like It*, a few years later. Both are examples of "Shakespeare's tendency to swerve back to his point of origin" (Bate 2008, p. 38), which is not quite the same thing as saying he loved and spent time with his wife and children.

Shakespeare's engagement with imaginative worlds far *from* his point of origin is equally evident in these years, whether understood as the journeys he took in his own reading (for *Romeo and Juliet*, Shakespeare worked from a 1562 English translation of a French version of an Italian story) or the journeys on which he took his audiences in his plays. To travel to the playhouses, whether by foot, horse, boat, or later coach, was to leave the everyday world behind. It was a form of travel. "It was at the theatre," the Swiss tourist Thomas Platter observed, that "the English pass their time, learning at the play what is happening abroad" (Platter 1937, p. 170). Such virtual travel in the realm of comedy was potentially limitless, unbound by time or place, with audiences finding themselves in ancient Ephesus or Athens, or contemporary Padua or Verona. In only one comedy, *The Merry Wives of Windsor*, did Shakespeare offer his audience a slice of English life.

In the year 1595, which brought a new Lord Chamberlain, Henry Carey, Lord Hunsdon (who succeeded his own son-in-law, Lord Howard of Effingham, who in turn had been made Lord Admiral – because this is how the world works), Shakespeare took his London audiences to Italy: *Two Gentlemen of Verona* centers on the erotically charged friendship between the two gentlemen and engages yet again with Ovidian metamorphosis. The fascination continued in *A Midsummer Night's Dream* from the same year – Greece the destination, this time - a play equally preoccupied with magic, transformation, and unnatural love(s).

Shakespeare had already played complicated gender games in *The Two Gentlemen of Verona*. Playgoers had seen an adolescent male acting a woman who pretends to be a boy. Shakespeare even has his characters Julia and Lucetta discuss the mechanics of cross-dressing, while later in the play Julia (in her boy's clothes) will recall how "at Pentecost" when "all our pageants of delight were played"

> Our youth got me to play the woman's part,
> And I was trimmed in Madam Julia's gown,

Which served me as fit, by all men's judgements,
As if the garment had been made for me;
Therefore I know she is about my height.
And at that time I made her weep a-good.

(4.4.158–163)

Garber (2004, p. 7) argues that Shakespeare's acknowledgment of the fact that boys played women allowed "both maleness and femaleness to be bodied forth in performance." This duality gives cross-dressing women characters such as Rosalind, Portia, Viola, and Imogen "liveliness and initiative" (ibid.). That may be an accurate assessment of those four characters, but on the Elizabethan stage it was maleness that was actually being *bodied*, whilst femaleness (or rather the idea of woman or femininity) was always and ever being performed. Nevertheless, cross-dressing touched raw nerves in many of Shakespeare's contemporaries, and became central to the culture wars between those hostile to theater and its defenders. The playhouses' position on the margins of city life, literally in the "liberties" in some cases, offered freedoms that were "at once moral, ideological, and topological – a freedom to experiment with a wide range of available ideological perspectives and to realize, in dramatic form, the cultural contradictions of its age" (Mullaney 1988, pp. ix–x). If the intention had been to keep the playhouses out of the city proper in order to discourage theatergoing, it appears to have backfired. Simply heading out of the city became an escape from everyday life and regulations, regardless of what foreign evils were being staged. Worse still, at some point in the 1590s it became normal for plays in public playhouses to start at 2 pm, clashing with the time for Evensong. Church or playhouse? It was a tough one for a Londoner's conscience.

This liberty of the liberties was just one of the reasons public theater was condemned. The antitheater lobby were driven by anxieties surrounding sex and gender roles, and specifically the specter of men turning into women. This was not simply a matter of cross-dressing. As Shakespeare dramatized, over and over again, men were humiliated and emasculated, transformed, by the experience of romantic love for a woman: Valentine in *Two Gentlemen* is mocked for being "metamorphosed with a mistress" (2.1.28). His servant Speed can now "hardly think" him his master (2.1.29). Cross-dressing didn't help, although the effect on the boy actors of wearing women's clothes was not as insidious as what might happen to the audience.

In response to these fears, the playwright Thomas Heywood insisted that audiences knew exactly where the boundary between boy actor and woman's part lay. The boy merely represented "such a lady, at such a time appointed." Heywood defends cross-dressing by insisting that any challenge to convention ceases when the play ends (Heywood 1612). Shakespeare's plays, however, often do quite the opposite, the endings of *Twelfth Night* and *As You Like It* being cases in point.

Is Shakespeare's interest in at least the performance of gender, perhaps even gender fluidity, rooted in the playwright's lived experience? Yet another question that we cannot answer. It is slightly less speculative to see the preoccupation as stemming from William's life as a dramatist in daily engagement with the power of theater to effect transformation and perception. These concerns are certainly to the fore in two of his works from this time which include a play within a play. *Love's Labour's Lost* has a scene in which a bunch of young, arrogant noblemen do their best to put off a group of amateur actors. They succeed, putting more than one "out of his part" (5.2.336). *A Midsummer Night's Dream* is rightly famous for its intensely funny (and strangely touching) rustic Mechanicals:

> Some man or other must present Wall; and let him have some plaster, or some loam, or some rough-cast about him to signify Wall; or let him hold his fingers thus, and through that cranny shall Pyramus and Thisbe whisper.
>
> *(3.1.52–55)*

In yet another metatheatrical moment, Shakespeare's choice of the star-crossed lovers Pyramus and Thisbe is not just any play-within-a-play: it directly echoes (or advertises) Shakespeare's own *Romeo and Juliet*. On a more practical level, these plays-within-plays are evidence, if we needed it, that Shakespeare was close to "the mechanics of a play's transfer to the stage" (Van Es 2013, p. 81), a man profoundly engaged, practically and creatively, with the mechanics and potentiality of performance. This level of control and involvement was new, special, and – from the evidence of Shakespeare's preoccupation with the relationships within companies of actors – exciting to the playwright.

Now that Shakespeare was writing for a more stable group of actors, he could tailor parts to showcase particular individuals. For Will Kemp, the Clown, he adds opportunities for his trademark "jigs" (which were not just dances, but songs, often bawdy). Knowing his leading actor's ability to handle long speeches, Shakespeare can create his wordiest king, Richard II.[1] More words, more psychological depth, more interaction between characters, what Van Es calls "relational drama," can be attributed to the remarkable stability of the Chamberlain's Men and Shakespeare's control over the casting of his plays. Unique amongst his contemporaries, Shakespeare even occasionally slipped the performers' names into his papers as he worked. Kemp's name is in the second quarto of *Romeo and Juliet*: he played Peter. All this suggests a tight-knit group, learning from each other. Kemp, clown and acrobat, musician and dancer, big earner, experienced European traveler, might even have been Shakespeare's source for the knowledge he displays in his plays of a world beyond England.

This picture of William Shakespeare, the literary dramatist in a stable company, confidently performing at and writing for multiple venues, including the court, does not take into account that theater remained an always precarious, sometimes dangerous, business – particularly if playwrights touched on topical issues. The various arguments advanced as to the date of composition of *A Midsummer Night's Dream* all have one thing in common: that Shakespeare is alert to a variety of social and political and cultural events around him.[2]

Take your pick from the following theories. Rustic Bottom, planning his performance for Theseus and Hippolyta and ruling out bringing in "a lion among ladies" (3.1.29) is an allusion to a court entertainment for the christening of Prince Henry, the son of King James VI in faraway Scotland in 1594. Therefore, Shakespeare is keeping up to date with theatricals in the Scottish court, perhaps with an eye on the regime change that will surely come when Elizabeth I dies. Or, the mention of an Indian king refers to the American Indian prince brought back to England by Sir Walter Ralegh from his voyage in search of the gold of El Dorado in 1595 (and whose best-selling account of that voyage was published the following year). Here, Shakespeare is tracking the adventures of Elizabethan England's most fascinating courtier. Or perhaps, Ralegh's unmarried (and never to be married) queen is present in Oberon's description of "a fair vestal throned in the west," whose "chaste beams" have quenched Cupid's fiery arrows (2.1.158, 162). Here, Shakespeare appears to shoehorn praise of Elizabeth's vestal chastity into what is, in essence, a marriage play, possibly one written for a specific wedding.[3] Maybe Shakespeare was simply interested in the weather: *Midsummer Night's Dream* references bad harvests, linking it to the year 1594. From flattering references to the monarchs of Scotland and England to an awareness of the weather, Shakespeare is undoubtedly engaged with the world outside the theater, but he is hardly playing with topical fire in these (suggested) allusions.

Then again, *A Midsummer Night's Dream* is a fantastical comedy. What of history? There is not as much distance between the two genres as we might think, given the importance of patrilineal inheritance and patriarchal control to the plots of both comedy and history. In an era in which the analogy between monarch and parent was a commonplace (Elizabeth was a mother to her nation, King James her successor would be its father), the succession of parents and children had deep metaphorical links with political structures. In his histories,

> Shakespeare quite naturally and conventionally treats political and familial issues as twins: the second tetralogy is as plainly organized in terms of fathers and sons as it is in terms of usurpation, rebellion, and legitimate succession. *King John* also takes up these forms of thought,

but the presence of three mothers – Eleanor, Lady Faulconbridge, Constance – and of a peculiarly freakish "son" – the Bastard – makes the play unique among the histories.

(Braunmuller 1998, p. 61)

History, nevertheless, was more dangerous territory than comedy, the more so if the subject was the deposition and death of a divinely appointed king of England. The textual history of Shakespeare's *Richard II* offers a glimpse of those dangers. The play was entered in the Stationers' Register in late August 1597, the year of the first edition. The next edition, a shorter version, had Shakespeare's name on it. Then, in 1608, well over a decade after the play's first performance, a longer version was published. This "later, longer version features the on-stage deposition of King Richard, a potentially controversial scene. The absence of 'the deposition scene' in the first three quarto editions has led critics to debate the possible censorship and revision of Shakespeare's plays" (Jacquez 2017). Was the deposition of King Richard performed – but not printed - during Elizabeth's reign? Or did Shakespeare add the scene when it was safe to do so, after the queen's death?

This may all sound like academic hair-splitting of the driest kind but the presence or absence of a potentially inflammatory historical scene (both in the text and in performance) could have very real consequences for playwrights and actors in the mid-1590s. The past could incite action in the present, as illustrated notoriously by the Earl of Essex's fascination with the deposition of English kings, specifically Richard II in the run up to his own attempt to depose an English queen, Elizabeth.

Essex was far from alone in linking the two monarchs. (The Jesuit Robert Parsons had used Ricardian history to justify his treasonous challenge to Protestant Queen Elizabeth.) It had been a common comparison from the late 1570s onwards, to the extent that the queen herself (allegedly) rebuked a courtier for his critique of Richard, saying "I am Richard II, know ye not that?" Whether Elizabeth actually said those words is debatable, but the conflation of past and present is utterly of its time. Since the accepted aim of all history was to look back in order to apply that knowledge to current circumstances, for political ends, it was a vital political tool – or weapon. This was precisely why it was rigorously censored, with strict prohibitions on explorations of recent English history. Playwrights who were seen to use historical events to comment on contemporary matters found themselves imprisoned, their plays banned.

The writer whose work Shakespeare was most indebted to when writing his *Richard II*, Samuel Daniel, had devoted an impressive 160 stanzas to the dangerous topic of the deposition and death of Richard, and the installation of

Henry Bolingbroke as King Henry IV in his 1595 *First Four Books of the Civil Wars*.[4] His strategy to avoid censorship or worse was, on the surface at least, to support conventional injunctions to obedience, even, perhaps especially when a king is behaving tyrannically. Channeling the Roman author Tacitus, he insists that aggrieved subjects must "admire times past, follow the present will / Wish for good Princes, but t'indure the ill" (Daniel 1601, stanza 76, ll. 7–8, p. 11). Shakespeare is similarly cautious, even evasive, in his approach to this potentially incendiary material. He ensures we do not see the king's military failures in Ireland and adds a churchman to the cast list to remind the audience that Richard is a divinely appointed monarch, and therefore his subjects cannot and should not remove him. Just as tactfully, Shakespeare creates a Richard who controls his own abdication scene (Potter 2012, p. 178): he is not removed, he removes himself, "thus emphasizing that no one else has the power to do it." Above all, Shakespeare chooses to follow the "more sympathetic and heroic" (ibid.) of the alternative accounts of Richard's death and, for good measure, makes the king killer repentant.

In this he takes a less high-risk approach than Christopher Marlowe, whose 1592 *Edward II* had dramatized the deposition and murder of a king. Both Richard and Edward show very human frailties and pettiness, which are in themselves a form of political commentary on their humanity – rather than quasi-divinity – but Marlowe's King Edward is open about his love for men (his sweet "minions," a word which recurs throughout the play [Marlowe 1997]); he treats his own nobles and churchmen appallingly; his murder, killed with a hot poker up his anus, is grotesque and demeaning; and his killer shows no remorse. In contrast, Shakespeare's play is assembled from less contentious historical accounts, which leads one historian (Gajda 2012, p. 245) to see *Richard II* as a deeply conservative work, one that warns against usurpation regardless of how terrible the reigning monarch might be. It is "a drama enshrining sixteenth-century homily while reflecting contemporary fears of a succession crisis."

But there is a faultline. Elizabeth's childless state had provided another writer, John Hayward, the chance to play with fire on the very first page of narrative in his retelling of the life of Richard's successor, Henry IV ("For neither armies, nor strong holdes are so great defences to a prince, as the multitude of children" [Hayward 1599, p. 1]), and Shakespeare is equally contentious. Richard's queen, Isabel, was – in reality – only 10 when her husband was deposed. Shakespeare transforms her into a woman, all to point up the couple's barrenness. She describes Bolingbroke, who usurps her husband, as "my sorrow's dismal heir." Samuel Daniel had created the character of a grieving queen but had at least apologized for not "suiting her passion to her years" (*The Civil Wars* [1609], Epistle Dedicatorie). Shakespeare does not even blink at this historical travesty.

Isabel's use of the word "heir" is a reminder that Shakespeare's dramatic depiction of the right to rule England is fundamentally dynastic. It works as follows. The Crown descends in the manner of real property, and he has best claim who can prove priority of descent. All others are usurpers. It's a clear, logical understanding of dynastic power and it underpins all Shakespeare's history plays. *Richard II* is certainly relevant to the political concerns of the mid-1590s, when the English monarch remained without an heir and anxious mutterings about the succession were becoming louder, but the play's message remains one of obedience. Richard may be a tyrant but this does not justify his overthrow. However dynamic he might be, the usurper Bolingbroke is given no moral legitimacy at the end of the play, and there are strong hints that the crown will lie uneasy on King Henry IV's head – as Shakespeare will explore in one of his next forays into English history.

As will be seen in the next chapter, none of this orthodoxy, caution, or tact was any use if other people understood your play (and the struggle between king and usurper) in a different way. Shakespeare could not prevent others imposing more radical interpretations on his work. He still can't.

At some point between 1595 and 1598, Shakespeare turned to English history again, writing *King John*. For Richard Dutton (2016, p. 8) the play provided an opportunity for Shakespeare to demonstrate, cautiously, his Catholic sympathies, and his treatment of the historical material provides an opportunity for us to glimpse "the pressure of his personal convictions." Most treatments of King John's struggle for power with the pope are "virulently nationalistic and anti-Catholic," Shakespeare is "more muted," keeping his badly behaving nuns and monks off stage, although retaining a meddling cardinal (ibid.). Others see this not so much as a reflection of Shakespeare's own loyalty to Rome, but his continued desire to appeal to the followers of the Earl of Essex, some of whom were Catholics or had Catholic sympathies. However, the most compelling character in the play – and the one given the most rousing patriotic speech of the play - is not the king, but the Bastard, whose natural father is Richard Lionheart. The audience hears his mother's apology for her seduction by the King, her plea that "God lay not my transgression to thy charge" (1.1.256) that it was a "dear offence / Which was so strongly urged past my defence" (1.1.257–258). There is enough here to justify the Bastard's rejection of any interpretation of his conception as sinful. As he says, his father was a real man, and women don't know how to say no. And Shakespeare gives his Bastard a remarkable speech about self-determination:

> For he is but a bastard to the time
> That doth not smack of observation,
> And so am I whether I smack or no;
> And not alone in habit and device,
> Exterior form, outward accoutrement,

> But from the inward motion to deliver
> Sweet, sweet, sweet poison for the age's tooth.
>
> *(1.1.207–213)*

Justifying, perhaps even celebrating, the rape that begot him; openly admitting to the audience his poisonous "inward motion"; the Bastard should, in simple moral terms, be as quickly dismissed and punished as Shakespeare's other illegitimate son from this period, Don John in *Much Ado About Nothing*. But Shakespeare, astonishingly, makes this bastard the mouthpiece for eloquent patriotic sentiment at the end of *King John*.

> O, let us pay the time but needful woe,
> Since it hath been beforehand with our griefs.
> This England never did, nor never shall,
> Lie at the proud foot of a conqueror
> But when it first did help to wound itself.
> Now these her princes are come home again,
> Come the three corners of the world in arms
> And we shall shock them! Naught shall make us rue,
> If England to itself do rest but true.
>
> *(5.7.110–118)*

Is this Shakespeare once again turning towards his roots? Jonathan Bate thinks so (2008, pp. 46–48). The Bastard (only a hint in the historical records) is a countryman, born in Northamptonshire, a good blunt fellow, who appeals to St. George: he "is the voice of Shakespeare's own place of origin, the midlands, deep England," even a voice for "William of Warwickshire": "an entrepreneur, a player, a man who idealises the shires even as he leaves them to enter the theatre, the market, the emergent empire" (ibid.).

Shakespeare's next bastard, Don John in *Much Ado About Nothing*, is, it has to be said, hardly a compelling character, something of an evil nongenius who attempts to sow discord amongst the young lovers, fails, and is captured: "your brother John is ta'en in flight" (5.4.123). The play as a whole insists on a simplistic construction of identity which is utterly of its time: just as wicked Conrad is born under Saturn, Don John is born a bastard. Brought back by armed men, Don John remains offstage at the denouement and is dismissed by Benedick: "Think not on him till tomorrow. I'll devise thee brave punishments for him. Strike up, pipers" (5.4.125–128). If *Much Ado* follows *King John*, then this is a serious rowing back from any celebration of the eloquent, center-stage Bastard. And it seems not all bastards are Shakespeare.

If *King John* was written after *Much Ado*, then we return to comforting literary biographical territory. Shakespeare is becoming more complex, creating in the Bastard a character replete with interiority, a man who has thought hard about his own status – and well on his way to creating two further, remarkable bastards, Thersites and Edmund. More generally, *King John* demonstrates a "major development" in Shakespeare as a dramatist, in his creation of an "extended and subtle dialogue which lets the audience perceive the moral implications for itself" (Potter 2012, p. 174). For many critics and audiences, this is what makes Shakespeare Shakespeare, what Garber has called his contrapuntal approach to his material, the way in which he allows characters to disagree, refusing to give the audience a clear moral steer. If "Shakespeare's job as dramatist is to present opposing sides with rare insight," then his way of going about his job is rare for his time (Bevington 2010, p. 4). Accordingly, another play from this period, *The Merchant of Venice*, has been mined for Shakespeare's ability to present opposing sides, specifically in its representation of the Jew of Venice, Shylock.

Shylock hovers between a straightforward comic villain and an intriguing protagonist. As with the Bastard in *King John*, Shakespeare is playing with audience expectations, both in terms of complexity of character, but also in the formal structure of the play. The Bastard ends the play with an eloquent, rousing speech. Admittedly, there's not much competition, but he's looking like a better leader than any of the other men in the play, and the take-home message seems to be: better an English bastard than a legitimate foreigner. The reverse is true for the later comedy. In the case of *The Merchant of Venice*, the closing romantic scenes have come to be seen as bathetic, with Shylock's defeat, humiliation, and forcible conversion three quarters of the way through *The Merchant of Venice* understood as far more compelling theater.

Shylock may disappear from the play, suggesting that he should not be viewed as a significant disruption to its comic business, but Shakespeare – as is so often the case – develops his sources and models in ways that ensure that Shylock cannot remain a one-dimensional villain. Compare a contemporary play, Haughton's *Englishmen for My Money*), in which a set of lovers are kept apart by a usurious, foreign, blocking figure, Pisaro. The character has "more than a little of Shakespeare's Shylock" (Van Es 2013, p. 133). But Shakespeare makes the conflict between Shylock and Antonio have a history. In *The Merchant of Venice* it is significant (ibid.) that

> Antonio has a history of slighting Shylock, that Bassanio has long been indebted to Antonio, and that Bassanio has pledged his troth to Portia. All those relationships are put under stress by the dramatist in the fourth act. In *Englishmen for My Money*, in contrast, behaviour is governed by the mechanical logic of farce. It is therefore much easier for Pisaro in *Englishmen* to conclude by embracing the young gentlemen who have outdone him. In *The Merchant of Venice* the laws of comedy cannot just sweep Shylock along in their wake.

This is an eloquent description of Shakespeare's practice, but it does not explain why he represents Shylock in the way he does. There will always be those who want William Shakespeare to be a nice guy, or at least one able to understand the root causes of what the Duke of Venice calls Shylock's "strange apparent cruelty" (4.1.20), one able (as a "stranger" originally himself in London, and therefore "well acquainted with both sides of that world") to show sympathy for the outsider (Potter 2012, p. 212). There were many outsiders in London, with some 4000 to 5000 foreigners driven to the city by economic and religious factors in Protestant Europe, in addition to those who had made the journey from Warwickshire. Perhaps, argues Smith (2013, p. 214), Shakespeare is less interested in Shylock's Jewishness, more interested in "the difficulties of human interaction in a multicultural city." Venice, on one level at least, stands for London: Jew vs. Christian stands for a more generalized cultural friction, perhaps the impact of Huguenot refugees.

And our contemporary (and proper) awareness of anti-Semitism is not imposed on the play, for Shakespeare is emphatic in his construction of Shylock the Jew, a man consumed with awareness of his "tribe." Even in its own time the Jew of Venice was of equal interest to Antonio, the Merchant of the title. The play is noted in the Stationers' Register of 1598 as "the Marchaunt of Venyce or otherwise called the Iewe of Venyce." Later, in 1600, the title page promised "the extreame crueltie of Shylocke the Iewe towards the sayd Merchant, in cutting a iust pound of his flesh."

A few years earlier, in 1594, there had been a marked growth in hostility towards Jews in the aftermath of the celebrated trial and execution of Queen Elizabeth's Portuguese physician, Roderigo Lopez. The good doctor had been accused by the Earl of Essex of plotting to poison the monarch. Lopez was a Marrano (that is, a Jew who had converted to Christianity), hardly surprising because, since 1290, when King Edward I expelled the Jews, it had been impossible to practice the Jewish faith openly in England. Recently, it has been recognized that some continued to observe Jewish customs in private, although there is no direct evidence that Lopez himself did so. His ancestry was enough to demonize him as "Doctor Lopez a Jew" (Carleton 1627, p. 163). And the Admiral's Men duly cashed in, giving three performances of Christopher Marlowe's *The Jew of Malta* between 4 February and 4 June 1594, with Lopez executed on 7 June of that year.[5]

Was Shakespeare doing the same thing? He had been satirizing, if not demonizing, the non-English for years, the xenophobia of his plays the flipside of his loyalty to "deep England," to appropriate Bate's phrase. Audiences had laughed at or condemned the French, the Scots, and the Moors in earlier plays. Now, in *The Merchant of Venice*, they could mock a black African, a Spaniard, and Shylock the Jew. In early performances of the play, it is highly likely that Shylock was played in the tradition of Pantalone, the avaricious merchant/

moneylender of the *commedia dell'arte* Venetian tradition, with beard, cloak, and humped back – with an added large false nose, just to make the racism even more physical. Make no mistake, *The Merchant of Venice* is a bawdy, romantic comedy (albeit with an awkward guest, Shylock): Portia's Belmont and the double marriage plot provide the frame and focus for the play, which ends with an obscene pun: "I'll fear no other thing / So sore as keeping safe Nerissa's ring" (5.1.306–307).

Moreover, *The Merchant of Venice* was a bawdy comedy with a substantial part for a boy actor who was getting too big for female roles, prompting the plot device whereby Portia conveniently cross-dresses as a young man. Once again, Shakespeare's writing is being driven by the people around him. And by pressure. The more successful the Chamberlain's Men were, the more their leading playwright needed to be productive, and flexible, ready and willing to tailor his plays for different venues and different audiences. The text of *A Midsummer Night's Dream* appears to have two endings, a fairy masque probably for private performance, perhaps at an actual wedding, and an epilogue spoken by Puck probably for public performance in a London playhouse. These alternatives strongly indicate two early performance venues and audiences. Another strategy appears evident in *King John*, in which Shakespeare takes over the plot of another play, scene by scene, at least for the first three acts. But the company needed plays, and fast, and *The Troublesome Reign of King John*, a two-parter published in 1591 and probably belonging to another company until now, was available. (Braunmuller [1998] provides a detailed comparison of the two John texts, showing that there are only minor variations, although some difference in emphasis, between the two plays up until the end of act 3 of Shakespeare's *King John*.) Another way to produce work quickly was to collaborate and it is now generally accepted that Shakespeare was one of the playwrights involved with *Edward III*,[6] which was anonymously published in 1596. Taylor (2016, pp. 148–149) is certain that Shakespeare is the author of the two Countess of Salisbury scenes in the play, and admires them unreservedly, whilst acknowledging that *Edward* might nevertheless be the "work of a talented Shakespeare admirer who had intricate knowledge of the Bard's works."

Were these collaborations solely driven by the need to speed up the production process, or did Shakespeare recognize the artistic value of collaboration? Examining the (later) case of *Timon of Athens*, Taylor suggests that Shakespeare understood his own limitations as a dramatist. To write *Timon*, he needed Thomas Middleton's satirical ability, whereas he could rely on his own talent for the "misanthropic tirades" of the second half of the play. As Taylor insists (Taylor 2016, p. 148): we "should not assume that soloist Shakespeare is always better than Shakespeare in company."

Meanwhile, the everyday attacks on theater continued. There was new trouble for the Lord Chamberlain's Men in the summer of 1596. Henry Carey,

Lord Hunsdon and Lord Chamberlain, died on 22 July. Now the players "are piteously persecuted by the Lord Mayor and the aldermen, and however in their old lord's time they thought their state settled, it is now so uncertain they cannot build on it" (Nash 1904–1910, Volume 5, p. 194). After a relatively settled two years, would Shakespeare's creative alliance with the Chamberlain's Men survive?

Biographers remain more interested in another death that summer. William and Anne Shakespeare's only son, Hamnet, was buried in Stratford-upon-Avon on 11 August 1596. The post-Romantic biographical project struggles with the fact that there exists no further information about Hamnet's passing other than the record of burial. We don't know where his father was (possibly acting with the Chamberlain's Men who were performing in Faversham, Kent, on 1 August), let alone what he felt about the death of his son. The silence of the archive disturbs us, so much so that even the otherwise cautious and revisionist *Shakespeare's Circle* book (Wells 2015, p. 11) claims "the greatest sadness in Shakespeare's life was the death of his son, Hamnet, in 1596." Lois Potter (2012, p. 225) is certain that "Shakespeare had been absent from home while his family needed him" and believes that "as elsewhere in his work, personal experience and feeling are diffused among several characters and are inseparable from literary influences and the demands of drama."

We need therefore to turn to the plays for a father's grief, and if not a father's, a mother's will do. Stanley Wells, for example, glances at Constance's lament for Prince Arthur in *King John* ("Grief fills the room up of my absent child," 3.4.93–105), but has to acknowledge not only that the dating of the play might not work (it is, like most Shakespeare plays, uncertain), but Arthur is not dead, merely absent.[7] Stephen Greenblatt (2004, p. 318) believes it took four or five years for Shakespeare to transmute his grief for Hamnet into drama: "the death of his son and the impending death of his father – a crisis of mourning and memory – constitute a psychic disturbance that may help to explain the explosive power and inwardness of *Hamlet*."

For Lois Potter (2012, p. 288) *Twelfth Night* is a more likely expression, or working out, of Shakespeare the father's grief, and again a delayed reaction. "It was perhaps five years since the death of Hamnet, whose twin was a girl, and the plot of *Twelfth Night* calls for each twin to think the other dead until their reunion in the final scene. If Shakespeare found the subject painful, this might be why Viola is the saddest comic heroine that he had created up to this point, and why both she and Olivia are introduced grieving for the loss of a close relative."

Smith (2012) offers a stringent critique of this kind of thing because, as Tromly (2010, p. 243) neatly puts it, "there is not a firm enough base of biographical fact to confer much substance on these hauntings." Instead, only three references to William Shakespeare survive from the autumn of 1596.

One has him living in parish of St. Helen's, Bishopsgate, where he was assessed for 5 shillings worth of tax. The second document tells a far less respectable story, exciting for those who find taxpaying (or even tax-avoiding) Shakespeare disappointingly dull. In the autumn of 1596, one William Wayte swore before the Judge of Queen's Bench that he stood in "danger of death, or bodily hurt" from "William Shakspere" and three others, including Francis Langley, one of the owners of the Swan Theatre. Predictably, in a second writ, Langley made the same accusation against Wayte, described in another case as a "loose person of no reckoning or value." William Shakespeare is suddenly "a dangerous thug," perhaps even "heavily involved in organized crime" (Dash 2011; see Nelson 2018b).

The third document offers yet another view of Shakespeare in 1596, no gangster now, but a newly minted gentleman. It is a grant of arms, gold with a black banner bearing a silver spear, to John Shakespeare and his children. The motto is "Non sanz droict" (not without right). Actor-playwright Shakespeare's new status as gentleman-writer may just be being mocked by Ben Jonson (1927) in the character of the social-climber, Sogliardo, in *Every Man Out of His Humour*, whose motto is "not without mustard" (3.4.86).

Heather Wolfe (2016) of the Folger Shakespeare Library has demonstrated incontrovertibly that while "the heralds at the College of Arms in England made the grant of arms to his father, William Shakespeare himself was intimately involved in the application and the ensuing controversy over their legitimacy." Perhaps he arranged matters because he was on the spot, but for those who see John Shakespeare as in dire financial straits in the 1590s, it was William rather than his father who had the money to deliver on the process. John had unsuccessfully applied for "gentle" status back in the 1570s. Now in the 1590s, perhaps William was engaged in "a form of reparation" towards his father, pursuing, without luck, the return of the Arden property lost by his father but, with luck, the coat of arms, "another symbolic wound his father had suffered" (Tromly 2010, p. 253). It may have been a hollow triumph in one sense. Hamnet's death meant the death of any hope of preserving Shakespeare's name "according to the common way of mankind" (Schoenbaum 1991, p. 12) or, more precisely, the common way of patriarchy.

There's another way to read the 1596 coat of arms, focusing less on William the father, more on William the playwright seeking recognition. The design specifies that the tilted spear is to have a silver tip ("the point steeled argent"),[8] offering a visual suggestion of a writing pen with a silver nib. Is Shakespeare nodding towards his success with the pen, rather than the spear? Actors and playwrights could be, and were, gentlemen but not many.

Perhaps the attacks on theater as a disreputable business conducted in disreputable neighborhoods were getting to him. "When the soul of your plays is either mere trifles, or Italian bawdry, or wooing of gentlewomen, what are we taught?" asked Stephen Gosson (1582, n.p.), one hostile voice amongst many. John Northbrooke, one of the public theater's most vitriolic opponents, saw no harm in permitting scholars "to play good and honest Comedies," but warned readers that all the public theater could teach them was "how to be false and deceive your husbands, or husbands their wives" and "how to disobey and to rebel against Princes" (Northbrooke 1577, pp. 94–95). As for the neighborhoods, public theaters were known to be hubs for crime and disease, which was precisely why the civic authorities insisted that playhouses were built in the suburbs.

Shakespeare's work and workplace needed defending, and writers like Thomas Nashe rushed to draw comparisons between the playhouses of Shoreditch and those of ancient Rome: "our Scene is more stately furnished than ever it was in the time of Roscius, our representations honourable, and full of gallant resolution" (Nashe 1842). Shakespeare himself may have been more ambivalent. Scholars have read his epilogue to *A Midsummer Night's Dream* (which refers to the play's "weak and idle theme" [5.1.414]) and his *Sonnet 111* (which alludes to the stain of "the dyer's hand," l. 7) as acknowledgments of his discomfort with his profession. The fact is, though, that countless play prologues and epilogues are drenched in false modesty, whilst – putting aside the questionable validity of reading *any* sonnet autobiographically – in context, the reference to a "brand" (l. 5) and "harmful deeds" (l. 2) in *Sonnet 111* could just as easily refer to a sexual misdemeanor which needs forgiveness, rather than the playwright's embarrassing trade. Yes, the theatrical profession would never be completely vindicated as a legitimate industry, would never gain a separate guild of its own, but ambition, a desire for respectability, pride in, perhaps even defiant pride in, his achievement with his pen are all present in Shakespeare's new coat of arms (Bednarz 2018, p. 24).

And with good reason. Over the course of 1597, more and more of Shakespeare's plays appeared in print. *Richard III*, *Richard II*, and *Romeo and Juliet* all came out in quarto editions. It is probable that a now lost edition of *Love's Labour's Lost* even carried the playwright's name. Being acknowledged as sole author in an era of such pervasive collaboration was a sign both of success and status.

Nevertheless, 1597 would bring a new challenge for Shakespeare. Since 1594, the Chamberlain's Men had been settled at the Theatre. Then, in April 1597, their lease on that playhouse expired. Just over a year earlier, James Burbage had bought "Seven Great Upper Rooms, the rooms on the floor below, and the rooms to the west in the Duchy Chamber" (Wolfe 2020a) in Blackfriars and begun creating a new playhouse there. He chose Blackfriars because it was a Liberty, one of the anomalous pockets of territory mostly within the city walls but outside the control of the City of London authorities due to their previous status as church property. Burbage's new theater would be easier to get to for the London audiences than the suburban playhouses in Shoreditch, but still evade mayoral oversight.

That was, presumably, the theory. In reality, the location of the early playhouses, such the Theatre and the Curtain, reflected a compromise between players and the authorities and that compromise was being threatened by Burbage's newbuild in Blackfriars. The playhouse immediately ran into problems with the Privy Council. With the enforced closure of the Theatre, and unable to move to Blackfriars, the Chamberlain's Men moved to the Curtain in Shoreditch and, probably, the recently built Swan on Bankside.[9]

It was a precarious lifeline for, in 1597, "theatre in London seemed to be in danger of being obliterated altogether" (Dutton 2018, p. 221). An order was sent out, signed by the very patrons of the theater companies, that "those playhouses that are erected and built only for such purposes shall be plucked down" in Shoreditch and Southwark (Wickham, Berry, and Ingram 2020, pp. 100–101). All playing was suspended in the Theatre and Curtain, the Rose and the Swan. The playhouses were not in fact "plucked down," but it was a significant warning shot. The Swan was the most obvious casualty, remaining unused for a number of years. The same summer, Ben Jonson got into serious trouble over his play *The Isle of Dogs* which, according to the authorities, "contained very seditious and slanderous matter" (Chambers 1923, Volume 4, p. 323). Topcliffe, renowned as a torturer or inquisitor was brought in. Pembroke's Men, the company who performed Jonson's play, went out of business.

And yet, the Chamberlain's Men went from strength to strength, and their leading playwright was about to enter a quite remarkable period of in his career, one in which he produced his greatest works.

Chapter Four

William Shakespeare in 1597: he's living in London, behaving badly (or the closest he'll get to behaving badly), a playwright and poet fascinated by the dark side, outsiders, the deviant: Bastards, Jews, Master-Mistresses.

William Shakespeare in 1597: he's a husband and father, the purchaser of New Place, the second largest house in Stratford-upon-Avon, with three stories, 10 fireplaces, two barns, two gardens, and two orchards.[1]

There are more glimpses of Shakespeare around this time, but still no consensus as to whether Stratford or London defined him best. We do know that William was ploughing the money earned in London back into his hometown and he certainly wasn't declaring his wealth to the authorities in the capital (Edmondson and Wells 2015a, p. 329). He's listed as a tax defaulter in November 1597, failing to pay five shillings. This might be about right for an actor (Shakespeare is listed as a "principle Comedian" in Ben Jonson's *Every Man in his Humour* that year) but hardly indicates the wealth needed, and obviously being accrued, to pay for New Place back in Warwickshire.

A year later, Shakespeare's name crops up again in the records. This time he appears to have been hoarding corn. These documents don't tell "a terrible story, but it is not uplifting either. It is merely and disagreeably ordinary" (Greenblatt 2004, p. 383). This, in itself, presents a problem for many biographers and readers of biography, forced to turn to the plays for the extraordinary or uplifting.

Such is not the case with, say, Ben Jonson. In just one episode from an appropriately colorful life, he murders a fellow actor from a rival troupe; he is imprisoned, branded on his thumb, his property confiscated and, if that were not enough, converts to Catholicism while in prison. This is the stuff of biography, not the avoidance of five shillings of tax and the acquisition of a large house in your home town. The irony is that it is Jonson who writes about the mundane. His *Every Man in his Humour* is yet another play "that brings a number of stupid or eccentric people together in order to allow a few clever ones to see

The Life of the Author: William Shakespeare, First Edition. Anna Beer.
© 2021 John Wiley & Sons, Ltd. Published 2021 by John Wiley & Sons, Ltd.

how ridiculous the others are," in the words of Lois Potter (2012, p. 192) who is clearly no fan of Jonson's comedy.

Being dull has its benefits, particularly if you were an actor/playwright whose social status remained perilously marginal. A statute of early 1598 focused its energies on the "Punishment of Rogues and Vagabonds" and included a restriction on travel by professional players, unless said players carried with them a sealed warrant from their noble patron. The statute further decreed that only the Admiral's Men and Lord Chamberlain's Men were permitted to use and practice stage plays. Even though William Shakespeare trod very carefully around his social and political superiors, things could still go awry. His two *Henry IV* plays offered the public patriotic battles and the "humorous conceits of Sir Iohn Falstalffe" (as the title page of the 1598 edition of Part II puts it), but those "humorous conceits" were still to get the playwright into trouble. The character of Falstaff was originally called Oldcastle, referring to Sir John Oldcastle, who was burned at the stake in the reign of Henry V for being a heretical Lollard (that is, a proto-Protestant). Sir John Oldcastle had held the title of Lord Cobham by right of his marriage into the Brooke family. Now, in the 1590s, William Brooke, Lord Cobham, objected to Shakespeare's representation of his ancestor on the grounds that instead of a brave, Protestant soldier, Oldcastle/Falstaff is a drunken, promiscuous, cynical coward.

What on earth was the usually cautious Shakespeare doing caricaturing Oldcastle in this way, perhaps even at the very time that Lord Cobham had his brief stint as Lord Chamberlain (August 1596–March 1597)? The Admiral's Men wisely staged two far more respectful plays about the man. Schoenbaum (1987, p. 194) thinks Shakespeare was simply being casual with his sources, rather than seeking to attack the family, taking the Oldcastle name "without a second thought" from *The famous victories of Henry the Fifth*. Nevertheless "second thought would have been advisable." Or perhaps Shakespeare, "unsettled" by his son's death, "briefly succumbed to the dangerous belief that he could do no wrong" (Potter 2012, p. 209). The lapse in judgment was quickly remedied however. An apology of sorts was added, in the form of an Epilogue to Part II ("Oldcastle died a martyr and this was not the man," Epilogue, ll. 31–32) and the character was named Falstaff by the time the play got into print. The rest is history. Or comedy. Soon after, in *The Merry Wives of Windsor*, a play built around Falstaff's character,[2] Shakespeare may even offer a knowing nod to the Oldcastle affair. The jealous husband Ford adopts the family name of Brooke when attempting to fool Falstaff, but "only for a jest" (2.1.194).[3]

So, once again, the danger passed. William Shakespeare, playwright, was doing well. So well that, in 1598, a quarto volume of *Love's Labour's Lost* advertised itself as "By W. Shakespeare" (although not *so* well as all that since his hugely popular *Richard III*, also published that year, remained anonymous). And Francis Meres's *Palladis Tamia, Wits Treasury*, praised Shakespeare in print: "the sweet witty soul of *Ovid* lives in mellifluous & honey-tongued *Shakespeare*, witness his *Venus and Adonis*, his *Lucrece*, his sugared Sonnets among his private friends, etc." (Chambers 1930, Volume 2, p. 194), a reminder that in his own time, Shakespeare was known far more as a poet than a playwright.[4]

The volume, "Shakespeare's Sonnets" would not be published for another 11 years, but the majority of the 154 poems praised by Meres were written in the first half of the 1590s, although the timeline for their creation is not exactly linear – and the subject of much scholarly contention (see Hammond 2012, pp. 8–9).[5] Given the difficulty of dating individual poems, biographical inference remains fraught, but since his sonnets appear to offer up a direct line to "Will," the man, few of us are able to resist.

Before capitulating to speculation, a word of skepticism, rooted in my own understanding on Shakespeare as a writer. For all that he was known more as a poet, at least in the first part of his career, Shakespeare – whenever he picks up a pen – is, I believe, thinking first and foremost as a dramatist. So, for me, his character "Will" is just one more of his superbly ambivalent, psychologically complex creations. To read the sonnets as straightforward autobiography is to be seduced by the confessional voice into a reductive correlation between text and life. For some critics, a stern reminder that the poems are literary constructs still does not put enough distance between the works and the man. We must completely separate what Shakespeare wrote from any questions about his lived experience, or more precisely, his sex life: "With few exceptions, those who write about his life continue to obsess over a handful of issues that have little to do with what or how he wrote – from his sexual inclinations to his pursuit of status to his decision to leave his wife a 'second best' bed" (Shapiro 2005b, p. 9).

And yet, the content of many of the sonnets is sexually explicit (which does not exactly dissuade the reader from asking questions about their author's "sexual inclinations") and the genre itself is notorious for playing with (auto) biographical readings. The greatest sequence of the era, Philip Sidney's, *Astrophil and Stella*, is on one level a self-portrait, if a very sophisticated, witty, and elusive one. Sidney makes it easy to identify the object of desire, "Stella": she is Penelope, Lady Rich, as numerous tiresome puns make it all too clear. At the same time, Sidney warns the reader that to make direct parallels between author and speaker would be crass: "I am not I, pity the tale of me" says Astrophil (Sonnet 45, l. 14; Sidney 1962).

Moreover, as with his drama, Shakespeare is as much in negotiation with contemporary writers such as Samuel Daniel and Edmund Spenser, or the overtly homoerotic Richard Barnfield, as he is with his own psyche. In this context, Sonnet 20, with its explicit references to male genitals (and what the speaker might or might not do with them) becomes both a sophisticated literary game, as well as a somewhat gauche exploration of male–male desire. Enigmatic and "shiftily comic," the surface argument (for chastity, given the fact that this is two men under discussion) is undercut by both the form and wordplay. At the very point in the poem that a sonnet reader would expect a thesis to be proved, the rhyme "fails to clinch the point it is ostentatiously supposed to register." The result is that the speaker's "claim to chastity is covertly endangered." Although the poem "can hardly prove Shakespeare homosexual, it cannot be invoked, as it so often is, to demonstrate his unwavering heterosexuality" (Kerrigan 1986, p. 51). What Kerrigan captures here, eloquently, is the built-in ambivalence of the sonnet form, the way in which, in particular in the hands of English sonneteers, the form will so often deconstruct itself – and its desires – in front of our very eyes.

Shapiro's stern warning (less persuasive to me than Kerrigan's reminder that the sonnets cannot, or can, be used to "prove" or "demonstrate" anything) is a response to some of the more reductive biographical takes on Shakespeare's sonnets. Back in the eighteenth century, William Oldys saw sonnets 92–95 as addressed to Shakespeare's "beautiful wife on some suspicion of her infidelity." This reading (characterizing Shakespeare as a jealous husband) entered the critical mainstream, surviving despite individual readers' understanding that the sonnets in question were addressed to a beautiful, unfaithful man. Every age finds the Shakespeare it is looking for in his sonnets, so we now see him no longer as a jealous husband, but as a man in conflict with his era's insistence on sex in the service of reproduction; its valorization of sexuality within marriage; its understanding of desire as sin. Desire for Shakespeare is "blind, amoral, and self-serving" (Chedgzoy 2001, p. 36). The body and its desires is also far more fascinating than those traditional sources of drama, military and political crisis.

That interest in the body is, however, very different to that of Latin poet Martial and his Italian successors. Shakespeare avoids Martial's "explicit language, as well as classical norms of male desire which see penetration as the essence of male sexuality" (Moulton 2017, p. 102). Instead, his sonnets "incorporate romantic and affectionate feeling in ways that are absolutely alien" to the earlier Latin and Italian writers, who were absorbed with the physical penetration of social inferiors: women, boys, and slaves (ibid.). Less interested in penetration, Shakespeare is transgressive in the ways in which his (or perhaps his characters') desires cut across the lines of gender and sexual identities against contemporary expectations.

"Shakespeare is queer because his language is queer" asserts Stanivukovic (2017, p. 5), but is the "Shakespeare" here the man or his texts? In this example, it remains unclear but elsewhere there is a slide into the biographical turn.

Shakespeare (writer *and* man) is preoccupied with transgressive desire, interested in "sexual relationships with well-born young men," and conversely found sexual relations with women "more functional than sentimental" (Duncan-Jones 2001, p. xi). Put bluntly, his sonnets show Shakespeare to be bisexual but he preferred men to women.

Or not. Shakespeare was "highly heterosexual" (Rowse 1973, p. 58) and "loved his wife and children" (Levi 1988, p. 101). Or, less categoric, but equally refusing to out the Bard, Shakespeare could *imagine* homoerotic feeling (Honan 2005), but did not experience it himself; or the sonnets are *"imaginings of potential situations which might have grown* from the initial Southampton situation" (his italics, Bate 1997, p. 53); or Shakespeare loved Southampton, but it remained an emotional not a physical attachment (Dutton 2010, pp. 123–124); or "profound homosexual attachment of a scarcely sensual, almost unrealized kind" is "registered" in the *Sonnets*, but Shakespeare remains uninterested in the physical qualities of the male lover (Kerrigan 1986, p. 51).

The slightly desperate heteronormativity at work here seems to say more about the critics than it does about the sonnets' exploration of male–male love and sex. We cannot know what sexual acts William Shakespeare enjoyed, nor what he believed or felt about those acts, but – although homoerotic writing was more prevalent in his era than one might think reading traditional criticism – his decision to write about male–male sexual acts in an era in which the terminology of "buggery," "sodomitical grossness," and "ingling" muddled these acts "hopelessly with bestiality and child abuse" (Kerrigan 1986, p. 47), and, more saliently, an era in which same-sex desire was viciously punished, does tell us something about the man. It also tells us something about the writer. If Shakespeare lived in a culture in which "there was no language for coping with" what we now call homosexuality, "even as a misdemeanour" (Kerrigan 1986, p. 47) (although that word "coping" is problematically charged), then his sonnets, for all their ironies and enigmas, are doing something remarkable. They offer just such a language and not just a ramped-up version of male–male friendship.

Most of Shakespeare's contemporaries were content to compare (favorably) the comradely love between men to the shallowness of desire of men *for* women, to laud friendship between men. Here's Ficino in full neo-Platonic flow: "The youth enjoys the beauty of the man with his Intellect." It is "a wonderful exchange. Virtuous, useful, and pleasant to both" (Ficino and Jayne 1985, p. 58). Ficino is saying no sex please, we're humanists. Shakespeare is saying something very different – but also very hard to pin down.

Reading the sonnets is complicated by the wide range of meanings that significant words (like love and friend) had at the time: "a servant would assure his master of his love, a subject do the same for his sovereign." "As with the word "friend," we have to allow the poems themselves to tell us what "love" means" (Hammond 2012, p. 18). The oblique expression of sexual feeling, in language which "permits alternative, non-sexual readings" (Hammond 2012, p. 19) is all part of the literary game, but it may also be a very wise form of self-protection. It was very rare for a writer to push an exclusively sexual interpretation on the reader, although the "blatantly homoerotic" Richard Barnfield comes close.[6] But that need not prevent us, in the relative safety of the twenty-first century, and after centuries of de-sexing the sonnets, from exploring the full range of sexual innuendo, as Jeffrey Masten (2016, p. 75) does with the phrase "make sweet some vial," or Helen Vendler, who glosses "conscience" as "knowledge of cunt" (1999, p. 639).[7]

In one respect, Shakespeare is actually more daring than Barnfield. The latter frames his homoeroticism within a pastoral setting, and therefore invokes the literary precedent of Virgil's *Second Eclogue* (Hammond 2012, p. 44). Running into criticism of his first volume of poetry, Barnfield used Virgil as a shield. To those who "did interpret The Affectionate Shepherd otherwise than in truth I meant, touching the subject thereof, to wit, the love of a shepherd to a boy" (Barnfield 1595, p. 3), the poet defends himself by arguing that he was only imitating Virgil. Shakespeare's lovers exist very much in the here and now. Then again, the outlook is poor for the possibility of consummating same-sex desire in Elizabethan London rather than the Sicilian sunshine. Barnfield permits us to imagine there "might be some form of time and place in which sexual love between men might be permitted" (Hammond 2012, p. 44). Shakespeare in contrast "focuses on the near-impossibility of male lovers sharing a space" (ibid.).

The de-sexing of the sonnets does serve to make them less uncomfortable reading, particularly when it comes to the descriptions of sex with a woman. Sonnets 135 and 136 are a "bit sleazy," 138 is "clever and devious," then 140 is "openly menacing, manipulative and downright nasty – precisely the kind of irrational, immoral, predatory behaviour" (Bell 2010, p. 300) predicted earlier in Sonnet 129: "till action lust / Is perjured, murd'rous, bloody, full of blame, / Savage, extreme, rude, cruel, not to trust" (ll. 2–4). In poems that can be thoroughly enigmatic as well as thoroughly obscene, some things are straightforward: disgust with the female body and with the sexual act with women.

The misogyny of the sonnets can be explained as Shakespeare's attempt to be heard in a homosocial world, the world in which the earliest anecdotes about Shakespeare place him, as Alan Stewart (2016, p. 73) shows: the "table-talk, chamber-talk, [and] tavern-talk," reveal a coherent Shakespearean "character" who appears in scenes of male emulation, sexual and intellectual rivalry, and masculine camaraderie. It would make sense, therefore, if "upwardly mobile male friendship" was where Shakespeare's "deepest emotions are invested"

(Duncan-Jones 2001, p. 133). Ambition does still does not quite explain the disgust with women's bodies. We perhaps need to admit simply that either Shakespeare subscribed to his era's misogyny, or that, at least in the sonnets, he was not interested in questioning it.

It is problematic enough to use the 1590s sonnets to consider William Shakespeare's preoccupations, if not his sexual preferences and desires. Things get even more speculative when biographers attempt to identify the historical figures behind the characters.

A slightly less challenging biographical question might be to ask why Shakespeare was circulating sonnets amongst his "private friends" in the 1590s, in manuscript, despite having published two volumes of poetry and received acclaim as a poet. Manuscript circulation "was a normal form of transmission for much lyric poetry in the period" (Orgel 2007, p. 139), so all this may signal is that William was successfully enmeshed in an elite literary coterie of poets and patrons. In this world of intimate exchange, moreover, mystification and playfulness are entirely appropriate: the readers would understand the references without them needing to be spelt out (following Burrow 2002 quoted in Orgel 2007, p. 143). Or maybe not merely appropriate, but necessary – and a way to understand and explain Shakespeare's determination to provide no clues as to any real-life objects of desire. Perhaps the enigmas of the sonnets (at line level and at the level of identities) are intentional on the part of Shakespeare, to protect both the poems' author and their object of desire (Kerrigan 1986).

If the circulation of Shakespeare's "sugared sonnets" in manuscript were part of an ongoing quest for noble patronage, then either that patronage was not forthcoming, or Shakespeare chose to leave the world of coterie poetry and concentrate on playwriting. An anecdote from the time shows that class as much as anything else might have been a factor in this decision. Poet Shakespeare is the butt of an entertainment at St. John's College, Cambridge. He may write "sweet" verse but the university wits' verdict is that he is fundamentally "a talented crowd pleaser who has not yet made his mark as a major writer" (Hadfield 2015, p. 200).

Meres (the man who noted those sugared sonnets in the first place) is kinder to Shakespeare, both as poet and playwright, praising his drama in high terms: an English Plautus for comedy, a Seneca for tragedy. For biographer James Shapiro (2005b, p. 13) that Shakespeare continued to write *plays* through until 1599 – unlike most of his generation – is significant in and of itself. He discusses a document in the hand of George Buc who, in line for the job of Master of the Revels that year, was making notes on plays and in one case was assisted by "W. Shakespeare." Buc's note tells us about Shakespeare the man in a way the sonnets simply cannot, argues Shapiro, offering a glimpse, if only a fleeting one, of a Shakespeare in 1599 who was recognized as an authority on the increasingly distant Elizabethan theatrical past – he alone of all the dramatists at work at the end of the previous decade was still writing plays. This is also one of the earliest indications that authorship mattered and plays were worth collecting. But more than this, it's a flesh and blood encounter that tells us something about Shakespeare's habits, his approachability, what it was like to talk with Shakespeare, what kinds of details stuck in Shakespeare's memory, even where he may have spent time and collected ideas for his plays. Not all of Shakespeare's encounters have to be invented.

(ibid.)

Yet he still remains elusive and, it seems, cautious. Following a period when he had been writing about master-mistresses (in poetry) and had boys playing girls playing boys (in drama), Shakespeare chooses to play it safe, at least with regard to gender, in *Much Ado About Nothing*. No cross-dressing, and a familiar, uncontroversial Italian story for his source with "no implications for English history" (Potter 2012, p. 222). Perhaps he was preoccupied at this time with the purchase and setting up of his new house in Stratford, or smarting from the fallout from his depiction of Oldcastle, aka Falstaff. If Shakespeare was attempting to keep a low profile (in his own time), then he's certainly succeeded with regard to ours. It seems strangely fitting that the only surviving letter addressed to the man, penned on 25 October 1598, was not actually delivered to him. It also seems fitting that the letter should ask for a loan.

However, William Shakespeare emerges from the archival mist on 21 February 1599, and what a moment it is. He signs a tripartite lease for, and contributes £70 towards, the construction costs of a new playhouse: the Globe. Once up and running performances would begin at 2 o'clock in the afternoon, six days a week, all year long, except for Lent. The start time allowed the audience to return to the city before dark, since running times were between two and three hours, and plays could not start earlier because that would interfere with the main meal of the day (dinner), at 12 noon. The "actors were trapped between the audience's eating schedule and the limits of daylight" (Dutton 2018, p. 267). Three "soundings" from a trumpeter, perched high above the theater, would signal the start of the play, calling the 800 groundlings and the 2000 seated spectators to attention. If the playhouse was filled to capacity, this would mean up to 17 000 people attending a single theater in just one week of playing.

This was Shakespeare's world, and he understood its working very well indeed – including the competition. The Admiral's Men remained nearby, old rivals, but later in 1599 the boy players would return, much to Shakespeare's interest. Later, he would give Hamlet a famous speech about the children's companies, one showing insider knowledge (unsurprisingly) and suggesting the whole set-up was "shortsighted, endangering the future livelihood of the boys who want to go on to be adult actors" (Dutton 2016, p. 286). But Shakespeare was not only critical of the ethos of the children's companies, he fears their competition too. When Rosencrantz responds to Hamlet's question about the "boys" carrying it away, with the affirmative "that they do my Lord. Hercules & his load too," he is referring to the symbol of the Globe Theatre: Hercules (*Hamlet*, Folio edition, 2.2.358–360). In an uncharacteristically topical, specific reference, Shakespeare draws attention to the real threat the fashionable boys' companies were to his own theater (see Stern 2004, p. 17). As the first published edition of *Hamlet* put it: "I'faith my Lord, novelty carries it away, For the principal public audience that Came to them, are turned to private plays, And to the humour of children" (scene 7, ll. 271–273).

Yet, despite or because of the competition, the Globe period proved to be one in which Shakespeare began to move away from both imitation and collaboration. Not entirely of course, that would have been impossible in the world in which he worked, perhaps for any writer, in any world. He continued to pick up ideas from contemporaries, and he borrowed heavily from the plots of earlier dramatists "wholesale." But there is a change at work. In his early works Shakespeare displays a mental habit that James Shapiro calls "assimilative imitation" (quoted in Van Es 2013, p. 28): a faithful following of a path set by other poets that is distinct from either Shakespeare's "later knowing parodies (such as the 'rugged Pyrrhus' speech in *Hamlet*) or the total digestion for his own purpose that we find with source texts (such as the original *Leir*)" (Van Es 2013, p. 28).

With hindsight, the change can be seen, but day by day, on the ground, life was not quite so coherent. When writing *Henry V*, for example, Shakespeare would have been unsure for which actual theater building he was writing. The Chamberlain's Men were only temporarily installed at the Curtain because their own playhouse, the Theatre, was off limits. It was all very unsatisfactory. But then – in one of the best stories in this book – action was taken. The actors (probably including Shakespeare, certainly including the brothers Richard and Cuthbert Burbage) went into Alleyn's field by night on 28 December 1598. With the help of the master-builder Peter Streete, they dismantled the Theatre and, as the legal documents put it, carried "all the wood and timber therof unto the Banckside in the parishe of St. Marye Overyes, and there erected a newe playehowse with the sayd timber and woode" (Chambers 1923, Volume 2, p. 415).

St. Mary Overies was to become an actors' church; it still stands, though it is now known as Southwark Cathedral. William's young brother, Edmund, would – probably – be buried there. The new theater would – definitely – be called the Globe.

That Shakespeare was writing for *public* theater is, however, never in doubt. More than that, Shakespeare celebrates that theater, in justly famous lines, in *Henry V*. The Chorus not only offers a defiant challenge to the theory of the unities but sets out something approaching a manifesto for drama: "this unworthy scaffold" can indeed "bring forth / So great an object." This "cockpit" can hold "The vasty fields of France." The actors, "us," are "ciphers" who work on the audience's "imaginary forces" (Prologue to act 1, ll. 10–18).

> Suppose within the girdle of these walls
> Are now confined two mighty monarchies,
> Whose high upreared and abutting fronts
> The perilous narrow ocean parts asunder:
> Piece out our imperfections with your thoughts;
> Into a thousand parts divide one man,
> And make imaginary puissance;
> Think when we talk of horses, that you see them
> Printing their proud hoofs i' the receiving earth;
> For 'tis your thoughts that now must deck our kings,
> Carry them here and there; jumping o'er times,
> Turning the accomplishment of many years
> Into an hour-glass.
>
> *(Prologue, ll. 19–31)*

Shakespeare's passion for drama comes across here, loud and clear. For many years, so too did his uncomplicated patriotism (at least in this play). Henry V's military heroism was indeed the "mirror of all Christian kings" (Prologue to act 2, l. 6), called upon to bolster British morale, most famously in Laurence Olivier's film version during World War II. Shakespeare never wrote anything as violent, simplistic, and immediately relevant to playgoers in the city as the anonymous *A Larum for London*, performed by his company, a rallying cry in the face of fears of a new Spanish invasion in the summer of 1599, a play which chronicled the 1576 and 1585 sieges of Antwerp. But in this period of his life he came close, writing with new energy about violence, as here in *Julius Caesar*.

> And Caesar's spirit, ranging for revenge,
> With Ate by his side come hot from hell,
> Shall in these confines, with a monarch's voice,
> Cry havoc and let slip the dogs of war,
> That this foul deed shall smell above the earth
> With carrion men, groaning for burial.
>
> *(3.1.270–275)*

"The artifice of rising rhythms, with the forecast of uncontrollable slaughter as revenge," the "release of such beyond-human bloodlust in war," are all to be found in *Henry V* (Daniell 1998, p. 250). Ten years earlier, Shakespeare had been more concerned to show the horror and futility of war and violence, notably civil war and rebellion. Even then, however, Shakespeare's real men are also soldiers, unlike Henry VI whose "bookish rule" (*Henry VI, Part II*, 1.1.271) is dragging England down. Talbot, a prototype for Henry V, rouses his men with rhetoric worthy of Agincourt in *Henry VI Part I*:

> Turn on the bloody hounds with heads of steel
> And make the cowards stand aloof at bay.
> Sell every man his life as dear as mine
> And they shall find dear deer of us, my friends.
> God and Saint George, Talbot and England's right,
> Prosper our colours in this dangerous fight.
>
> *(4.2.51–56)*

And even Henry VI looks up from his books long enough to realize that the English need to stop killing each other and start killing the French.

> And like true subjects, sons of your progenitors,
> Go cheerfully together and digest
> Your angry choler on your enemies.
> *(Henry VI Part II, 4.1.166–168)*

For Henry V, beating the old enemy in war is not enough, he must marry the French princess. Henry V, "all king, all soldier" (Garber 2004, p. 395) – and eventually, all husband – is the quintessential manly prince, a rare beast in Shakespeare's work. The Chorus unequivocally celebrates and anticipates the audience's enjoyment of the "warlike Harry," who will

> like himself,
> Assume the port of Mars; and at his heels,
> Leash'd in like hounds, should famine, sword and fire
> Crouch for employment.
> *(Prologue, ll. 5–8)*

And critics remain both dazzled and impressed by him, and his creator. The "completion of a process of maturation has brought Hal to the point when he can and must marry. Being fully a man, he is now ready to take to him a wife. He does so as his due, his prize, his possession. Yet even here Shakespeare does not forget what he has been learning about mutuality from his writing of romantic comedies." Thus writes the much-missed David Bevington (2005, p. 95) in one of his later surveys of Shakespeare's work.

Times change, however, and our Shakespeares change. For the generation following Bevington, the "triumph of Henry V is only a temporary one, momentary in terms of the scope of history," a mere "spectacle of victory, and a concept of kingship, that is finally only an idea, precariously achieved and too easily lost" (Garber 2004, p. 408). *Henry V* is a play with an "obsessive preoccupation with insurrection," one which questions foreign wars and traditional ideas of masculinity (Dollimore and Sinfield 1992, p. 118).

So much for Shakespeare the straightforward patriot. Equally unresolved is the playwright's view of one of the leading soldier-courtiers of the era, the Earl of Essex – the only living figure ever referred to directly in any of Shakespeare's plays. The context was the earl's return from a military expedition to Ireland on 28 September 1599. He was disobeying the orders of his queen by doing so, and he had failed in the task he had been set: the quelling of rebellion. However, Shakespeare has the Chorus to act 5 of *Henry V* describe "the General of our gracious Empress" (l. 30) coming home, "Bringing rebellion broached on his sword" (l. 32). The crowds welcome him:

> London doth pour out her citizens.
> The Mayor and all his brethren in best sort,
> Like to the senators of th'antique Rome
> With the plebeians swarming at their heels,
> Go forth and fetch their conquering Caesar in.
> *(5.0.24–28)*

The language recalls "the rain-soaked crowds that cheered Essex's departure for Ireland" (Gajda 2012, p. 205). It also seems to link Essex to Caesar, whose return from Gaul led to the civil wars that in turn ended the Roman Republic. And, as Essex's biographer points out, "the regal comparison of Essex with Henry V was hardly more comfortable. Popular acclamation ... was the province of the monarch, not the subject" (Gajda 2012, p. 204).

In reality Essex was far from an all-conquering hero, and on his return was swiftly imprisoned by his furious queen. The praise was premature and unwise, but perhaps the misjudgment merely shows the strength of Shakespeare's sympathy for the earl, even that he wished to see him on the throne. Others see the topical reference as an active intervention on the part of playwright, a "well-meant but ill-advised attempt at mediation" between Essex and Elizabeth (Patterson 1999, p. 338). It seems unlikely that the queen would to listen to the Lord Chamberlain's playwright's political advice, far more likely that she and her Privy Council would view the intervention as meddling in dangerous matters. It is unsurprising that the Chorus referring to Essex was cut from the quarto version, and the play itself drastically simplified to create "a Lancastrian history that would pass the closest inspection" (Patterson 1999, p. 331).

Shakespeare's (and his Company's) sympathy – or otherwise – towards the earl would be tested in February 1601. The Lord Chamberlain's Men were asked by Essex and his followers, who had for some time, "exhibited a sensitive awareness of the history of the reigns of Richard II and Henry IV" (Gajda 2012, p. 236) to "have the play of the deposing and killing of King Richard the Second to be played the Saturday next" (Wickham, Berry, and Ingram 2020, p. 197). The actors were promised "forty shillings more than their ordinary to play it" (ibid.). What the players did not know (or said they did not know) was that, the following day, Essex and his followers would launch a coup against Queen Elizabeth I.

The coup failed, not least because London did not "pour forth its citizens" to support him. But the Chamberlain's Men were implicated and duly questioned. Augustine Phillips, spokesman for the players, made it clear that they were reluctant: he and "his friends were determined to have played some other play holding that play of King Richard to be so old and so long out of use as that they should have small or no company at it" Wickham, Berry, and Ingram 2020, p. 197). Perhaps the play was "old" and "long out of use" (then again, you would say that if you were implicated in treason), but no matter: the players were overruled by the earl's supporters and "played it accordingly" (Dionne 2007, p. 222). It might have helped that they were paid 40 shillings more than their usual charge to perform "the deposyng and kyllyng of Kyng Rychard the Second" (Nelson 2017). This time the Chamberlain's Men got away with performing murder: Augustine Phillips was released, and there were no further consequences for his company of players.

What was Essex (Bolingbroke) seeing in Shakespeare's play as he plotted against Elizabeth (Richard)? Paul Hammer (2008, p. 34) believes *Richard II* works as a warning against following Bolingbroke's dreadful courses. Bolingbroke had intended to purge the state of evil counsel but had become carried away. The Earl of Essex would now "do it *properly*," without the awful consequences of 1399 – the deposition of the monarch. But as Gajda points out (2012, pp. 51–52), Shakespeare does not make Bolingbroke's usurpation clearly unintentional. As ever, the play is ambiguous, Bolingbroke himself "taciturn; the audience must itself decide if he acts at first only to claim his confiscated inheritance and to thwart the evil counsellors, Bushy, Bagot, and Green, or if he entertains ambition for higher powers from the point of his return from exile" (ibid., p. 52).

Essex's failed coup was still in the future when Shakespeare returned to the relative safety of comedy. *As You Like It* may be his response to the repertoire of the rival company, the Admiral's Men, who performed at least three plays based on the court-in-exile of Robin Hood and it may have been written quickly. There are mistakes and confusion over names, both suggesting hurry, and the play recycles "a number of devices used by Shakespeare in previous romantic comedies. These include a structural division between court and country, a green world that is as much a realm of the imagination as a natural environment, and, driving the play's action, a voluble, witty, and resourceful cross-dressed heroine" (Shaughnessy 2018, p. 15).

   As You Like It can also be seen as a nostalgic play, generically – and personally for its author. Its main source, Thomas Lodge's prose romance *Rosalind*, "was a product of a golden moment in Elizabethan history, the period following England's great triumph over the Spanish Armada in 1588" (Shapiro 2005a, pp. 232–233): the

> nostalgia exercised its hold on Shakespeare as well. Like many of the other sources Shakespeare turned to this year, *Rosalind* dates from around the time that he moved to London and began writing. A decade into his career, as his work began to turn in new directions, Shakespeare needed to take his bearings. He found himself reflecting back to that time when he had first fully immersed himself in the literary culture, measuring how much had changed, what kind of writing was no longer possible.

Or perhaps what kind of *new* writing was possible. Shapiro has Shakespeare responding to the rise of Ben Jonson. The creation of the "enigma" that is Jaques demonstrates a playwright "motivated to try his hand at satire for the first time." And the experiment that is the "melancholy, brooding and sentimental" Jaques becomes "a rough sketch for Hamlet" (Shapiro 2005a, p. 245). It is Rosalind, however, the "voluble, witty and resourceful" heroine of *As You Like It*, who is truly exceptional, not quite like any other Shakespeare woman, although she has her forerunners in Romeo's off-stage, pre-Juliet love interest and the most articulate and charming of Shakespeare's early heroines, Rosaline in *Love's Labour's Lost*. For starters, the part of Rosalind is a huge challenge for a young actor. The boy playing her has some 201 speeches with a total of 680 lines. Moreover, "by scripting Rosalind predominantly in prose, Shakespeare adds a further, formidable technical challenge to what is already an unprecedentedly demanding role" (Shaughnessy 2018, p. 21). McMillin (2004) (through a detailed analysis of cues, amongst other things) demonstrates that Shakespeare, the dramatist, does everything he can to help the actor tackle the part, one that is longer and more challenging than many male roles, from Romeo through Macbeth to Prospero.[8] As for the writing itself, it "marks a significant advance in his handling of character and intimacy" as "Shakespeare lifts a conventional heroine out of popular story and transforms her into someone we feel we know or want to know. How he does so, and how he then endows her with the ingenuity to educate the 'untutored youth' she loves about who she is and what intimacy means, is one of the mysteries of literary creation" (Shapiro 2005a, pp. 228–229).

If even the literary techniques required to create "someone we feel we know or want to know" are mysterious, then how much more so the psychology of the man who created her. Or him.

Because William Shakespeare, the generous, experienced playwright, remains preoccupied with gender and performance in *As You Like It* and his Rosalind assumes a boy's disguise very early in the play:

> Were it not better,
> Because that I am more than common tall,
> That I did suit me all points like a man?
> A gallant curtal-axe upon my thigh,
> A boar-spear in my hand, and in my heart,
> Lie there what hidden woman's fear there will,
> We'll have a swashing and a martial outside,
> As many other mannish cowards have
> That do outface it with their semblances.
>
> *(1.3.111–119)*

Famously, Rosalind (or more precisely the boy actor playing her) ends the play, foregrounding the operation of theater itself, encouraging the audience to understand sex and gender as both innate *and* a performance. He/she/he addresses the audience directly. This is no mere nod to the erotic transactions in and around the theater. Now, "the boy playing the girl who played a boy who played a girl appears in a girl's dress and coyly flirts with both sexes. The epilogue thus continues the protagonist's intricate drag act, providing Rosalind with one last chance to arouse, amuse, unsettle, and charm us" (McCoy 2015, p. 80).[9]

That "intricate drag act" has involved Rosalind choosing Ganymede as her alias. The name "is richly provocative of the fears of anti-theatricalists because of its homoerotic associations," for, in classical myth, Ganymede is the beautiful Trojan shepherd boy abducted by Jove and enslaved as cup-bearer to the gods (Orgel 1997, p. 51). In Shakespeare's London of the 1590s, it was also a contemporary slang term for a catamite, a boy used sexually by an older man. The most explicitly pederastic literary text of the period, Richard Barnfield's 1595 sonnets, address "sweet Ganymed" (19.2), a "sweete youth" (20.5), and "sweet boy" (14.5) with "hony-combs" (8.14) dropping from his lips. Rosalind/Ganymede is as much a "master-mistress" as the young man of the sonnets, and the epilogue only the final gesture in a play which has played provocatively with gender and sexuality.

Whereas at the end of *As You Like It* (as elsewhere in Shakespeare) all the characters are returned to his or her appropriate *social* position – the duke is now again a duke and not a forest outlaw, Rosalind is now Rosalind and not

Ganymede, and so forth – there is no such stability when it comes to sex or gender. The Epilogue undercuts any "neat convergence of biological sex and culturally constructed gender" (Howard 1988, p. 435) since "if a boy can so successfully personate the voice, gait, and manner of a woman, how stable are those boundaries separating one sexual kind from another, and thus how secure are those powers and privileges assigned to the hierarchically superior sex, which depends upon notions of difference to justify its dominance?" Howard notes, "the Epilogue playfully invites the question" (ibid.).

Does this mean that William Shakespeare was also preoccupied with the question and its more subversive answers, particularly at this time? I think yes, in part because he is (as hinted by Howard) far *less* interested in asking those questions of traditional social hierarchies. Emma Smith agrees: "in Shakespeare's comedies, gender can be played with and impersonated, but class distinctions are absolute" (Smith 2012, p. 17). *Why* he, personally, was particularly interested remains, to take Shapiro's word, mysterious.

Shakespeare's creation of Rosalind suggests he was a risk-taker in a different way. As noted above, he would not have created such a demanding role unless he was reasonably confident that there was a boy actor with the ability to do it justice. Therefore, we can infer that there were a number of extremely talented apprentices learning their craft with the Chamberlain's Men in the late 1590s.

This is good news if you need an actor who can take on the part of Rosalind, but commercially and artistically it is a high-risk strategy in the volatile and precarious environment of the public theater. That Shakespeare and his company invested in these young actors reveals an "entrepreneurial adventurousness that not infrequently expressed itself as sheer recklessness," concludes Shaughnessy (2018, p. 30). James Burbage, erector of the Theatre back in 1576, and his sons, dismantlers and rebuilders of the Theatre's timbers some 20 years later, were adventurous in this way, and it is possible that their colleague, William Shakespeare, was too. However, it seems that *As You Like It* was an adventure too far for the Chamberlain's Men. No record survives of a performance. Perhaps the play was too naturalistic (Shapiro 2005a, p. 229) for audiences. Perhaps the satirical links between the character Jaques (there are lavatorial echoes of "jakes") and the courtier Sir John Harington, creator of the water closet, or something about the Earl of Essex touched a raw courtier nerve.

If this were the case, however, *As You Like It* would have had a "topicality and direct (not to mention reckless) contemporary allusiveness that was generally uncharacteristic of its constitutionally circumspect and non-aligned author" (Shaughnessy 2018, p. 11). It's also a play which can be quite easily mined for autobiographical allusions on the part of its constitutionally self-effacing author. That the play is set in the Forest of Arden, Shakespeare country, is a biographical gift. That the witty clown Touchstone (stone being testicles) is a self-portrait of Shakespeare (spear being penis): one needs to think through the pun. Less bawdily, there's a young William in the play, so the dialogue between the clown and the boy "can be read as an exchange between the wealthy and quick-witted playwright and the provincial youth he has left behind him in the Forest of Arden" (Bate 2008, p. 45).

The allusions are so discreet as to be easily missed, and, as ever, there are other suggestions. The name Touchstone (rather than applying to Shakespeare) may reference the company's new clown, Robert Armin, once a goldsmith. A touchstone is a tool, and Armin had played a character called Tutch in an earlier play. For me, the lack of consensus merely confirms Shakespeare's circumspection. His tendency to placate rather than challenge those more powerful than him is evident from the textual history of another play from this period, *The Book of Sir Thomas More*. To the story of More "calming a London riot against immigrants, and then his stoic refusal to submit to King Henry VIII's will despite the pressure put on him by his family," Shakespeare adds (in a section known by scholars as "Hand D") "a rousing speech about tolerance which encourages the rioters to imagine themselves as refugees in an inhospitable land." It seems that his material was "rather too topical in early modern London – the marks of the Master of the Revels, the Elizabethan censor, suggest this" (Smith 2012, p. 236), and *Sir Thomas More* never saw the light of Elizabethan day. Shelved, it was revised a few years later (ibid.) and it is possible that the passage in Hand D, a plea for tolerance, was added as part of an attempt to placate the censor.

As You Like It didn't appear in print until 1623. Did Shakespeare, more generally, lose interest in, or decide against, the publication of his drama after 1600? Was he simply not motivated by seeing his name in print? It may have been simply a matter of printing house economics, at least when it came to publication of comedies, and old-fashioned comedies at that. Shaughnessy (2018, p. 12) thinks so: "Shakespeare's pastoralism, his habit of locating his comic intrigues in fantasy worlds elsewhere, and the fondness for cross-dressed boys that he shared with courtly forebear John Lyly in his 1580s heyday, had come to seem rather old-fashioned, especially when set against the emergence of the sharp, cynical, London-set, money-driven civic comedies of Jonson, Thomas Dekker and Thomas Middleton."

Shakespeare's romantic comedies may have been going out of fashion on London stages but, by 1600, "fifteen or all but five of the first twenty plays" Shakespeare wrote "were in print" and "more than half of them had reached at least a second edition" (Erne 2013, p. 80). Shakespeare may not have been concerned to publish his plays, but someone was. His histories were the best-sellers, but five of his comedies were in quarto by 1602, including a 1600 edition of *A Midsummer Night's Dream* of "the very highest textual authority, since it bears many marks of having been printed from the author's 'foul papers': that is, his autograph draft (in this instance evidently in its final state; simply not a fair copy). Certainly this *Dream* was not printed from the prompt-book which would be transcribed from the autograph" (Brooks 2007, p. xxii). For Lukas Erne (2013, p. 135), this suggests that if Shakespeare was holding back his work, it was not out of lack of interest in publication but because he was one of the few writers who could envisage "an ambitious collected edition" of his writings, such as the folio of *Works* that would be produced by Jonson in 1616. In an age when there was no copyright law, an author would not make money from the printed playtext, but he would make his name.

What's at stake here is a debate about Shakespeare's own understanding of his writerly status, whether he saw himself as a man of the theater or as a poet, a popular or literary dramatist, writing for the moment or for posterity. If Shakespeare was not indifferent to his plays' publication and was actively seeking fame – by any means (Erne) – then he would have been pleased by the various allusions to another play of 1599, *Julius Caesar*, parodied by Jonson twice in *Every Man Out of His Humour* and recorded by Thomas Platter, a Swiss doctor from Basle, visiting England in the autumn:

> On the 21st of September, after dinner, at about two o'clock, I went with my party across the water; in the straw-thatched house we saw the tragedy of the first Emperor Julius Caesar, very pleasingly performed, with approximately fifteen characters; at the end of the play they danced together admirably and exceedingly gracefully, according to their custom, two in each group dressed in men's and two women's apparel.
>
> *(quoted in Greenblatt 2004, p. 293)*

Apart from the reminder that plays ended with a dance, Platter's "fifteen characters" suggests there was a lot of doubling, and a sophisticated tiring-house set-up to achieve all the costume changes. With regard to "apparel," Platter would have seen actors in an eclectic mix of dress, old and contemporary. The play's famous anachronisms, such as the "sweaty nightcaps" worn by the Roman plebians, or a clock striking in ancient Rome, both offer further evidence, if it were needed, that historical accuracy was not a high priority for Shakespeare or his contemporaries. More importantly, the audience were being asked to draw parallels between the past and the present. Shakespeare was offering his audiences a play "about resonant regime-change at a time when the sands of the Tudor regime were inexorably running out" (Dutton 2018, p. 268). He was playing with fire, but once again he avoided trouble.

Shakespeare wrote at least three new plays for the Chamberlain's Men in 1599: *Henry V*, *Julius Caesar*, and *As You Like It*. The company also performed one from Jonson, *Every Man Out of His Humour*, with *An Alarum for London* the fifth play we know for sure from that year. All, writes Shaughnessy (2018, p. 34) are "large-scale, resource-intensive works." *Every Man Out of His Humour* has a cast of more than 30 – though no Shakespeare acting – and "an intricate metatheatrical structure which runs to 4,526 lines," more than double the length of most plays in the period. This is a confident, ambitious theater company at the top of its game and Shakespeare was their leading dramatist. And, perhaps by June, the Globe playhouse was their new home, just over a hundred days after the signing of the ground lease on the site in Bankside on 21 February.[10]

Some believe that *Julius Caesar*, Shakespeare's "tragedy of the first Emperor," was chosen for the first afternoon, with 12 June as a likely date, because it was "astronomically useful and astrologically significant" Daniell 1998, p. 16). On that day there was a new moon, "and a high tide at Southwark at 1 p.m., more than convenient for the arrival of an audience of three thousand. (The alternative, arriving at a low tide, would have meant a long slog through smelly mud.) ... Astrology suggested that a new moon on the summer solstice made 12 June unusually propitious for a new venture, and readings of the stars supported this. To open a theater on the summer solstice, coinciding with the sun–moon–earth conjunction and exceptional high tides, on a date which was as well astrologically promising, would show wisdom" (Daniell 1998, p. 16).

The Globe tied Shakespeare "even more closely to a small group of theatre owners (or 'housekeepers'), a circle even more exclusive than that of the Chamberlain's fellowship" (Van Es 2016, p. 262): Shakespeare himself, Richard Burbage, John Heminges, Augustine Philips, and Thomas Pope and the new man, Robert Armin, who took over from Will Kemp. By all accounts, Armin was not an easy colleague, but he was new and he was different. In the tradition of the courtly wise fool, he had a command of languages (Italian, Latin), and could mimic the logic chopping of the scholars. (Some have argued that Shakespeare himself could read Italian.)[11] For Shakespeare, Armin represented an opportunity. Kemp had contributed to the subplots of his plays, with the clown scenes alternating with the serious action. Now, things would be different. In what was probably his first role, that of Touchstone, the fool, instead of bouncing and tumbling, offers a long speech on the seven degrees of the lie. Armin's arrival in the company may have hastened Shakespeare's move away from building his comic plots (and characters) from the materials of disguise and cross-dressing. Instead of resolving the chaos with sometimes implausible marriages, Shakespeare's comedies entered some darker, more skeptical, worlds.

These worlds were already familiar to Ben Jonson, whose *Every Man Out of His Humour* was performed that winter of 1599/1600. Shakespeare was not in the cast list for Jonson's play but he is the object of some (reasonably good-natured) satirical digs. What is Jonson laughing at? Shakespeare's pretensions to gentle status (the coat of arms); his tendency towards hyperbole and romantic plot formulas, so different from Jonson's own satirical comedy; and – perhaps not in laughter but in admiration – his ability to create a comic character like Falstaff. Jonson's Bobadill may, indeed, be a fellow dramatist's homage to Sir John.[12]

In contrast to Shakespeare, there is no doubt at all that Jonson was serious about getting his plays into print. Indeed, the quarto edition of *Every Man Out of His Humour*, which appeared the following year, emphasizes "the superiority of the printed work" (Riggs 2015, pp. 188–189), adding material not designed for the stage, and advertising that it contained "more than hath been publicly spoken or acted." This is a play quarto designed to be read.

Meanwhile, all we know of William Shakespeare at this time is that he was busy avoiding taxes – again.

Chapter Five

October 1600, and Shakespeare is still avoiding taxes. He may be living in the Clink. And he may be starting to write *Hamlet* because in that play he refers to the Children of the Chapel (the "eyrie of children" who are "now the fashion" and "berattle the common stages") who had just begun performing at the Blackfriars playhouse. This was galling because James Burbage had acquired parts of the old Blackfriars monastery in 1596 and converted them into a rectangular indoor theater, only to find that residents in the area would not countenance professional performances there, going so far as to get an injunction to stop the theater being used by adult players. Unable to mount productions in Blackfriars himself, he was forced to lease his theater to the Children of the Chapel, who were allowed to perform there because they were not considered as professional players, despite audiences being charged to see them play. Any and all productions were part of their education. Ever alert to developments in the theater world, always conscious of competition, Shakespeare saw the boys doing well, and dragged them into his *Hamlet*.

What better play to open the second half of these chapters than Shakespeare's most iconic work? But, we need to pause for a moment. What do we mean by *Hamlet*? This may seem like a foolish question, but it goes to the heart of Shakespeare's practice as a dramatist and challenges our own creation of certainty where there is none.

We could start with a play called *Hamlet* which was probably written between 1587 and 1589, therefore over 10 years earlier, and therefore belonging in Chapter One of this book. This *Hamlet* was probably written by Shakespeare, or so its editors (Taylor and Loughnane 2017, p. 547) argue: Shakespeare's authorship of the play is "more convincing than any alternative explanation."

The Life of the Author: William Shakespeare, First Edition. Anna Beer.
© 2021 John Wiley & Sons, Ltd. Published 2021 by John Wiley & Sons, Ltd.

Then there's the first quarto edition (Q1), which was registered for publication in the summer of 1602 and appeared the following year. The title page announced that the play had been "divers times acted … in the City of London: as also in the two Universities of Cambridge and Oxford, and elsewhere." This is probably not the same play as the *Hamlet* that was performed in the late 1580s, but it could be a rough draft, or a recollection of a performance of a play by Shakespeare. It is fast, plot-driven, and not particularly ruminative: the play's "emotions are raw rather than mediated and it is more of an ensemble piece, not a showcase for a single star performer" (Thompson and Taylor 2006, p. 16), the kind of play that would suit a company with "limited rehearsal time" (ibid.).

And then there's the "real" *Hamlet*, or more precisely, the second quarto version of the play (Q2), "Newly imprinted and enlarged to almost as much againe as it was, according to the true and perfect Coppie," and which appeared in print over New Year, 1604–1605. Some think this version may have been based on Shakespeare's own papers (the "true and perfect copy"), but there is no certainty. Q2 is a much more thoughtful play than Q1. Whilst the later play seems to be exploring the very idea of the revenge tragedy, Q1 simply *is* a revenge tragedy. The fascination with revenge is nothing new. Indeed, if Shakespeare wrote his first version of the play back in the late 1580s, it's something old. *Titus Andronicus, Romeo and Juliet*, and *Julius Caesar*, all three of "these generic predecessors had contained revenge as a motivation for the narrative, as had many of the English history plays," Shakespeare wrote in the 1590s (Thompson and Taylor 2006).

Gary Taylor and Rory Loughnane (2017) think Shakespeare wrote Q2 in 1603, after the death of Queen Elizabeth I in March of that year. Their argument is that, if Shakespeare did not collaborate with Ben Jonson on the tragedy *Sejanus* and he did write *Hamlet* in 1602, then he would have done no playwriting at all in 1603 – an unlikely scenario. They go on to suggest that it is also unlikely that "Shakespeare would have permitted a failed collaborative play (*Sejanus*) to be his only 'new' offering at court in the first theatrical season of the new reign" (p. 548). They do honestly admit that this is all speculation. The date range for this, the most familiar version of *Hamlet*, remains 1599–1604, with even money on early 1602 or mid-1603. (Just to make things more interesting, the Royal Shakespeare Company website has the play written in 1600, because of its allusions to *Julius Caesar* which we know for sure was performed, if not composed, in the autumn of 1599.)

Finally, there's the text of *Hamlet* that appears in the Folio of 1623. It is longer than Q1 but based on a transcript differing in numerous details from Q2, omitting more than 200 lines found in the quarto from 20 years earlier. Editors over the years have adopted different approaches but usually it comes down to the phrase used in Bevington (Hamlet: Online Shakespeare Edition; Bevington n.d.): "The Editor's Choice version combines the most effective passages from all three texts."

So, when attempting to map *Hamlet* onto Shakespeare's lived experience, the first question needs to be: which *Hamlet*? The straight-up revenge tragedy, perhaps written in the late 1580s? Or the more complex psychological drama, written (or created by revision) at some point in the early 1600s? The later play is the work of choice for most biographers, although the precise dating of the writing of the second quarto and therefore its relation to Shakespeare's life remains contested, and rightly so.

Uncertainty as to what Shakespeare wrote and when he wrote it means that sweeping claims, or even fascinating questions, which center on a particular play can flatter to deceive. Shapiro (2005b, p. 11), for example, expressing exasperation with traditional biographies of Shakespeare, concludes that "we remain almost as far as ever from answering the question of how, in the course of a year or so, the author of competent but unspectacular plays like *Much Ado* and *The Merry Wives of Windsor*, went on to write *Hamlet*."

That question drives his remarkable and enjoyable study of the year 1599, but not only does it rely on an early, unprovable dating of *Merry Wives* and the privileging of just one of the versions of *Hamlet* that survives, but it downplays the ambition and complexity of plays like *Henry V* and *Julius Caesar*.

Do we really need to see some kind of mysterious transformation, some hidden trigger, that will bring *Hamlet* into the world? It seems we do, whether that trigger is understood as Shakespeare's religious angst or the death of his son, Hamnet.

First, then, the religious angst which (whether seeing Shakespeare as a first-generation Protestant or a closeted Catholic) is tied up with his relationship to his father. Greenblatt (2001) shows that Hamlet's question – "*Hic et ubique?*" – as he seeks his father's ghost under the stage – is an echo of a Catholic prayer to be said when entering a graveyard.[1] Hamlet meets his father, William meets (Catholic) John. In a more general sense, the play dramatizes the poetics of purgatory, "the shift from a culture in which the living could do something for the dead (specifically, they could shorten their time in purgatory by prayers and other actions) to one in which nothing could be done – or in which revenge becomes a problematic substitute" (Thompson and Taylor 2006, p. 42).

Or Shakespeare is intrigued by the paradox that "a young man from Wittenberg, with a distinctly Protestant temperament, is haunted by a distinctly Catholic ghost" (Greenblatt 2001, p. 240). And for Shakespeare (and Greenblatt 2001, p. 249), it's personal: the "Protestant playwright was haunted by the spirit of his Catholic father pleading for suffrages to relieve his soul from the pains of Purgatory."

There are a couple of problems with this. If the play was mainly completed *before* John Shakespeare's death in September 1601 then the dates don't work. And to insist on a not-so-hidden Catholic agenda in *Hamlet* is to dismiss the "range of religious associations" (Maguire and Smith 2012, p. 50) at work in the play:

> Hamlet is a student of Wittenberg, strongly associated with the reformer Martin Luther (and with Hamlet's strongly anti-Catholic stage predecessor, Marlowe's Dr Faustus). He describes death in orthodox Protestant terms, as the "undiscovered country from whose bourn / No traveller returns" but then encounters the distinctly Catholic ghost of his father, returned from the distinctly Catholic location of Purgatory, "doomed for a certain term to walk the night, / And for the day confined to fast in fires / Till the foul crimes done in my days of nature / Are burnt and purged away."

Shakespeare draws attention to precisely these interpretive problems. His characters know their ghost theory. Hamlet himself decides to use theater to test if

> It is a damned ghost that we have seen,
> And my imaginations are as foul
> As Vulcan's stithy.
>
> *(3.2.78–80 [Q2])*

or more simply in scene 9 of Q1, to discover if "It is a damnèd ghost that we have seen" (l. 58). That the ghost was the figment of a diseased imagination, that any vision was the work the devil, who preys upon the weak – women, children and those who were depressed or melancholic – was accepted Protestant wisdom at the time in which Shakespeare was writing. The powerful irony is that neither Hamlet's nor Shakespeare's use of theater serves to prove anything, and we the audience are left uncertain – about Hamlet, the Ghost and, as ever, about Shakespeare's personal beliefs.

What we are faced with is a playwright who allows different religious beliefs to coexist in a single play. Earlier, in the mid-1590s, he was quite comfortable writing plays with widely differing understandings of crucial theological positions, such as the nature and significance of grace and free will. In *Love's Labour's Lost* Berowne, a charming but unlikely catechist, insists that without heavenly help, without "special grace," a "war" against the "affections" cannot be won.

> For every man with his affects is born,
> Not by might mastered, but by special grace.
>
> *(1.1.149–150)*

But in *Romeo and Juliet*, written just before *Love's Labour's Lost*, Shakespeare creates the Friar, a character who insistently but quietly implies "man's freedom to choose 'grace' or 'rude will,' to offset the dehumanising effect of his pervasive and strong emphasis on the operation of Fate" (Blakemore-Evans 2003, p. 25). Shakespeare's opportunist rather than consistent use of the Bible, his willingness to explore the faultlines and inconsistencies of religious belief within and between plays, may show pragmatism or skepticism or caution. As ever, his own beliefs remain astonishingly difficult to decipher. Or perhaps not astonishingly. It has been argued that, if

> uncovering the specific beliefs of most people is hard enough, it is especially true of writers. Writing could, of course, be used as evidence against people when religious policy changed. Poets who circulated verse in manuscript might evade censorship, but work for the public stage was another matter. There were strict prohibitions, as well as checks through the office of the Master of the Revels, on the declaration of particular beliefs in plays, which is why so few are about religion and why it is almost impossible to link particular dramas to an individual's religious belief (which has not stopped some critics from trying).
>
> *(Hadfield 2019, p. 18)*

The fascination with faultlines and inconsistencies may stem from the world in which Shakespeare lived and worked, a world in transition, poised between Catholicism and Protestantism. Hadfield offers a roll-call of Shakespeare's contemporaries to demonstrate the complexities. Ben Jonson? Converted to Catholicism but "at the end of his long life it was hard to know which side" (ibid.) he was on; Thomas Dekker? Trenchant anti-Catholic, but even so he might have been "covering his tracks or simply wanted to take the money" (ibid.); Edmund Spenser? "Protestant poet" (ibid., p. 19). But both of his sons were suspected of Catholicism in the mid-seventeenth century.

Shakespeare's mind and world are both informed by these religious changes, and for some this allows a conflation, at one level at least, of character and playwright: Hamlet and Shakespeare shared with their transitional Elizabethan generation the experience of having Catholic fathers who had been born before the Reformation, of living through the fervent anti-Catholicism of the second half of Elizabeth's reign, and of leaving their successors with the new religious politics of James. Shakespeare's religious beliefs become "less a matter of individual biography and more a snapshot of contemporary doctrinal shifts, uncertainties, and overlaps; the 'bare ruined choirs where late the sweet birds sang' (Sonnet 73, l. 4) epitomize a general rather than a personal, cultural nostalgia amid the debris of English monastic architecture" (Maguire and Smith 2012, p. 52).

Shakespeare's father allegedly gets two more mentions in the play, in the Graveyard scene. First, there's the Gravedigger's somewhat gratuitous reference to Adam as a "gentleman" on the grounds that he was "the first that ever bore arms" (5.1.32–33). This is, apparently, a reminder of the coat of arms William had helped John acquire in 1596. Then there's the reference to a tanner: as a glover, John Shakespeare's work involved tanning skins which would then be transformed into gloves. John Shakespeare's social standing, rather than his death, is the focus here, which perhaps supports the Arden editors' suggestion (determined as they are to keep John in the biographical frame) that Shakespeare's father "had been in poor health for some years before his death, so the play may anticipate rather than reflect that event." But do we need Shakespeare to be responding to the death (or indeed the life) of John Shakespeare for the play to reflect concerns about the "lost world" of traditional Catholicism? Historian Susan Brigden (2000, pp. 364–367) ends her superb survey of the sixteenth century with her understanding of *Hamlet* as a work marking the end of an era, an era defined by religious and political upheaval, a pre-echo of Maguire and Smith's argument about the workings of a more general than personal nostalgia.

If not William and John (plus Catholicism), then what about William and Hamnet? Park Honan (1998) is certain that Shakespeare's son was known as Hamnet *and* Hamlet. If so, the play is a working out of a father's grief for his son, although it is less clear what Shakespeare might be saying about his relationship with Hamlet/Hamnet.

Skepticism aside, Shakespeare's relationship with his own father and his own son must surely be relevant to a play in which a father and a son, both called Hamlet, die. Perhaps as Garber (2004, p. 479) argues, a play which is "almost obsessively concerned with the relationships between fathers and sons, seems poised" between the death of Shakespeare's own son and father. Even before Hamlet is told that his father has returned as a ghost, he is utterly preoccupied with him: "My father – methinks I see my father" (1.2.183) he tells Horatio, before reassuring his friend that he sees his father only in his mind's eye.

Hamlet is not the only play to be preoccupied by "patrilineal identity": from *Henry VI Part I* on this is "the central thematic, political, and formal concern of such plays" (MacFaul 2012, pp. 64–65). Braunmuller (1998, p. 62) suggests that *King John*, from the mid-late 1590s, reveals most clearly a pattern common to many of Shakespeare's plays. By rearranging historical facts and redistributing historical emphases, the playwright creates a characteristic sequence. At first, the royal heir is dominated by his father; he then enters the social and political arena through marriage; submits to the guidance of another older male, and "finally emerges as an independent character, striving to achieve a monarchy to rival his now-forgotten father's." The pattern can play out tragically (with the father's displacement requiring regicide) or comically, "if the child's maturation into adult sexuality predominates."

The roots of this displacement lie in patriarchy itself. The father has proved himself a "man" by having (male) offspring, but having fulfilled his function, must necessarily be displaced by his heirs. The necessary tension between a son (who to be a man himself must displace his father) is heightened by Shakespeare, who often explores a conflict between duty and autonomy.

Whether these tensions and conflicts are not merely implicit to the workings of patriarchy but are rooted in William's own relationship with his father is another question. There is, according to Tromly (2010), a pattern to, or emphasis laid upon, the father/son dynamic that suggests lived experience. A dutiful son is pressured to conform, "to perform an action that he senses is foreign to his values and threatening to his autonomy" (p. 243). This pressure creates ambivalence in the son, but an ambivalence that is hard to express. Shakespeare's fictional sons "do eventually act, and the action usually involves the rescue of the father from his enemies." Significantly, "without exception, these filial restorations figure more largely in Shakespeare's plays than in the sources they are based on. They are also considerably more complex, being expressions of filial autonomy as well as deference" (ibid.). All this, for Tromly, suggests that William is bringing his troubled relationship with John to his plays.

But what of William and mother Mary, Hamlet and Gertrude? Shakespeare's use of his sources does offer some hints as to his attitudes towards women, at least in this middle-period of his writing, at least in this play. He took most of the plot of *Hamlet* from a very popular sixteenth-century French writer, François de Belleforest. He, in turn, had taken the Hamlet story from a chronicle of the life of Amleth of Denmark, compiled in the late twelfth century by Saxo the Grammarian.

There are two major differences between Shakespeare's *Hamlet* and his two main sources, and one striking similarity. In their versions of the Hamlet story, Saxo and Belleforest both have a long delay, of years, before the revenge is achieved. However, this delay is not a concern, as it is in Shakespeare's play. Instead, it is a sign of the determination of the revenger. And their hero triumphs. Amleth justifies his actions to the people in a long speech, is made king, and, most importantly, he is alive. In Elizabethan revenge tragedies, the avenging hero was not permitted to live, once he (and occasionally she) had achieved revenge, since it would have been too shocking, morally, politically, and theatrically if the character was seen to be rewarded for their decision to take justice into their own hands. In this instance, therefore, Shakespeare is following the dramatic and moral conventions of his time, rather than being faithful to his sources.

Where he sticks close to his sources is in the representation of Gertrude and, in particular, the level of disgust expressed concerning her sexual activity. Both the twelfth-century Saxo and the sixteenth-century Belleforest wrote long passages about the queen's repulsive, animalistic sexual appetites. The queen is, for example, described as a "brute beast" by Saxo, whilst Belleforest has his hero say to his mother that she is

> a vile wanton adulteress, altogether impudent and given over to her pleasure", who "runs spreading forth her arms joyfully to embrace the traitorous villainous tyrant that murdered my father.
>
> *(Belleforest n.d.)*

From Hamlet's response to his mother (and snubbing of Claudius) at the start of the play, through the infamous closet scene, Shakespeare creates a son over-involved with his mother. Hamlet's primary focus is Gertrude's sexual relationship with Claudius, rather than Claudius's murder of his father. Indeed, that the play is as much about sex as it is about death has dismayed some readers. Writing in 1920, T. S. Eliot expressed his era's discomfort with the play's (and specifically its protagonist's) preoccupation with sexual acts: "Hamlet is up against the difficulty that his disgust is occasioned by his mother, but his mother is not an adequate equivalent for it; his disgust envelops and exceeds her"; hence the play lacks an "objective correlative" – an appropriate matching of emotion to object (1997, p. 58).

Biographers are far less willing to map Hamlet and Gertrude onto William and his mother. They prefer, if pushed, to see the representation of Gertrude as "a kind of meditation on the ageing and passing of the Virgin Queen" (Thompson and Taylor 2006, p. 38). In a similar move, Shakespeare's preoccupation with fathers is a sign of his engagement with the politics of the era – and specifically the notion that the king was a father to his people – rather than his familial ties. Church and state taught and enforced the God-given authority, the divine right of the father/king. Rebellion against the father/king was sin. Obedience even when he did wrong, even if he was a tyrant, was a virtue. So, when Claudius says to Hamlet, "Think of us / As of a father" (1.2.107–108), he is saying, in practice, think of me as your king. One of the (many) reasons that Hamlet has such a problem with revenge is that it would mean killing his new father/king. If Claudius's killing of Old Hamlet has the primal curse upon it (as Claudius himself admits, in his soliloquy in act 3, scene 3), then killing one's king/father on the word of a Ghost who might or might not be the devil is almost as bad. But then we enter the usual biographical cul-de-sac. The *Hamlet* plays foreground king-killing, but the death of the avenger (a change from his sources) hardly suggests a radical defense of tyrannicide.

Back to sex, then. Yet another way to map the play onto Shakespeare's life is to consider its depiction of the intimacy between Horatio and Hamlet, dramatic creations who embody the multiple understandings of the word "friend" in Shakespeare's time. Is this friendship another expression of William's bisexuality? Hamlet and Horatio certainly speak the language of same-sex desire. There will be those who disagree with a resolutely queer reading of Hamlet's death ("The rest is not silence, but Horatio," Masten 2016, p. 82), but reading Shakespeare's own sexuality from the plays is just as plausible, or implausible, as reading his grief for his son or his anxiety about his father's illness, his love for his mother, or his affection for his friends.

Because, as ever, the biographical facts are sparse. On 25 March 1601, Mary, William's mother, is mentioned in a will as owing a debt. And on 9 September, John, his father, was buried. Despite his previous financial problems, John still owned his large double-house in Henley Street, and this William inherited. His mother, and his married sister (Joan), continued to live there after John Shakespeare's death. But there are no direct records referring to William himself.

In sharp contrast, we have a satirical account of Ben Jonson courting theatrical acclaim in 1601. A fellow playwright mocked him for venturing on stage when his play had ended, "to exchange courtesies, and compliments with Gallants in the Lords' rooms" (the expensive box seats adjoining it) in order "to make all the house rise up in Arms, to cry ... that's he, that's he, that's he" (Dekker 1602). These kinds of comparisons between Shakespeare and Jonson are illuminating, but they can also mislead. As Andrew Hadfield notes (2019, p. 25), considering the relationship between biography and belief, "Jonson leaves numerous traces of his stated beliefs, identity and allegiances." In contrast Shakespeare "remains, *like most* Elizabethan and Jacobean writers, conspicuously elusive" (ibid., my italics). Jonson is the anomaly, not Shakespeare.

One final thought on *Hamlet*. Shakespeare might just have parodied his great tragedy in his great comedy, *Twelfth Night*. If so, do we catch a glimpse of a man willing to laugh at his own seriousness, even his own suffering? Is he a playwright willing and able to satirize his own creation, Prince Hamlet? Potter (2012, pp. 287–288) thinks so, and I do too.

> That Malvolio was a steward and not a prince would be clear from his costume, but, played by a leading actor, he would have drawn all eyes when, like Hamlet in 1.2, he entered with the rest of Olivia's court but remained silent until he was addressed. Like Hamlet, he refuses to be part of the jollity of those around him. Like Hamlet, he makes negative comments on clowns. Like Hamlet, he soon changes to an antic costume. He then is confined – as a prince could not be – in a dark

room, the usual recommended cure for madness. When, in his last scene, he threatens "revenge on the whole pack of you," his attempt to turn the comedy into a revenge tragedy is the final absurd touch.

This "final absurd touch" comes at the end of a very, very funny play. The earliest mention of Shakespeare's *Twelfth Night* is by law student, John Manningham, in February 1602, and focuses on the gulling of Malvolio by Feste. It was another superb part for Robert Armin, the new, more sophisticated fool in the playing company.[2]

> A good practice in it to make the steward believe his lady widow was in love with him by counterfeiting a letter, as from his lady, in general terms, telling him what she liked best in him and prescribing his gesture in smiling, his apparel, etc. And then when he came to practice, making him believe they took him to be mad.
>
> *(Wolfe 2020b)*

Manningham saw a private performance of the play in the Middle Temple, another reminder, if one were needed, that Shakespeare's plays were written for, and performed at, venues other than the public playhouses and the court. He was not quite sure of the title, first writing "Mid," crossing it out and inserting the correct title, suggesting he was going to write *Midsummer Night's Dream*. Despite this slip, "Manningham was in many ways an ideal spectator: young and well educated, he brought to the performance an impressive array of precise literary and theatrical knowledge, enabling him to place the comedy culturally" (Elam 2008, p. 4). He knows Shakespeare's earlier work, recognizes his Latin and possibly his Italian sources: Plautus's *Menaechmi* and a play called *Gl'Ingannati* ("inganni" means deceits), one of the Italian versions of the story which, in a typical late sixteenth-century move, had been translated into Latin for performance at Cambridge University in 1595.

For contemporaries like Manningham, placing Shakespeare within a literary heritage was much more important than understanding him as a man. Similarly, in our own time, it is less biographically fraught to write about Shakespeare as a competitive playwright or indeed a competitive poet: what "rouses Shakespeare to unalloyed anger is not sexual infidelity but the exaggerated 'praise' and 'false compare' of rival poets" (Kerrigan 1986, p. 25).

Shakespeare's literary competitiveness or, more gentleman-like, his engagement with other writers, is apparent through the 1590s, not least in his depiction of lovers-turned-poets, who are all, to a man, terrible writers. In *Love's Labour's Lost* the male courtiers pen execrable sonnets in praise of their mistresses, to laughable effect. Demetrius in *A Midsummer Night's Dream* is not much better at recycling romantic clichés: "O Helen, goddess, nymph, perfect,

divine! / To what, my love, shall I compare thine eyne?" (3.2.147–148).
Shakespeare gives the best lines about the poet-lover to his melancholy Jaques:

> and then the lover,
> Sighing like furnace, with a woeful ballad
> Made to his mistress' eyebrow
>
> *(2.7.148–150)*

But the most pointed literary put-down is given to Rosalind in *As You Like It*. Orlando, with all his poetry, all his "accoutrements" of the lover, merely reveals himself as loving himself rather than any other. Only fictional lovers (Troilus is mentioned) die of love: "Men have died from time to time and worms have eaten them, but not for love" (4.1.97–99).

Twelfth Night is all part of this, a nod towards Shakespeare's younger rival Ben Jonson, but a generous one, fueled perhaps by William having performed in Ben's *Every Man in his Humour*. The subplots in which Puritan Malvolio is tricked and humiliated, and the idiotic Andrew Aguecheek is relieved of his cash and dignity, reveal that Shakespeare had "an intimate grasp of the relationship between Jonson's gulls and the wits that exploit them" (Riggs 2015, p. 190). Shakespeare will never be Jonson, however, because the gulling of Malvolio, a character sick of self-love, is achieved by the fool Feste, who like Touchstone, conceives of "folly as the universal condition of human experience" and is given the last words by Shakespeare (Riggs 2015, pp. 190–191). Despite the prospective marriages which close the story, the play itself finishes with Feste's song ("the rain it raineth every day" [5.1.382ff.]), a wistful, poignant, melancholy moment, a world away from Jonson's urban edginess.

The tone of the ending is not the only element of *Twelfth Night* that suggests to some that the play was as much born of Shakespeare's experience of grief as *Hamlet*. William was the father of fraternal twins. At the end of *Twelfth Night*, Viola and Sebastian believe the other one dead but are joyously reunited. But, "if Shakespeare found the subject painful, this might be why Viola is the saddest comic heroine that he had created up to this point, and why both she and Olivia are introduced grieving for the loss of a close relative" (Potter 2012, p. 288). "There's something deep in the psychology of a twin, when the other twin dies, which would make her want to keep that twin alive by acting out his life as well as her own" (Billington 1990, p. 40), observed the theater director John Caird, talking about the character of Viola, when he directed the play for the Royal Shakespeare Company in 1983. Maguire and Smith (2012, p. 82), who quote Caird, note that the

> psychology is not, as it happens, confined to twins (it was identified by Freud as a classic component of grief), but they provide a striking visual

illustration of it. In Shakespeare grieving twins are mistaken for each other not because (or not just because) they are twins but because mourners temporarily incorporate the lost one in themselves.

The revelation that Sebastian has survived the shipwreck that separated the twins lives not only marks the end of Viola's mourning for him, but also the end of her cross-dressing. Caird again: "The brother turns up, which means she doesn't have to be a boy anymore" (Billington 1990, p. 40).

As Maguire and Smith point out, *Twelfth Night* doesn't quite "give up the frisson of Viola's sexually ambiguous persona that easily" (Maguire and Smith 2012, p. 82). She ends the play still dressed, and addressed, as Cesario. Only at this stage of the play do we find that she is called Viola: "until this point no one, including the audience, has known what to call her" (ibid.). Or him. This small detail, hardly noticeable in performance, is just one element of the homoerotic, gender-bending feast that is *Twelfth Night*.

Shakespeare even creates a double time scheme (does it take place over three days or three months?) to allow the relationship between Antonio and Sebastian to mature. Sebastian stays for "months" with "an ordering older man who is frankly desirous of him, who showered him with "kindnesses" (3.4.348), and who, moreover, saved him from death at sea and nursed him back to health. It is the classic homoerotic relationship, wherein the mature lover serves as guide and mentor to the young beloved" (Pequigney 1992, pp. 204–205).

Sex (in all its meanings) is as significant as grief to *Twelfth Night*, and the character of Viola is pivotal to both concerns. Shakespeare "takes the most remarkable risks" with the character, who "occupies a place which is not precisely masculine or feminine, where the notion of identity itself is disrupted" (Belsey 1985, pp. 185–187). For his contemporaries, especially those who viewed theater as a dangerous space, in which males could morph into females, Viola/Cesario is inflammatory writing. It is in fact impossible in real life for a set of male/female twins to be identical except for gender – but not in drama. Viola is cut from the same bi-gendered cloth as Rosalind, and considering the erotic spark between Viola/Cesario and Olivia (and earlier between Rosalind/Ganymede and Orlando) it seems evident that "with their provisional trying on and discarding of identities" Shakespeare's plays "offer tremendous opportunities for the investigation of how provisional gender categories can be and how volatile the workings of erotic desire" (Chedgzoy 2015, p. 417).[3]

That Shakespeare "made the most of these opportunities throughout his career" may not tell us anything about his own sexual identity, but it does reveal what interested him. *Twelfth Night* would be the last (and best?) of his four cross-dressing comedies (after *The Two Gentlemen of Verona*, *The Merchant of Venice*, and *As You Like It*). From this point on, Shakespeare's exploration of gender took a different dramatic form.

With hindsight, *Twelfth Night* marks a turning point for Shakespeare, as playwright. It is the last of his so-called "romantic" or "happy" comedies, the first of his "dark" comedies, and perhaps even foreshadows in "its representations of actual and feared deaths the later development of tragicomedy" (Elam 2008, p. 3). Even a critic who eschews "developmental narratives" sees *Twelfth Night's* insistence on the

> darkness and arbitrariness of desire to such a degree that it marks a consummation of Shakespeare's criticism of conventional love – and an almost inevitable end to his romantic comedy. Although his plays continue to explore sexuality and often contain some of the same motifs, they do not attempt to maintain the balance that the straightforward comedies do between nature and artifice, play and seriousness, union and dissolution. They become so dark as to be considered deeply problematic (*Measure for Measure*) or simply tragic (*Othello*). Then, at least for a while, the tragic vision takes over.
>
> *(Haber 2018, p. 296)*

Whether "happy," "dark" or "romantic," *Twelfth Night* is most assuredly a comedy. The same cannot be said for *Troilus and Cressida* from a similar period: a generically indeterminable play, mixing history, comedy, and tragedy into a skeptical analysis of war-politics, sex, and sexuality, all washed down with disillusionment.

For once, one of Shakespeare's Prologues survives, and it is hardly cheery. And hither am I come,

> A Prologue armed, but not in confidence
> Of author's pen or actor's voice, but suited
> In like conditions as our argument,
> To tell you, fair beholders, that our play
> Leaps o'er the vaunt and firstlings of those broils,
> Beginning in the middle, starting thence away
> To what may be digested in a play.
> Like or find fault; do as your pleasures are;
> Now good or bad, 'tis but the chance of war.
>
> *(Prologue, ll. 22–31)*

"Good or bad," take your pick. There's a desperate nihilism to this play which is new. Reading all the plays in order (or what we think of as the order), *Troilus and Cressida* feels different, feels darker.

It is also the play that has been most mined for Shakespeare's philosophy, on account of an eloquent defense of the need to maintain a stable social hierarchy from the character Ulysses. This, for many years, was viewed as a reflection of the playwright's own sociopolitical views. "Take but degree away – untune that string, / And hark what discord follows" argues Ulysses (1.3.109–110), ventriloquizing his creator's trenchant conservatism. "Observe degree, priority, and place" (1.3.86) or else the terrifying transformations begin:

> Power into will, will into appetite
> And appetite, an universal wolf,
> So doubly seconded with will and power,
> Must make perforce a universal prey
> And last eat up himself.
>
> *(1.3.120–124)*

It is a nightmare vision of the anarchy or "cultural cannibalism" (Garber 2004, p. 545) that ensues when authority collapses.

Today, we are less inclined to view a single character as a mouthpiece for Shakespeare himself. The playwright refuses to offer audiences a single "conducting authorial voice," therefore Ulysses's arguments remain but one element in a contrapuntal structure, goes Garber's argument (2004, p. 543). For her, this is a uniquely Shakespearean view of the world, but it may equally derive from the changes occurring in his world, in which new and changing economic patterns and practices were disrupting traditional hierarchies, exacerbating fears of (quite literally) disorder. In response, the church regularly reminded the nation's subjects (as in this Homily of 1571) that "obedience is the principal virtue of all virtues, and indeed the very root of all virtues, and the cause of all felicity" (Jewel n.d.).

Time to pause for a moment and consider Shakespeare's political beliefs. If you've come this far, you'll know there are no documents in the case, only the plays and poems. And you'll know that to attempt to read Shakespeare's beliefs from his plays is fraught with dangers, from the uncertainty about the dating of many of the plays to the instability of the texts themselves (from the different editions to the presence of collaborators). All this is compounded by what we know and love as Shakespeare's use of multiple perspectives, the way in which his plays refuse to offer simple answers to simple questions. Here, for example, is an analysis (Kahn 2011, p. 212) of the politics of *Julius Caesar,* "an enigmatic play, representing the assassination of Caesar from shifting perspectives that frustrate any certain judgement of either the victim or his assassins."

Cicero's statement, "But men may construe things after their fashion, / Clean from the purpose of the things themselves" (1.3.34–5), better suggests how we experience the play, for though it poses many questions it provides no clear answers, leaving us to "construe things" for ourselves. Was Caesar a tyrant who deserved to die, or a ruler whose greatness provoked the envy of lesser minds? Was Brutus "the noblest Roman of them all," or a misguided idealist? How can we tell? By making the motives and the personalities of Caesar, Brutus, and Mark Antony so richly ambiguous, Shakespeare involves us in their political dilemma as if it were our own.

Shakespeare provides no direct political steer. This does not necessarily mean he is politically neutral. His individual characters are conflicted, their dramatic presentation is often ambivalent, but the fear remains the same: chaos. That fear drives, dominates, at least two of Shakespeare's tragedies (*Macbeth* and *King Lear*) in which the death or disintegration of a king leads to unspeakable horror, the triumph of the "universal wolf." Even the stability of tyranny is preferable to anarchy.

Over the years, I for one have wanted to find a radical Shakespeare, the rebel discovered by cultural materialist or feminist critics in my youth (maybe in all our youths). For those critics, Ulysses's celebration of degree is a cynical piece of political rhetoric, and one not necessarily endorsed by the play as a whole, or its author. But against that it is important to recognize the all-pervasive insistence on social and political obedience, underwritten by Christian doctrine, in Shakespeare's own time. The fifth of the Ten Commandments from the Bible, "Honour thy father and thy mother," demanded respect for those in authority generally, from one's father to the monarch. The superior, all-powerful, and crucially, God-given, position of the father/king was, therefore, absolutely accepted. Obedience, as per the Homily above, was the only possible response, even if the father/king behaved badly. For playgoers in Shakespeare's time there was no escape from this view of authority. Any performance ended with prayers for the monarch. Even if one of Shakespeare's plays appears to criticize a particular monarch, offers an "exploration of troubled kingship," questions "everything the monarch stood for" (as, it is argued, do *Henry IV Parts I and II*), the theatrical event itself would end with a rousing, monarchical prayer (Stern 2010, p. 124). Indeed, it is possible that the knowledge that the playgoing experience would end with a very public display of loyalty paradoxically created a space for more complex treatments of political topics such as (failures of) kingship. This "prayer moment" (ibid., p. 127) made clear that players "performed under the auspices of an authority (and hence were not rogues or beggars)." The judgmental audience might feel that "liking the play and company was the duty of a loyal subject." Put simply, "potentially, whatever king or queen may have been questioned or slaughtered within the fiction, the reigning monarch of the time ruled the end of some versions of every Shakespearean drama - and perhaps every history play altogether" (ibid., p. 124).

For all the political games being played, theater supported the status quo and was used to instruct the people and keep them obedient. The stage could be, and was, compared to the scaffold, where public executions unfolded like theater, and the crowd would enjoy the spectacle whilst being shown evil being punished. The playwright Thomas Heywood summed the situation up when he wrote that plays were written and performed to teach "subjects' obedience to their king" (Heywood 1612).

Heywood wrote these words in a work called "An Apology for Actors" precisely because the acting profession needed defending from the charge that plays encouraged disobedience, even rebellion. Theater was dangerous because it could demystify the workings of power, it could make great ones familiar, and therefore make an audience question the (God-given) authorities and hierarchies that kept people in their place.

Is there any room in this picture of early modern drama in which to place a politically radical Shakespeare? If there is, then it seems he did everything he could to minimize the risk to himself. When *Richard III* was printed anonymously in 1595, Shakespeare may have been glad that his name was not on the title page because in the aftermath of the publication of *The Rape of Lucrece* "it would have been easy to position the playwright as a critic of monarchy." This is precisely what Shakespeare did not want to be so, within a few years, both plays were revised, possibly to remove some of their implications (Potter 2012, p. 158).

Yet Shakespeare is relentlessly drawn to explorations of kingship (and occasionally queenship), and even more problematically, tyranny. And he seems fascinated by one particular understanding of the workings of monarchical power. He remains strangely uninterested in political concepts or systems, and, rare for his time, not too preoccupied by the problem of corrupt advisors. He is far more interested in the individual person, and his (and occasionally her) responsibility, their "will." So, most accounts of the reign of Richard II foreground his "reliance on evil counsel," his "propensity to listen to the poisonous advice of flatterers at the expense of advisers of virtue, or of ancient noble lineage" (Gajda 2012, p. 241). Indeed, the evil favorite flourished as a character in the dramas of the early 1590s. Samuel Daniel, the author of Shakespeare's main source for the play suggests that Richard's youthful reliance on evil counsellors was an almost inevitable response to being dominated by his uncles: "Minions too great, argue a king too weake." The theme is less interesting to Shakespeare. Certainly, Richard's England is overgrown with "noisome weeds which without profit suck / The soil's fertility from wholesome flowers." Compared, though, with the treatments of other writers, we do not see Bushy, Bagot, and Greene exercise poisonous influence over Richard's decision making: the king's seminal action, the confiscation of the Lancastrian estates on Gaunt's death, is a decision sprung from his own uncounselled *will*, making Shakespeare's Richard directly and singularly culpable for the acts that precipitate Bullingbrook's rebellion. Richard *rejects* the virtuous and prophetic counsel of Gaunt on his deathbed.

(Gajda 2012, pp. 241–242)

Or put more bluntly, it is Richard's "personality, not his political situation, that dominates the play" (Potter 2012, p. 176).

So, for Shakespeare, political crises are caused by the individual's failings, not the system that produces the individual. In "all his political plays," Shakespeare portrays the struggle between nations and empires "in terms of the central personalities engaged in it" (Wilders 1995, p. 2). In *Antony and Cleopatra*, "Caesar ultimately wins and Antony loses because of the kind of people they are and because of the irresistible power which Cleopatra exercises over Antony. This gives to the relationship between the lovers a sense of unusual weight and risk" (ibid.). It is the relationship between two people that matters. Later in *Troilus and Cressida*, the great warrior Achilles is roused, not by love of country, but by the death of his lover, Patroclus. He wants revenge on Hector, the "boy-killer." These men are motivated by personal passion not abstract ideals.

I believe this does tell us something about Shakespeare's perspective. The focus on the individual has political implications in a world which understood monarchical power in terms of divine right, and divine right in terms of the king's "two bodies," human and divine. Even if a monarch was a tyrant, their authority remained God-given. The task of the loyal subject was to encourage the monarch away from tyrannical behavior. And the task of a leader was to suppress emotion. In *Henry V*, Shakespeare's vision of kingship is "as a role that necessitates coldness, rigid self-control, and fettered passions," a vision he will return to in later plays, such as *Antony and Cleopatra* (Garber 2004, p. 397). Self-control on the part of the leader is the bulwark against tyranny, as Henry V insists:

> We are no tyrant, but a Christian king;
> Unto whose grace our passion is as subject
> As are our wretches fetter'd in our prisons.
> *(1.2.242–244)*

Throughout Shakespeare's work, there is a recurrent call to be true to one's self. When a king is not himself, that complicates things. Richard II is not kingly, he fails to be one of his two bodies. But that the personal is the political is not as apolitical (or nonideological) as it sounds. It is an ideology in and of itself.

Chapter Six

Ulysses does not end *Troilus and Cressida*. Nor does Troilus, although he is given a superb speech, which includes a rhyming couplet (which some argue suggests that the play was *supposed* to end with): "But march away. / Hector is dead. There is no more to say" (5.11.21–22). It is Pandarus who is last man standing and Shakespeare, as he had done in *As You Like It*, written around the same time, breaks the fourth wall. In the body of the play, Pandarus has been dismissed by Troilus, but now he turns to the audience and talks directly to them – about syphilis. Promising to see them again in two months' time, until "then I'll sweat and seek about for eases, / And at that time bequeath you my diseases" (5.11.55–56). With this reference to two months, is Shakespeare alerting his audience to "a never-written or lost sequel" which would be staged after another eight-week term at the Inns of Court (Kerrigan 2016, p. 289)? Or is Pandarus (still in character, rather than acting as a pimp for Shakespeare's work) pointing up the playhouse's proximity to the brothels, and thus disease? It's a dark, dark ending to a troubling play and this is clever, strange writing.[1]

What has happened to William Shakespeare? Creatively, he seems to be moving in a completely different direction to his day-to-day existence. The life events we know about (and admittedly we don't know about many) are taking him one way, towards respectability, stability, wealth, in Stratford-upon-Avon, but the drama seems to be heading in another direction entirely: towards darkness.

It could be that he was living two lives: decent family man in Stratford, promiscuous troublemaker in London. On the one hand, the archive (specifically, Shakespeare Birthplace Trust Records Office, MS ER 27/1) tells us that, on 1 May 1602, Shakespeare bought 107 acres of land and 20 acres of pasture in Old Stratford from William and John Combe; that more land was bought in September; that New Place was reconveyed to him. He's a man consolidating his property and status. On the other, there's a story about actor William in London. Admittedly, it's old news, but it is doing the rounds in 1602:

The Life of the Author: William Shakespeare, First Edition. Anna Beer.
© 2021 John Wiley & Sons, Ltd. Published 2021 by John Wiley & Sons, Ltd.

Vpon a tyme when Burbidge played Rich. 3. there was a citizen greue soe farr in liking with him, that before shee went from the play shee appointed him to come that night vnto hir by the name of Ri: the 3. Shakespeare overhearing their conclusion went before, was intertained, and at his game ere Burbidge came. Then message being brought that Rich. the 3.d was at the dore, Shakespeare caused returne to be made that William the Conquerour was before Rich. the 3.

(BL MS Harley 5353, fol. 29)

The man who wrote the anecdote notes that "Shakespeare's name William," just in case we don't get the joke, whilst modern scholars assure us that "citizen" might mean a widow or a prostitute, or perhaps a married woman. The good news, at least for those troubled by Shakespeare's fascination with beautiful young men, is that the anecdote has him having sex with a woman.

Two different lives? I am not so sure. I think it more likely that Shakespeare moved between Stratford and London, that he lived, geographically at least, what has been called a "much more porous reality" (Edmondson and Wells 2015a, p. 330). And somehow, he (and his family) continued to thrive. Even the death of Queen Elizabeth I in March 1603 provided an opportunity for Shakespeare rather than a crisis. He was still an actor, listed as "principle tragedian" in Jonson's *Sejanus*, but now with the new monarch, he becomes a "King's Man," under the direct patronage of James I.

The new King authorized William Shakespeare and his associates, the King's "servants," "freely to use and exercise the Art and faculty of playing Comedies Tragedies histories Enterludes moralls pastoralls Stageplaies and suche others like as theie have alreadie studied or hereafter shall use or studie aswell for the recreation of our lovinge Subjectes as for our Solace and pleasure when wee shall thincke good to see them duringe our pleasure."[2]

The company were the recipients, in the spring of 1604, of four yards of red cloth to wear "against his Majesty's royal proceeding through the city of London" (Nelson 2018a) a year late, because the plague that closed the theaters in 1603 had also prevented James's formal coronation. (The theaters had been closed during the final illness of Queen Elizabeth in the early spring of 1603, and then remained closed due to plague, only to reopen again in April 1604.) From then on, Shakespeare and his colleagues were busy "servants," performing for the special envoy from the king of Spain in August 1604, and preparing for their first court season. Presumably to save time, they dug out plays from over 10 years earlier (there was a Whitehall performance of *The Comedy of Errors* in December 1604) or revived recent successes, such as *Othello*.

Othello, set in Venice and Cyprus, and focusing on a Turk-defeating, wife-murdering Moor, was well-judged to appeal to King James, whose poem on the

Christian victory over the Muslim Ottomans at Lepanto had been reprinted on his accession to the English throne. There were also the tastes of James's wife, Queen Anne, to consider. She was fascinated by people of color, or at least by the possibilities of blackface. For the court entertainments of 1604/1605, Ben Jonson wrote his *Masque of Blackness*, in which Anne and her ladies appeared as "daughters of Niger" (Prologue, l. 63) at "her Majesty's will" (Prologue, l. 24) (Barker and Hinds 2002).

Shakespeare's success was grounded not only on his well-judged appeal to his monarchs' tastes, but also on his appeal to different audiences, the convenient portability and adaptability of his plays, and the sheer emotional impact of his writing. In 1610, at a performance of *Othello* in Oxford, one Henry Jackson wrote that the play made the audience cry, most notably when "the celebrated Desdemona, slain in our presence by her husband ... entreated the pity of the spectators by her very countenance" (Shakespeare 1987, p. 18). A couple of years later, this everyday tale of wife murder was one of the entertainments chosen for the marriage of James I's daughter, Princess Elizabeth, to the Elector Palatine.

Some things didn't change under the new regime. Christopher Marlowe is still on William Shakespeare's mind, 10 or more years after his death, specifically his contemporary's last play, *Doctor Faustus*. Both *Othello* and *Faustus* explore a "fearful intimacy between the protagonist and his tempter," a "damnable symbiosis through which a literally demonic servant contrives to deliver his master 'body and soul' into Lucifer's possession" (Neill 2006, p. 17). "O what will I not do to obtain his soul?" says Mephistopheles (Marlowe 1989, scene 5, l. 73), relishing the moment when Faustus self-destructs by composing a deed of gift that places himself in the devil's power. Othello, confronted with the stupefying evidence of Iago's treachery, craves an explanation for his ensign's inexplicable malice: "Will you, I pray, demand that demi-devil, Why he hath thus ensnared my soul and body?" (5.1.297–298).

Shakespeare also continues to mess with his sources, taking and transforming the plots of both *Othello* and *Measure for Measure* from Giambattista Giraldi Cinthio's collection of novelle, *Gli Hecatommithi*, published just a year after his birth, in 1565. In *Othello*, Cassio (Desdemona's alleged lover) is promoted by Shakespeare from a lowly *capo di squadra* (equivalent to a corporal) to Othello's second in command, and thus made villain Iago's superior. At one stroke, Shakespeare complicates Iago's motives as he attempts, and succeeds, in destroying Othello. In Cinthio, the villain's plotting – in itself, directed primarily at Disdemona – is motivated by his mistaken belief that the reason she is not interested in him is that she is in love with the *capo*. Lust turns to hatred swiftly. Shakespeare may have remembered the *capo*'s desire, because he adds it – almost casually, and somewhat distractingly – to the long list of Iago's motives. That might be the point: we never do quite understand what drives

Iago to destroy Othello. It is their toxic relationship that dominates the stage: Desdemona becomes merely collateral damage.

Busy, wealthy, productive, close to royalty: Shakespeare is doing well. And yet, in their content, his plays continue their descent into some of the most disturbing parts of human experience. *Othello* offers the audience a relationship "between two figures who are infected with a more extreme version of the misogyny and sexual nausea that taint the hero" of *Hamlet* (Neill 2006, pp. 403–404). Both misogyny and sexual nausea are prevalent in *Troilus and Cressida* and *Measure for Measure*, whilst in *All's Well That Ends Well*, written at around this time, Shakespeare risks an exceptionally gloomy opening, with one leader dead, his widow mourning him and saying goodbye to her son, and news of the serious illness of the King of France. Even by its end, the play, like *Measure for Measure*, fails to offer the sense of "release or joy" delivered, to different degrees, by the earlier comedies. *Troilus and Cressida* may be a comedy, but it is "not of the kind that Shakespeare had previously written" (Thomas 1987, p. 14, quoted in Arnold 2018, p. 537), linked to *All's Well* and *Measure for Measure* by mood (gloomy), tone (bitter), and moral ambiguity, but also by genre. *All's Well That Ends Well* could be added to Neill's list of plays preoccupied with misogyny and sexual nausea. Shakespeare takes the familiar materials of the popular "patient wife" plays of the public stages, but focuses, as does *Measure for Measure*, on "complex issues of female chastity: not simply praising virginity but examining the acceptable conditions for its loss" (Van Es 2013, p. 222). "Dowries, pregnancy, and sexual gratification – almost untouched upon as serious topics in the earlier writing – are now the primary drivers of plot" (ibid.). *All's Well* is a play that contains, at least for me, one of the most poignant questions in Shakespeare's plays. Helena asks Parolles about virginity: "How might one do, sir, to lose it to her own liking?" (1.1.49–50). The answer the play gives suggests that this is impossible for Helena, impossible for any woman, but at least the question has been asked. This is pretty much as far as Shakespeare will go when considering female desire.

There's worse to come from this uneasy period in Shakespeare's dramatic productions. *All's Well* ends with one of the least promising marriages in Shakespeare – and it's a low bar – that between Bertram and Helena. But at least there's a marriage. *Timon of Athens* is a strange play, even for this strange time in Shakespeare's writing life.[3] Preoccupied with death, disillusion, and sexual disease, the only two women in the play are syphilitic prostitutes, calling to mind Pandarus at the end of *Troilus and Cressida*.

Did this "obsession" with disease (evident also in Shakespeare's allusion to "seething baths," a treatment for syphilis, in his Sonnet 153, l. 7) grow out of "personal experience of syphilitic symptoms" or, less sensationally, "the mere observation of them"? According to a medical historian (Stone 2003, p. 9) there is a horrible accuracy to Timon's descriptions of the ravages of tertiary syphilis, in the speech in which he urges the women to go and infect their customers. Or is the question itself a "gross example of this fallacy of reading Shakespeare's fictions as biographical fact"?: "since *Timon of Athens* expounds so knowledgeably about syphilis, Shakespeare must have been suffering from a venereal disease when he wrote the play" (Charney 2009, p. 165). This emphatic rejection of the relation between fiction and lived experience when it comes to syphilis is compromised by the following statement from the same critic: "One thing, however, is certain. The fact that aging is such a significant theme in Shakespeare is proof of his own anxieties about growing old" (ibid.). We all tend to take the biographical turn that fits our own view of Shakespeare, and morality for that matter. Others extrapolate *Timon* on to the marriage of William and Anne. Did Shakespeare fear his own wife's fidelity, or was he unfaithful to her – and (Bate 2008, p. 191) "did he then feel remorse as his career came towards its end and he contemplated spending more time back home in Stratford?" More often, however, as with Shakespeare's take on politics, there is a reluctance to read his beliefs and experiences as foundational to his drama, more willingness to see him reflecting the *mores* of his time. His era's growing obsession with fidelity is the driver for these plays, rather than the state of his marriage or his sexual health.

This obsession with fidelity was rooted in a changing understanding of marriage which had implications far beyond the joining of any individual husband and wife. Patriarchy, understood as a specific political theory, insisted that the family and the state were parallel structures, governed by father and monarch respectively. Over the course of Shakespeare's lifetime, the nature and extent of a husband's power over his wife would come to be disputed far more than the powers of fathers over their children. Underpinning any husband's control were assumptions about women's essential inequality with men, their physical and moral inferiority. The marriage contract was predicated on his inequality, with a dash of feudalism thrown in. Women "exchanged their material production and labour for promises of love and protection, in the same way that, in feudal society, tenants had rendered food and services in exchange for their landlords' protection" (Briggs 1997, pp. 47–48). The word "love" is in there, somewhere, but more important is the economic and social transaction and the maintenance of hierarchy within the home. Or at least that was the understanding of marriage when William and Anne were wed back in 1582. Over the course of his adult lifetime, voices began to call more strongly for, and to celebrate, a more "companionate" marriage, not quite a marriage of equals (impossible to imagine, given the assumptions made about women), but more of a partnership, more of a marriage of true minds.

Protestantism increasingly valorized the nuclear family as a microcosm of the state, with women more likely to be idealized as chaste and obedient wives rather than as virgins. But how to manage the tricky business of marital chastity? It seems that this new conception of companionate, consensual marriage created anxiety in men, primarily about the fidelity of their wives. "The husband was expected to give his wife enough satisfaction to avoid her being obliged to go elsewhere, but not to arouse her so much as to provoke extra-marital sex – a recipe for masculine anxiety if ever there was one" in the words of Mark Breitenberg (1996, p. 26). He further argues that, compounding this anxiety, was the belief that women could not conceive without orgasm. Therefore, women's sexual pleasure was fundamental to the perpetuation of the family, but also profoundly threatening to the male imagination, since women were believed to be less able to govern their rampant sexual desires. All this anxiety contributes to "extreme depictions of women's sexuality as either monstrous or excessive or, in the case of the 'good' wife, little more than a necessary aspect of procreation" (ibid.).

Before getting too excited about Shakespeare's depictions of male sexual anxiety at the turn of the century and jumping to the conclusion that they are a reflection of his own rocky marriage, we need to throw *The Merry Wives of Windsor* into the mix. The play is an outlier in many respects, not least because it is set in England, but primarily because a jealous husband is reformed and reeducated by his virtuous (and quite feisty) wife.

Pardon me, wife. Henceforth do what thou wilt:

> I rather will suspect the sun with cold
> Than thee with wantonness. Now doth thy honour stand,
> In him that was of late an heretic,
> As firm as faith.

> *(4.4.6–109)*

Shakespeare also gives his young male suitor an eloquent defense of marriage based on love, and a trenchant critique of "forced marriage," which results in "a thousand irreligious cursed hours" (5.5.223–224).

Merry Wives stands as one of the few Shakespeare plays which portray marriage as "a locus of erotic pleasure and satisfaction" (Chedgzoy 2015, p. 417), and is particularly striking in the context of this middle period of this work, when the institution is hardly celebrated. Marriages are, of course, still part of the plot. Shakespeare's social conservatism and his professional caution may both be evident in his continued use of the romantic comic form and its concluding marriages, since, as Rose argued back in 1988 (p. 88), these dramas represent "neither a mythical nor a revolutionary society, but a renewed traditional society, whose stability and coherence is symbolized by marriage and is based on the maintenance of traditional sexual roles." That's the theory anyway, and there are still those who attempt to reassure us that, say, the message at the end of *The Merchant of Venice* is that "sex is subservient to a romantic ethos and focused on the sanctity of marriage as the foundation of family and society" (Dutton 2018, p. 220). For me, in contrast, the marital alliances that end these plays seem more like empty gestures towards comic form than convincing conclusions to love stories.

The problem is that the marriages which end Shakespeare's comedies (or destruct in his tragedies) suggest that only formal lip-service is being paid by the playwright to the idea of marriage as a symbol of "stability and coherence." In *Measure for Measure*, Isabella retains her chastity despite the best efforts of the appalling hypocrite Angelo ("who will believe you, Isabelle?" 2.4.153), but only by giving up another woman to him. Isabella is rewarded for her virtue by a proposal of marriage from the Duke, and Angelo punished for his sin by marriage to Mariana. This ending was, for centuries, viewed as a happy one for all. Isabella is saved from the unnatural life of a Catholic nunnery and offered the glory of wifedom and being a duchess, every Protestant woman's dream. Angelo's marriage to Mariana "falls like a spring sunbeam – tentative but hopeful – across the bleak last act of the play" (Kerrigan 1982, p. 17). But Isabella's fate is imposed upon her. Shakespeare has the all-powerful Duke say: "Give me your hand and say you will be mine" (5.1.492), but gives Isabella no right of reply. Her silence speaks volumes to modern critics and directors, but it is harder to see it as resistance to the patriarchy in Shakespeare's own era. In fact, like so many of Shakespeare's outspoken, feisty women, Isabella may be being applauded for dwindling into a (silent) wife.

For the two transgressive men in *Measure for Measure*, marriage is more overtly punitive. When Angelo is found out, he asks for death. Instead, he gets marriage to Mariana, the woman he has betrayed. Lucio, whose only redeeming feature is his friendship for Claudio, is sentenced to be whipped then hanged, only to be told that, instead, he must marry the woman by whom he has a child.

A dramatic diet of punitive marriages, all washed down with infidelity, prostitution, and disease, does suggest a jaundiced view of the institution on the part of Shakespeare – or at least a reappraisal of marriage as a happy-ever-after closing device for his drama. But it still tells us nothing about the state of (possibly syphilitic) William's marriage to Anne.

It might tell us something about theaterland in the early years of James's reign. All of the plays discussed here may have been prompted by the "friction between the new cynical and misogynistic comedies of the boys' stage and the more gynocentric drama of the adults. Shakespeare, given his secure association with the players was more consistently tied to this woman-centred drama than his contemporaries" (Van Es 2013, p. 222). This is a cautious biographical move, explaining a playwright's choice of subject matter not through his individual experience as a man in his forties, but in terms of professional competition. It has the public theaters driving him in one direction ("the heroics of marriage"), whilst his consciousness of the values of "court and coteries cir-cles" [(Van Es 2013, p. 221)] (indoor theater of various kinds) and their "fash-ionable literary culture" and "caustic cynicism about the fate of the married man" are driving him in another. This is what leads to the distinctive "mixed" quality in Shakespeare's writing at this time, "in which the popular female voice often sits side by side with the expression of a new, harsher, misogynistic fear of sexual betrayal" (Van Es 2013, p. 222). William writes about that fear not because he had experienced it, but because it will see off the competition.

Which is precisely what the King's Men were managing to do. The Rose Playhouse, home of the Admirals' Men, was slowly getting pushed out of business, helped by the fact that the building was literally sinking into the marshland on which it had been built. Back in the 1590s, the Chamberlain's Men's repertory consistently matched that of the Admiral's Men but with the new century Shakespeare's work was even more closely related to that of his contemporaries, even more alert to the changing tastes of his audiences who wanted more gritty, urban, and satirical drama. *Measure for Measure* provided just that – and a healthy dose of flattery of the new monarch.

Measure for Measure played at court on 26 December, the King's Men's sec-ond contribution to the revels of the winter of 1604–1605. Shakespeare chose another Cinthio plot because it was as equally well-calculated to appeal to the new king as *Othello* had been. The representation of the ruler of Vienna, a Duke who claims "I love the people, / But do not like to stage me to their eyes" (1.1.68–69), may well have been a homage to the king in his first season of revels. James claimed to dislike crowds, and the Duke's discreet solution to the problems revealed in *Measure for Measure* is an exemplary display of true power.

Those problems were very close to home despite the nominal setting of Vienna. Shakespeare depicts a sexually and politically corrupt city and sub-urbs, a city and suburbs rather like London. That distance had never been great anyway. In the earlier *Twelfth Night* a seemingly casual mention of a pub-cum-brothel "in the south suburbs" (3.3.39) near the Globe collapses the distance between fictional setting (Illyria) and London. England, and specifically London, is usually present, wherever Shakespeare sets his plays. The early *Comedy of Errors* has the Phoenix, a London tavern and also a shop in Lombard Street. Helen of Troy becomes Nell in *Troilus*. There's a reference to Mile End in *All's Well That Ends Well*. But casual topicality becomes strategic political commentary in *Measure for Measure*. The fictional brothels of the Vienna sub-urbs are due to be torn down in an attempt to enforce the law against prostitu-tion and to stop the spread of sexually transmitted disease. King James ordered the destruction of the tenements of the real London suburbs in April 1604, ostensibly to prevent the spread of plague.

William Shakespeare was at or near the height of his success as a playwright in this first full year of Jacobean rule, with seven plays and eight performances at court. He remained responsive to developments in his own industry, alert to competition, sensitive to the changing world around him, and an astute flatterer of monarchs. It therefore seems implausible to me that he would actually set out to challenge the political legitimacy of his monarch and patron, James. Nevertheless, some see him doing so. *Troilus and Cressida, Measure for Measure*, and *All's Well That Ends Well* (long called "problem plays") can also be viewed as "comedies of rule," in which young lovers seeking romantic felicity share the stage with rulers seeking power (Arnold 2018). Shakespeare's previous comedies "feature rulers such as dukes or kings, but in these the political interests of (mostly) benevolent rulers are aligned with the romantic interests of young lovers. In *Troilus, Measure*, and *All's Well*, rulers, far from felicitously reconciling the assertion of their own power and the liberation of lovers from oppressive parents, consolidate political authority by regulating romantic desire" (Arnold 2018, p. 537). This new take, Shakespeare's "darker version of the comic ruler" is a "response to James I's absolutist construction of the relation between *rex* and *lex*" (ibid.), that is, the king and the law.

In this reading of man and life, Shakespeare, in his first plays for King James, is challenging his monarch's alleged absolutism. Alleged, because in recent years, this view of James's reign has been challenged. James's reign was no more absolute than his predecessor's, and not much different in tone. The king's lack of money, rather than his surfeit of powers, would create the fault-line in his rule, a crack that would widen and lead to civil war and the execution of his son. But even this was all to come in the optimistic early months of James's rule, when England welcomed a male king, and not just that: a married male king with heirs.

Further, we know that James so admired Shakespeare that he commanded a repeat performance of *The Merchant of Venice*. The King's Men were so successful that they ended up with a double-booking of *Love's Labour's Lost*. Sir Walter Cope, a friend of Robert Cecil (the Principal Secretary), was trying to find an entertainment for Queen Anne. The King's Men offered him the old play but then they realized it was already "appointed to be played tomorrow night at my Lord of Southampton's" (quoted in Dutton 2018, p. 136). The parties ended up coming to an agreement. Both Cecil and Southampton would entertain the queen, but two nights apart in early January 1065. Which night *Love's Labour's Lost* was performed remains unknown.

It was all going so well. So well, indeed, that some have seen Shakespeare and Burbage as close to being knighted or offered formal positions at court. If his grappling with courtly discourse in poems like *Venus and Adonis* some 20 years earlier is anything to go by, Shakespeare's social aspirations still burned strong.

But if that was the case, something went wrong. Katherine Duncan-Jones (2001) sees Shakespeare's disillusion and disappointment reflected in his creation of (or revision of) some of his sonnets. Sonnet 110 (ll. 2–3) alludes to something that has been "sold cheap" that is "most dear." The following sonnet has "harmful deeds," and a name which has received a "brand" of his "strong infection" (111, l. 2, l. 5, l. 10). Ten sonnets on, and the interest continues: "false adulterate eyes" "give salutation to my sportive blood" (121, ll. 5–6). These references, put together, according to Bate (2008, p. 232), have "the whiff of some sexual misdemeanour which may have sullied Shakespeare in the eyes of the Herbert brothers." (The Herbert brothers, William and Philip, would – 20 years on – be the dedicatees of the First Folio of Shakespeare's works in 1623. William was a significant patron of the arts, the supporter of, amongst others, Ben Jonson. There is no direct evidence that the Herberts were patrons of Shakespeare during this period, nor that they had an opinion, good or bad, of Shakespeare's sexual activities.)

Meanwhile, Shakespeare kept turning out plays. The demands upon him as principal playwright to a successful company may explain the scrappy state of the text of *All's Well That Ends Well*. It has numerous disparities, which point "to revision, but may also be attributed to normal carelessness in the playwright's drive to finish" (Snyder 1993, p. 206). Revisions, carelessness, perhaps collaboration: the picture is of a hard-working playwright who, for whatever reason, does not have complete control over the play text. And, lest we forget, a playwright who does not have control over his audience's and fellow writers' responses. So, there may be a "proliferation of allusions to" *Hamlet* in other plays of the period – suggesting celebrity – but these allusions are "as often as not facetious or satirical" (Thompson and Taylor 2006, p. xx). Renown is not quite the same thing as respect. The knighthood didn't materialize.

All we know is that by 1604, Shakespeare was living with an émigré French Huguenot family, the Mountjoys, in Silver Street near St. Olave's Church, Cripplegate. The Mountjoys were tiremakers, so probably theater people, which seems fitting. (Tire is an abbreviation of "attire," so the Mountjoy family could have made any kind of garments, for the playhouses and beyond.) But then the biographical mists descend once more. There is no archival evidence that Shakespeare was even in London from autumn 1604 to the early summer of 1612, and he is absent from the list of King's Men's players in 1607, one of the years suggested for *Timon*. The winter of 1607 was one of the bitterest on record, and plague was ravaging London during these years. Perhaps (and we are back to syphilis) the "stain" mentioned in the sonnets kept a diseased Shakespeare out of London. Or "*Shakespeare may never have fully retired, but he may well have semi-retired much earlier than we suppose*" (Bate 2008, p. 359, his italics). *Timon* then becomes evidence of his "first semi-retirement, his flirtation with the possibility of handing over more of the day-to-day writing duties to a Londoner" (ibid.).

Semi-retirement may be too strong a word, but Shakespeare does slow down his production of plays, with Shapiro (2015) even suggesting that *Timon* is

Shakespeare's only offering over an entire three years. One way to cut down one's workload is to collaborate. One way to stay in touch was to work with a younger playwright. Good reasons for 40-year-old veteran, William Shakespeare, to collaborate with the rising star Thomas Middleton, who was already adept at creating citizen comedies. Shakespeare did go on to write another tragedy with a strongly urban feel, since *Coriolanus* is as much about Rome as *Timon* is about Athens, and he had already written a comedy, *Measure for Measure*, set in a corrupt Vienna, but Middleton's influence – as much as the experience of plague in London – might explain the grittiness of the satire.

The editors of the Arden edition have Shakespeare, the senior playwright in the creative partnership, driving the *Timon* project, imagining him reading up his Plutarch (in preparation for *Antony and Cleopatra*) and coming across Timon's story. Plutarch would also suggest the later *Coriolanus*.[4] Shakespeare, they argue, delegated certain sections of the writing of *Timon* to Middleton, such as the "tawdry masque," but kept the "meatiest scenes for himself." Meatiest here means opportunities for ambiguous characterization and the great speeches of the fourth act, as well as the "elegiac and muted ending" (Dawson and Minton 2008, p. 5). This ending is so muted (with the anti-hero dying offstage) that some see the play as unfinished, or at best unpolished, set aside for revision but then forgotten.

These years saw Shakespeare returning to collaboration (abandoned since joining the Chamberlain's Men in 1594); slowing down his production of material; perhaps ill; perhaps in semi-retirement. And if *Timon* is an indication of Shakespeare's state of mind in these years, then he appears to be a very, very bitter man, ripe for the writing of his most harrowing tragedy, *King Lear*, a play packed with "pre-echoes" (or simply echoes) of *Timon*.[5]

Once again, there is a perplexing discrepancy. The content of *King Lear* tells one story of a writer's life and mind. Its performance history suggests another. William Shakespeare remained a very successful man, a King's Man. *King Lear* took pride of place in the Christmas season of 1606, staged in the Great Chamber of the Palace of Whitehall on 26 December, an intimate, attractive venue. The high ceiling, wooden floor, and tapestry-covered walls would have created a good acoustic, indoor theater at its best. In this playing space, Shakespeare did something extraordinary. The 300 spectators, including the most important spectator of them all, the king, sat back expecting to be entertained at the end of a traumatic year for the country, a year of fear in the aftermath of the Gunpowder Plot.

For the "recreation" and solace of his absolute monarch, King James, Shakespeare offered *King Lear*. An astonishing play, it dramatizes the disintegration, madness, and death of a once-absolute monarch (and his kingdom). Even if we accept that Shakespeare started writing the play when the idea of the Union of England and Scotland "seemed all but assured," making *Lear* timely but "unthreatening," the utter destruction of Lear's kingdom is hardly the most obvious way to celebrate that union (Shapiro 2015, p. 35). Not only that. *Lear* (like *Timon*) shows a concern with the suffering of the poor and marginalized. Edgar, in *Lear*, becomes Poor Tom, a redemptive transformation, allowing him as a beggar to understand the suffering of the ordinary people, indeed his future subjects according to one ending of the play.

Five years on from writing his last romantic comedy, Shakespeare revisits a moment in *Twelfth Night*. In what had been an early role for Robert Armin, the playwright had him end *Twelfth Night* with song:

> But when I came unto my beds,
> With hey, ho, the wind and the rain,
> With tosspots still had drunken heads,
> For the rain it raineth every day.
> *(5.1.394–397)*

Now the song (and Armin as The Fool) return in *Lear*. The Fool sings the refrain just before the king enters the hovel on the "blasted heath" (3.2.74–77). The boundaries between comedy and tragedy dissolve in these moments, but throughout Shakespeare adapts his historical sources in ways that surely reveal his fascination with the border between laughter and tears. Twenty years earlier he had written a remarkable passage in *Love's Labour's Lost* in which Rosaline seeks to educate Berowne in the purpose of comedy:

> You shall this twelvemonth term from day to day
> Visit the speechless sick, and still converse
> With groaning wretches; and your task shall be
> With all the fierce endeavour of your wit
> To enforce the pained impotent to smile.
> *(5.2.838–842)*

How can he "move wild laughter in the throat of death?" (5.2.843) asks Berowne.

Shakespeare appears to answer the question in *Lear*. In one of the play's most striking scenes, Edgar, disguised as Tom, leads his own, blinded, father across the stage and fools (serious fooling this) him into thinking he is throwing himself off a cliff, when all he does is fall to the floor – and live. This scene is not in the "anonymous play *The True Chronicle History of King Leir*, written in the 1580s and published in 1605, though Shakespeare drew extensively on its capable, affecting account of an ageing king who divides his realm between two uncaring daughters after rejecting his third and youngest for not flattering him in a love-trial" (Kerrigan 2018, p. 63).

There are hints of the story in Sir Philip Sidney's *Arcadia*, where a usurped king seeks death, but the scene on the imaginary cliff does not have a single, identifiable source. Instead, it contains "layers of imitation" which "resonate back to antiquity, to something like symphonic effect." *Lear* is "original in the early modern sense of going back to origins" (Kerrigan 2018, p. 64), in this case *Oedipus* (and *Antigone*) as written by Seneca, mixed with a passage from Montaigne's *Essais*.

Something made this play worthy of "commemorating, for its date, venue and royal audience were all recorded when the play was entered in the Stationers' Register and were then advertised on the title page of the 1608 quarto. This had never happened before with one of Shakespeare's plays nor would it again" (Shapiro 2015, p. 349). Perhaps it was that *Lear's* first audiences, or at least those who knew the story, were expecting a happy ending. In Shakespeare's source, the king is restored to power and his daughter Cordelia lives. Instead, Cordelia dies.

Nowhere is it more true than in its ending that the play *King Lear*, like *Hamlet*, is not a fixed entity. The quarto and Folio texts end differently, a change most likely determined not by Shakespeare as an individual, but by his acting company's awareness of venue and audience. Kerrigan (2018, p. 17) sets out the process. The 1608 quarto was probably written for a court performance, therefore "the crown of Britain is eventually taken by the Duke of Albany (one of the titles held by James VI and I)." In the later Folio version of 1623, the crown "goes to Edgar, who bears the name of an Anglo-Saxon king who laid claim to Britain," a change that would "satisfy the geopolitical bias of a London, public theatre audience." The Folio version also reflects (Shapiro 2015, p. 352) "a good deal of shrewd theatrical intervention." All this is yet another reminder that the text(s) through which we "know" William Shakespeare were and are constantly shapeshifting, with interventions and alterations occasioned by censors and editors, actors and prompters, as much as playwrights.

One of those interventions suggests that someone understood the first version of *Lear* as, perhaps, just "*too* dark, *too* unbearable": they "flinched and pulled the ending back from the abyss." Where the 1608 quarto has Lear's infamous "O, O, O, O" ("Shakespeare's shorthand for Richard Burbage to groan his last, followed a moment later by his dying words"), later the king's death is softened. The "O's disappear, and the heartbreak becomes Kent's not Lear's." Above all, Lear dies believing that Cordelia lives (Shapiro 2015, pp. 353–355).

Or perhaps not. I incline towards the possibility of an even darker reading, where Lear is aware he is deluding himself. Albany's replacement by Edgar, his social inferior, is another gesture of hope: the younger man has suffered, but his suffering has been purposeful.

A concern with the relationship between fathers and sons returns to the foreground in *Lear*, leading Tromly (2010, p. 263) to suggest that Shakespeare's lack of a living son, his sense of his aging, would have "sharpened his perception of Gloucester's suffering." This is possible, in that Shakespeare had passed 40 by the time of *Lear*, but he is as interested in illegitimate sons as much as legitimate. He had already created the Bastard of *King John* and Don John in *Much Ado* in the late 1590s, and the straight-talking Thersites in *Troilus and Cressida*, a man who revels in his own outsider status.

> Thersites What art thou?
> Margareton A bastard son of Priam's.
> Thersites I am a bastard too; I love bastards. I am bastard begot,
> bastard instructed, bastard in mind, bastard in valour, in
> everything illegitimate. One bear will not bite another, and
> wherefore should one bastard? Take heed, the quarrel's
> most ominous to us. If the son of a whore fight for a
> whore, he tempts judgement. Farewellt, bastard.
>
> *(5.8.6–14)*

Edmund in *King Lear* is not only the most evil but also the most eloquent bastard created by Shakespeare, given one of the great speeches by his creator.

> Thou, nature, art my goddess; to thy law
> My services are bound. Wherefore should I
> Stand in the plague of custom, and permit
> The curiosity of nations to deprive me,
> For that I am some twelve or fourteen moon-shines
> Lag of a brother? Why bastard? wherefore base?
> When my dimensions are as well compact,
> My mind as generous, and my shape as true,
> As honest madam's issue? Why brand they us
> With base? with baseness? bastardy? base, base?
> Who, in the lusty stealth of nature, take
> More composition and fierce quality
> Than doth, within a dull, stale, tired bed,
> Go to the creating a whole tribe of fops,
> Got 'tween asleep and wake? Well, then,
> Legitimate Edgar, I must have your land:
> Our father's love is to the bastard Edmund
> As to the legitimate: fine word, – legitimate!
> Well, my legitimate, if this letter speed,
> And my invention thrive, Edmund the base
> Shall top the legitimate. I grow; I prosper:
> Now, gods, stand up for bastards!
>
> *(1.2.1–22)*

On one level, Edmund's illegitimacy naturalizes his hatred of his brother, his despising of his father – the same essentialist maths done to come up with Don John's enmity towards his legitimate brother, Don Pedro (and to everyone else as well). It is a familiar literary trope. Sir Philip Sidney, for one, used it, offering the "story of the King of Paphlagonia who has symmetrical, binary sons: a kind, natural, legitimate son and a cruel, unnatural, illegitimate son" (Tromly 2010, p. 244). Cruel, unnatural, illegimate, but also compelling, resourceful, and eloquent when written by Shakespeare.

Few biographers have been brave enough to map Shakespeare's fascination with bastards onto his own life. (An illegitimate son, anyone? Davenant crops up as a contender every few years, usually in time for an anniversary of some kind, only to be dismissed by scholars as seventeenth-century fake news.) If the character is understood to have a real-life counterpart, it is Edmund, Shakespeare's younger brother, about whom we know nothing except that he was born in Stratford, and may have died, young, in London. More of Edmund later, but first, let us consider Shakespeare as Lear. That is more fertile ground, given that William was the father of daughters, with Hamnet dead for nearly 10 years. Of the daughters, Susanna, born in 1583, is often deemed the favorite, with Tromly (2010, p. 264) going so far as to see her as the inspiration for Cordelia, a woman who "risks her life to rescue her father, as sons had done in earlier plays, but unlike them she performs the act with a commitment of love that dissolves the ambivalence created by the pressure of duty and indebtedness."

Shakespeare's relationship with his children, dead or alive, favored or not, is almost impossible to recover from either archive or play, but *Lear* does offer further clues as to his political thinking. Indeed, to understand that the play is about family is not to depoliticize it in a world in which the king was understood as a father to his country. Therefore, "the image and horror of the collapse of the state and the obliteration of the royal family" witnessed by the audience at the end of *King Lear* worked as an echo of the "violent fantasy of the Gunpowder plotters a year earlier" (Shapiro 2015, p. 353). Then again, Shakespeare had already staged a shocking obliteration of the royal family in *Hamlet* a few years earlier, without needing a prompt from Guy Fawkes.

Susanna makes an appearance in the records in the aftermath of the Gunpowder Plot, a reminder that although Fawkes failed in his mission, there were repercussions for months and years afterwards. All through 1606, the authorities were anxious to round up Catholic sympathizers and in May, in Stratford-upon-Avon, William's daughter was one of 21 people reported to the ecclesiastical court for refusing to take Holy Communion at Easter. Of the 21, many were "known Catholics, including Margaret Reynolds, whose family had sheltered a Jesuit priest and who regularly paid fines for non-attendance. Also included in the list were Hamnet and Judith Sadler, well known to the Shakespeare family, perhaps close enough friends to have had William name his twins after them" (Hadfield 2019, p. 29). Susanna at first ignored the summons. Time passed, the case was dismissed. Perhaps she fell into line and took Communion: 10 of her co-defendants did just that. She has been seen as rebellious, careless, or with a very good reason for her actions, which the court accepted. But, as Hadfield (2019, p. 30) suggests,

> those would seem to be odd explanations of such behaviour at a particularly sensitive and dangerous time. Perhaps this is really the best biographical evidence we have of the Shakespeare family's religious stance, demonstrating that they had Catholic allegiances. Or, rather, that Shakespeare's eldest child, posthumously famous for being 'Witty above her sex,' may have been a Catholic before her marriage to the physician, Dr. John Hall, on June 5, 1607. Hall appears to have had Puritan inclinations, which further complicates the picture of allegiances and suggests that, if Susanna was a Catholic, differences in religion were not insurmountable obstacles to unions and could be overcome.

Opinion, unsurprisingly, remains divided. For Dutton (2016) and MacKinnon (2015, pp. 77–78) the episode is a clear sign of Susanna's secret Catholicism, whilst for Greg Wells (2015, pp. 91–92) it, ironically, shows her "Puritan leanings."

What the episode does indicate is the level of paranoia in the aftermath of the Gunpowder Plot. Whilst Catholics were forced to declare their loyalty to the king, in theaterland players were instructed to remove all "profanity" from their plays. The 27 May 1606 Act to Restrain Abuses of Players would be the only time Parliament legislated matters relating to the content and performance of plays. Shakespeare's Scottish play, *Macbeth*, may have been a product of this feverish time, showing how the Gunpowder Plot "struck very close to home for Shakespeare. The issues of regicide, providence, religious faith, political deviousness and fanaticism, which were all evoked by it, were inevitably in his mind as he wrote" the play (Dutton 2016, p. 139).[6] Dutton's knowledge of Shakespeare's mind relies on placing the play in James's reign. Most do, if only because the king was Scottish.

A Scottish theme was not, however, a guarantor of success or royal approval in Shakespeare's time, as is evident from "the tragedy of Gowrie." In 1604, the Lord Chamberlain recorded that

> the tragedy of Gowrie with all the action and actors hath been twice represented by the King's Players, with exceeding concourse of all sorts

of people. But whether the matter or manner be not well handled, or that it be thought unfit that princes should be played on the stage in their lifetime, I hear that some great Councillors are much displeased with it, and so is thought shall be forbidden.

(Chamberlain 1939, p. 199)

The play dramatized the Gowrie Conspiracy of 1600, in which the Earl of Gowrie apparently kidnapped and attempted to assassinate James VI, although some claimed the king had faked the crisis. The Lord Chamberlain was right. The play was suppressed after those two performances, almost definitely because James himself was being played on stage while still alive. The King's Men were, temporarily at least, in trouble, although Shakespeare, perhaps demonstrating his "instinct for caution and his track record of staying out of trouble" (Bate 2008, p. 345), did not appear in connection with the play. Maybe it was an ideal moment to head to Stratford.

Shakespeare does not go near contemporary Scottish history. His *Macbeth* is safely set in the eleventh century, so was not politically "unfit" for an early seventeenth-century London stage. But, bearing in mind the ways in which the past was understood to be only too relevant to the present, even events of the eleventh century could resonate with contemporary politics, contemporary events. *Macbeth's* Porter imagines a Catholic priest being escorted into hell for lying, which may allude to the trial and execution of Jesuit Father Henry Garnet, the leader of the English Jesuit community. Garnet had defended the practice of equivocation, that is, explains Bate (2008, p. 345), "paltering with double sense so as to avoid either incriminating himself or committing the sins of lying upon oath and revealing the secrets of the confessional" at his trial. Bate goes on to argue that Garnet's status as a male witch, and the awkward fact that the leading Gunpowder conspirators came from Warwickshire families, may lie close to the surface of *Macbeth*, but remain tactfully veiled: Shakespeare "had learned the lessons of Gowrie's closure. To dramatize contemporary event was too close to the bone" (ibid.).

Not only that, Shakespeare, yet again, tweaks his historical source and probably in the interest of safety, for the playwright and his company. In Holinshed, Shakespeare had read that Banquo was a co-conspirator with Macbeth. King James claimed to be descended from Banquo. So, conveniently, Banquo becomes virtuous and is provided with a son, Fleance, who amazingly survives. The line of kings is set out by the weird sisters, extending from "Banquo and Fleance to the living king who sat in the most prominent seat in the banqueting hall": all of the King's "preoccupations are in here: rights of royal succession, the relationship between Scotland and England witchcraft, the sacred powers of the monarchy, anxiety about gunpowder treason and plot" (ibid., p. 346). Shakespeare goes further, beyond simply adding material guaranteed to appeal to James (witches and ghosts), to ensure that his killer of kings, Macbeth, is a "butcher," his wife "fiend-like." Every mention of the English and the Scots dwells on the two nations' unshakeable alliance. Rarely does Shakespeare demonstrate "such blatant one-sidedness" (Potter 2012, p. 324). Then again, concludes Potter, "none of Shakespeare's subsequent plays would come so close to contemporary events" (ibid., p. 325).

Which is not to say that Shakespeare avoided politics. What may have been his next play, *Antony and Cleopatra*, was probably performed during the visit to England of King Christian of Denmark, Queen Anne's brother, in 1606, and the King's Men's lead playwright offers his royal patron, according to Shapiro (2015, p. 310), "a tragedy of nostalgia, a political work that obliquely (for there are never reductive and dangerous one-to-one correspondences between ancient and modern figures) expresses a longing for an Elizabethan past that, despite its many flaws, appeared in retrospect far greater than the present political world." At worst, Shakespeare is revealing King James's limitations, at best the play is ambivalent, giving with one hand and taking away with the other when it comes to parallels between James and Octavius, the latter, creator of the *Pax Romana*, the former, with his motto, *Beata Pacifici*, the first British monarch to portray himself as a Roman emperor on his coins. Pragmatic, capable, and infuriated by Antony's "lightness" (with good reason), Octavius is also rigid and, for audiences, unlikeable.

Yet again Shakespeare's unwillingness to be didactic, his willingness to give his flawed characters interiority, leaves critics divided: is he a subtle critic of the Stuart king or a flatterer of royalty? So much for politics. What of religion? For Potter (2012, pp. 340–341), *Antony and Cleopatra* marks a turning point as much as *Hamlet*. A masterpiece in a new genre, Shakespeare had for the first time "started to think seriously about dramatic theory." For years, Shakespeare had been interweaving comic and serious episodes, leavening history with often gratuitous romance. That was how playwrights wrote tragedy in his youth and he didn't change it, in contrast to the reformer Jonson.[7] But now Shakespeare fully explored the possibilities and meaning of tragi-comedy, a term "everyone already knew," because of Guarini's argument that only tragi-comedy was a properly Christian response to tragedy, dramatizing "the availability of salvation up to the last moment." Reading Guarini led Shakespeare to begin a move away from tragedy, made him think seriously, for the first time, about the fact that "most of the sources of his tragedies belonged to an alien religious culture" (Potter 2012, pp. 340–341). It's a big claim with implications for both *Antony and Cleopatra* and his final tragedy, *Coriolanus*. Both become plays designed to make the audience understand the difference between pagan worlds and future Christian redemption. One can't help but come to the conclusion that, for Potter at least, Shakespeare has found religion.

For some, he may also have taken a belated opportunity to offer a self-portrait in the character of Enobarbus, friend to Antony. Enobarbus is certainly more than a choric figure.[8]

Yes, he does at times ventriloquize Shakespeare's Latin sources, most notably in his rightly famous speech about Cleopatra in her barge (2.2.201–228), which is taken straight from Plutarch; he does open and close a number of scenes; and he offers a detached, at times, ironic commentary on the unfolding action. But he is also a character with depth, skeptical and pragmatic in a world of overblown gestures and unstable egoists. His flexibility is both his cardinal virtue and his tragic undoing, as he betrays Antony.

In Bate's admiring words (2008, p. 423):

> Intelligent, funny, at once companionable and guardedly isolated, full of understanding of women, but most comfortable with men (there's even a homosexual frisson with Menas and Agrippa), clinically analytical in his assessment of others, but full of sorrow and shame when his reason overrides his loyalty and leads him to desert his friend and master, he might just be the closest Shakespeare came to a portrait of his own mind.

It would be nice to think of Shakespeare the man in this way.

Chapter Seven

Enobarbus or Lear as self-portrait: take your pick between understanding Shakespeare the man in terms of friendship or family. There has been a lot so far in this book about the latter, less about the former, mainly because we do at least know that Shakespeare had parents, siblings, a wife, and children. A grandchild is even on the way in 1608. There are glimpses of William's friends: the tradespeople of Stratford-upon-Avon who stood as godparents to his children; his colleagues in the playhouses. Even John Milton, for whom no familial archive exists (not a single letter to any of his three wives, nor to his brother, let alone his daughters), wrote letters to his male friends, and his friends wrote back. More importantly, those friends kept his letters, and with good reason.

Friendship was for many men in Shakespeare's time and beyond the highest form of love. It could even occur (at least in a teenager's idealism) between men and women. When Juliet, after her one night with Romeo says, "Love, Lord, ay Husband, Friend" "that last word is no anti-climax, but rather a specially intimate term" (Hammond 2012, p. 18). It was more pertinent nevertheless to the intimacy between men. The relationship, for example, between Achilles and Patroclus in *Troilus and Cressida*, men who "share a tent and loll on a bed," is "both an heroic friendship and an erotic bond" (Garber 2004, p. 559). Such noble, idealized, and eroticized friendships between men were recognizable to Elizabethans as much as to classical writers. Not only that: they were recognizable, and preferable to friendships with women for some familiar reasons. "To compare the affection towards women unto [friendship], although it proceed from our own free choice, a man cannot nor may it be placed in this rank: her fire, I confess it to be more active, more fervent, and more sharp. But it is a rash and wavering fire, waving and diverse: the fire of an ague subject to fits and stints" (Florio's translation of Montaigne [Montaigne 1632]).

Bearing in mind the general belief in Shakespeare's time that women were second-class humans (not to mention unstable, emotional, and irrational), it is not surprising that friendships between men were often valued more highly.

The Life of the Author: William Shakespeare, First Edition. Anna Beer.

Women might be needed in order to create a family, but true love and friendship was only possible between equals: between men.

Misogyny was ingrained in Shakespeare's era. Even though there was a woman, Queen Elizabeth I, ruling England during the first half of his writing career, during his lifetime the majority of women had very limited rights, not only in the legal, political, and economic worlds, but also in their personal lives. Marriage, the production of children, and the management of the household were viewed as a woman's role and purpose. Underpinning the beliefs about what individual women were, or were not, supposed to do were some basic beliefs about all women. Women were understood to be morally, intellectually, and physically weaker than men. The Bible provided a justification for this understanding, specifically the Book of Genesis in which Eve caused the Fall of Man by disobeying God's command not to eat from the Tree of Knowledge. These religious arguments were reinforced by the writings of the classical writer Aristotle, who stated that the female body was an inferior version of the perfect male form. Medical theories further supported a strong sense of difference between males and females, which served to justify the dominance of men over women. Men were believed to be hot and dry, and women were cold and moist. It was this that made women passive, intellectually unstable, and lacking in courage.

Because of these essential differences, women were expected to obey all men in their family, including their father and brothers, with disobedience figured as a form of treason, a reminder if one were needed that the personal is always the political in Shakespeare's time. As important as, and closely connected to, obedience was the virtue of silence for women. This idea, like the others, had biblical authority.

> Let your women keep silence in the churches: for it is not permitted unto them to speak; but they are commanded to be under obedience, as also saith the law. And if they will learn any thing, let them ask their husbands at home: for it is a shame for women to speak in the church.
> *(I Corinthians 14:34–35)*

Many have tried to separate Shakespeare the man from the ingrained misogyny of his era. Take his creation of Cleopatra for example, which is used to demonstrate that the playwright is keen to depict a strong, complex, eloquent female character. The argument goes that having co-authored *Timon of Athens*, a play almost without women, Shakespeare – the balanced, fair-handed Bard – moves on to *Antony and Cleopatra*, a play that focuses on the Eqyptian queen at the expense of the Roman generals, and by doing so departs from his Latin Roman source, Plutarch. Even more inspiring to those who want to see a softening of Shakespeare's misogyny, the play might be a response to the work of a woman, Mary Sidney, the Countess of Pembroke. Her tragedy *Antonius* (1592) – itself an adaptation of Robert Garnier's *Marc Antoine* (1578) – offers a sympathetic portrayal of Cleopatra. It is Antony who is responsible for his own downfall, and the only condemnation of the Egyptian queen comes from woman herself. Could it have been reading Sidney's work that inspired Shakespeare to give Cleopatra more words than any other of his female characters? She certainly does not keep silence. More than that, it has been suggested that the play is quietly revelatory of Shakespeare's understanding of and compassion for women's position both in society and on his stage, in part because he has Cleopatra explicitly draw attention to the phenomenon of boys impersonating women in the playhouses of his time. The Egyptian queen fears a future "squeaking Cleopatra" who would "boy" her greatness "i'th' posture of a whore": "the ultimate degradation will be to be performed by a young male actor, like a whore. It is an astonishingly daring moment for that young male actor to deliver" (Smith 2019, p. 261). Shakespeare had made similar moves throughout the 1590s, to comic effect, but this is a tragedy, this is Cleopatra's tragedy, it is *her* fear. Shakespeare appears, for a moment, to acknowledge the situation of women in his own time, that they are only and ever represented (physically on the stage, but metaphorically in all aspects of life) by men.

And yet, these valiant attempts to recuperate Shakespeare from the misogyny of his time are hard to sustain. The landscapes of belief within which he lived and worked determine that we are encouraged to admire Brutus's virtuous wife, Portia, in *Julius Caesar* who, waiting for her husband and hearing bad news, kills herself ("with this she fell distract, / And, her attendants absent, swallowed fire"). This is what obedient wives do. And Portia matters so little to the play and the course of men's lives that her husband can callously dismiss her death ("Speak no more of her," 4.3.156), then turn – with brutal speed – to war: "Well, to our work alive. What do you think / Of marching to Philippi presently?" (4.3.194–195). With Portia out of the picture, ruthless Cassius moves equally swiftly to bond with Brutus: "I cannot drink too much of Brutus' love" (4.3.160). These moments are some of the most disturbing in Shakespeare's work, and perhaps we should understand them as a criticism of men's behavior. A similar question is raised by the earlier play, *Much Ado About Nothing*, in which Shakespeare creates a world in which women are categorized as virgins or whores, and in which men have (almost) absolute power over women, and in which a woman's sexual behavior is public business. It is a world rather like the one in which Shakespeare lived. Claudio is given every misogynist cliché you can think of by his creator (Hero is no Diana; she's Venus; like "pamp'red animals" that rage "in savage sensuality" [4.1.59–60]; a "rotten orange" [4.1.30] given to a friend). As with Brutus and Cassius, the play asks questions about male behavior and values. Claudio's responses to women oscillate between a cynical attitude to them as dangerous (a man must not get caught), seasoned with anxiety about cuckoldry, and a form of romantic idolatry learned from books.

But perhaps, by the end of the play, Claudio learns that these extremes are dangerous and destructive, both to women and to himself, and perhaps his creator believed this too. Further evidence that Shakespeare the man was, at least, sympathetic to women's position in his society can be found. For example, he is wont to add women to his plays, or to enhance their significance as he does in the very early *Comedy of Errors*. The rediscovered mother Emilia is Shakespeare's addition, and the character of Adriana, the neglected wife, is enlarged and given a sister, Luciana. There's even a powerful conversation between the sisters. The bitter resentful Adriana is chastised by Luciana, who has swallowed the patriarchal rulebook, hook, line, and sinker.

> Why, headstrong liberty is lash'd with woe.
> There's nothing situate under heaven's eye
> But hath his bound in earth, in sea, in sky.
> The beasts, the fishes, and the winged fowls
> Are their males' subjects, and at their controls;
> Man, more divine, the master of all these,
> Lord of the wide world and wild wat'ry seas,
> Indued with intellectual sense and souls,
> Of more pre-eminence than fish and fowls,
> Are masters to their females, and their lords:
> Then let your will attend on their accords.
>
> *(2.1.15–25)*

However, more women, more speeches by women, does not necessarily translate into more agency for women, let alone a critique of the values of silence, chastity, and obedience. Instead, these characters often serve to prove why they need to remain subject to their "more divine" men. Put another way, and looking at another early play, *Richard III*, it has been calculated that women (including the unhistorical character of Margaret) speak approximately 22 percent of *Richard III* (Howard and Rackin 1997, pp. 217–218). But, crucially, "prominence does not simply equate with empowerment" (Adelman 1992, p. 9). Sometimes desired, the women of Shakespeare's history plays are "more often resented, mocked, manipulated and marginalized" (Siemon 2009, p. 18). Shakespeare moves them "from positions of power and authority to positions of utter powerlessness, and finally moves them off the stage altogether" (Adelman 1992, p. 9).

Active female characters, at least in these early history plays, are invariably depicted in a negative way by Shakespeare. Eleanor in *Henry VI Part II* is a more bloodthirsty Beatrice, a woman who longs to be a man if only because she could then decapitate her enemies:

> Were I a man, a duke and next of blood,
> I would remove these tedious stumbling-blocks
> And smooth my way upon their headless necks.
> *(1.2.63–65)*

In contrast, the "more sympathetically depicted female characters, such as the victimized women in *Richard III*, never go to war, they play no part in the affairs of state, and they seem to spend most of their limited time on stage in tears" (Howard and Rackin 1997, p. 98). Yes, female tears can also be understood as "railing, lamentation and cursing, utterances that indeed constitute 'affairs of state'" (Siemon 2009, p. 18), but if women have power, it is only power to curse. Silence is safer. Beatrice in *Much Ado About Nothing* moves from being one of Shakespeare's most articulate characters to frustration at the limitations of being a woman ("O God that I were a man! I would eat his heart in the market place," 4.1.304–305), to silence. "Peace, I will stop your mouth" (5.4.97) says Uncle Leonato handing her over to Benedick, who most editors suggest promptly kisses her. We hear no more from Beatrice.

Women's stories usually end with marriage (in his comedies) or death (in his tragedies). But because this is drama, redirected, in every sense, by each new generation, it is now possible to understand and experience the ending of a play like *Measure for Measure* differently, to understand "Shakespeare's women" differently. Directors make Isabella reject the Duke's offer of marriage or have her remain resolutely unmoved and silent: both can be made extremely awkward moments for the ruler of Vienna. This glimpse of Isabella's independence, her refusal to dwindle into a wife in the final moments of the play, lies in a long tradition of reclaiming, in all sorts of creative ways, the agency of Shakespeare's women characters. His writing allows for it, even with, especially with, the minor characters such as a woman called Kate, who is almost always referred to in discussions of *Measure for Measure* as a "whore," because this is what Lucio calls her. His bitter, ironic comment when commanded by the Duke to marry Kate is that "marrying a punk, my lord, is pressing to death, whipping and hanging" (5.1.520–521). His line is yet more grist to the "marriage as punishment" critical mill, but his referring to Kate as "punk" is also significant, in that critics have been only too willing to parrot him.

Melissa Sanchez (2017) pulls this reading apart, line by line, her interpretation informed by an understanding of history as much as queer theory. She argues that Kate's circumstances trouble any easy definition of "whore." If her marriage to Lucio will transform her from "punk" to "wife," then it is equally possible that her pregnancy may have turned her from maid to punk for "Kate's actual status – maid or punk? – at the time she conceived Lucio's child is never clearly stated" (Sanchez 2017, p. 270) in the play. Instead, other details are provided to us. Mistress Overdone, the brothel keeper, says that Lucio promised to marry Kate; Lucio himself admits he got a "wench with child" (4.3.167–168), but denied his paternity because he would then have been forced to marry the "rotten medlar" (4.3.171–172). As Sanchez (2017, p. 270) points out:

> It seems unlikely that a paying client would promise a prostitute marriage: the whole point of prostitution is that men can have sex *without* marriage, commitment or progeny. It also seems unlikely, given the public shaming and harsh corporeal, carceral and economic penalties imposed on prostitutes, that a prostitute would take a client who has impregnated her to court in hopes of compelling him to marry her, more unlikely still that the court would rule in her favour if he acknowledged paternity.

She concludes by suggesting two things: that Kate did not have sex with Lucio as a prostitute – that is, in exchange for money, and that she had not slept with other men, as a prostitute or otherwise, for enough time before and after her encounter with Lucio that his paternity would have been unquestionable. Kate may, therefore, have been a "maid" at the time of conception, and she may be a "punk" (or at least an unmarried mother living in a brothel) at the time of the play's action precisely because of Lucio's insemination of her.

Shakespeare allows for these moments of interpretative freedom, so that we can release the characters from the circumstances in which they were created.

But place Isabella (and Kate for that matter) back in around 1604 and the walls close back in. Generically, the drive to romance endings (and romance means marriage – even in history plays when the sources don't offer them, even in Shakespeare's one attempt at a city comedy, complete with brothels and plague and rape) is omnipresent. In performance terms, it is hard to imagine the boy playing Isabella having the authority to usurp the precedence of the Duke in this final scene although, in a typically playful way, Shakespeare had done just that with the boy-girl-boy character of Rosalind in *As You Like It*.

For all the wonderful lines given to women characters by Shakespeare, for all the compelling situations in which he places them, he never quite gives women the interiority, the full humanity, the independent agency, the ability to work out their own salvation, that he gives to his men.

There are tantalizing sightings of what might have been, sometimes even when a character is *not* cross-dressed. It is as if Shakespeare opens a door into a world of possibility for women but then closes it. He had been doing this for years. Juliet "has a stronger personality than Romeo" and "she wins through to an almost frightening maturity more quickly." She is "poised and playfully serious" at the lovers' first meeting, and in the window scene she is "more thoughtful, prudent and realistic than Romeo" (Blakemore-Evans 2003, p. 27). But by the end of the play, Juliet is more than dead, she is turned into a symbol, a statue, a matter of competition between the surviving fathers.

> But I can give thee more,
> For I will raise her statue in pure gold,
> That whiles Verona by that name is known,
> There shall no figure at such rate be set
> As that of true and faithful Juliet.
>
> *(5.3.298–302)*

There are exceptions to the rule, because this is Shakespeare. In *Love's Labour's Lost*, the princess is more intelligent than the king, and the women control the drama and their men. The door is indeed opened, as it is in Shakespeare's depiction of female–female friendship in his plays of the mid–late 1590s. These friendships are as intense and loving and reciprocal as the friendships between men. Helena in *A Midsummer Night's Dream* speaks of her friendship with Hermia: "the sisters' vows"; "schooldays' friendship, childhood innocence" (3.2.199 and 3.2.202); that they created one flower with their needles

> As if our hands, our sides, voices and minds
> Had been incorporate. So we grew together
> Like to a double cherry, seeming parted,
> But yet an union in partition,
> Two lovely berries moulded on one stem.
>
> *(3.2.207–211)*

This beautiful image describes the two women's "ancient love," destroyed by erotic competition for a man, and then displaced by socially sanctioned love for their future husbands. A similar "ancient love" exists between Rosalind and Celia in *As You Like It*, who are dearer to each other "than the natural bond of sisters" (1.2.265). As Celia explains:

> We still have slept together,
> Rose at an instant, learned, played, ate together,
> And whereso'er we went, like Juno's swans,
> Still we went coupled and inseparable.
>
> *(1.3.70–73)*

Comic form (and social convention) dictates that Celia is married off, most implausibly, to the only suitable available male at the end of the play.

Things get more complex and troubling in *Measure for Measure*, written a few years after *As You Like It*. Chedgzoy (2000, p. 55) explains:

When Lucio brings Isabella the news that Claudio "hath got his friend with child" (1.4.29), she soon realizes that this must be "my cousin Juliet" (1.4.44). The relationship is not one of blood, though, but of choice: they are cousins "Adoptedly, as schoolmaids change their names / By vain though apt affection" (1.4.46–47).

Shakespeare offers a glimpse of a long-established friendship, similar to that of Helena and Hermia, or Rosalind and Celia, and a

> rare opportunity in this play to see women relating to each other outside the framework of patriarchal institutions such as the brothel and convent, or beyond the manipulations of the Friar/Duke. But after this brief acknowledgment of Juliet, Isabella seems to forget her entirely. Indeed, except for the last sixty lines or so of the play, they are never even on stage together, and so there is no dramatic space where the relationship between them could be developed.
>
> *(Chedgzoy 2000, p. 55)*

Shakespeare's forgetting of Juliet in *Measure for Measure* may seem a small moment, but it is symptomatic of these plays of the early 1600s, which reveal a playwright quite happy to trade in conventional tropes of women. The only female characters in *Hamlet*, Gertrude and Ophelia, end up as collateral damage, victims caught in the crossfire of the revenge plot driven by men. Shakespeare allows Ophelia and Gertrude to respond, to report, and occasionally to plead, but he rarely shows them thinking, or rationally discussing and interpreting situations. Instead they are told what to think, what to do, and, most importantly, what they are.

Laertes says, starkly, to Ophelia, that she is a fool to believe that Hamlet loves her and tells her to "think it no more" (1.3.10). Polonius, in the same scene, tells Ophelia that she has been behaving like a green girl and a baby in accepting Hamlet's tenders of love, and that she must remember she is his daughter and behave according to his command, not her own judgment or feelings. Later, Hamlet will continue the misogyny of his opening soliloquy by telling Ophelia that wise men know well enough what monsters you [women] make of them, whilst accusing her of being little more than a prostitute. In the closet scene, Hamlet tells Gertrude about her own sexual desires, and how disgusted he is by them. His tirade is only interrupted by the reappearance of the Ghost, who is also quite sure that women are weak: "Conceit in weakest bodies strongest works" (3.4.114). Hamlet may be calmer in his words to his mother after the Ghost's intervention, but he still instructs her what to do: she must not let the bloat king tempt her again to bed.

There may be only two female characters in *Hamlet*, but there is an immense amount of talk *about* women. From Hamlet's "Frailty, thy name is woman"

(1.2.146) to the moment when he turns Ophelia's comment on the short prologue to the Mousetrap into a judgment on the brevity of woman's love
(3.2.151–153), a female character and/or the nature of "woman" is regularly
defined by the words of the male characters around her.

This is most true of Gertrude. Hamlet talks much more about his mother
(and about women) than Gertrude talks about herself, and her son is one of her
harshest critics. Hamlet is obsessed with, and disgusted by, her sexual activity,
and extremely critical of her lack of judgment. How can she not see a difference
between Claudius and Old Hamlet? He answers his own question. Lust is
Gertrude's motivation – and has blinded her to the truth.

Which brings us back to Cleopatra. She (not silent, not chaste, not obedient)
may be good theater, but she is a dangerous woman. Cleopatra dresses drunken,
sleeping Antony in her clothes and wears his sword. Stern Roman Octavius
knows that the Egyptian queen is "manlike" and Antony "womanly." After
what Caesar initially sees as her betrayal in the final battle, he attacks Cleopatra

> verbally as a "foul Egyptian" (4.12.10), "[t]riple-turned whore" (13),
> "false soul" (25), "gipsy" (28), "witch" (47), "vile lady" (4.14.22). Other
> characters are no less abusive. Philo calls her "gipsy" and "strumpet"
> (1.1.10; 13), Enobarbus an "Egyptian dish" (2.6.128), Octavius a "whore"
> (3.6.68), and Scarrus a "nag" (3.10.10), a slang term for a prostitute.
> Scarrus also hopes Cleopatra will suffer from leprosy, believed to be a
> venereal disease.
>
> *(Klein 2016, p. 461)*

Misogyny will out. Anatomy is destiny for Shakespeare's female characters,
even his most compellingly realized creations. Rosalind faints when she hears
of Orlando's injury. Her woman's body betrays her, even as she begins and
ends the play thoroughly in command of herself and those around her.

Is it a coincidence that there is no record of Rosalind and Cleopatra being
performed in Shakespeare's lifetime? They are the female characters to whom
Shakespeare gives the most lines, the "women" who almost, but not quite, break
free from the misogyny of their context, whether understood as the early modern
stage or the social world beyond that stage. Yes, the amount of lines Shakespeare
lavishes on the boy actor playing Rosalind may have annoyed "his experienced
fellow sharers, used to playing the leading roles themselves" (Shapiro 2005a, p.
235) but it may be that – only half-consciously – Shakespeare had opened the
door onto a view of women that his contemporaries could not or would not see.

Shapiro's take on *As You Like It* is part of a view of a Shakespeare who was
beginning to lose his way, after a decade or more of success. Three years on, in
1606, Shapiro (2015) sees a playwright who, having struggled to find his footing
in the early years of the new king's reign, returned triumphantly to form with

the three extraordinary tragedies, *Lear*, *Macbeth*, and *Antony and Cleopatra*. Shapiro's approach to Shakespeare is compelling, sparking creative connections for the reader, and allowing us to immerse in the playwright's world, but it relies on assumptions about the dates of plays. *Antony and Cleopatra*, for example, was only registered for publication in 1608, so may not even have been in existence in the all-important 1606.[1]

For once we are on safer ground when it comes to matters of traditional biographical interest. In 1607, Susanna, William's daughter, married the physician John Hall. Hall was staunchly Protestant (making his new wife's run-in with the church authorities the previous year less likely to be a sign of her hidden Catholicism), and 10 years older than his bride. Which made him only 10 years younger than his new father-in-law, who proved generous. William gave his daughter Susanna the substantial gift of 107 acres of land in Old Stratford as a marriage settlement, while retaining a life interest. Most likely, the new couple lived in a house in the old town, now known as Hall's Croft. It was "a good match": marrying a doctor is apparently "just what every father wants for his eldest daughter" (Bate 2008, p. 50).

There's more. Despite the usual warning ("We must always be wary of attempts to map Shakespeare's life on to his work"), Bate believes that the "presence of several dignified, sympathetically portrayed medical men," coming after a couple of ridiculous, comic doctor characters in his earlier work, signifies Shakespeare's pleasure in the marriage and in John Hall, his doctor son-in-law (2008, p. 52). About nine months after the marriage, Susanna gave birth to a child. Elizabeth Hall, William Shakespeare's first grandchild, was baptized in February 1608. Her grandfather was not yet 44.

Pericles (written, perhaps in the final months of Susanna's pregnancy, "perhaps the first weeks of the life of Shakespeare's first grandchild, Elizabeth" [Bate 2008, p. 52]) has been viewed as a response to these family events. Reversing the Oedipus story, "the hero begins by solving a riddle but avoids the crime of incest, and his destiny leads him to a reunion that is happy rather than horrified" (Potter 2012, p. 345). Incest will return in the next chapter, but for now, Susanna's husband. This play about a father and a daughter, about death and rebirth, also celebrates the powers of the doctor Cerimon. "This is not to say that Cerimon *is* Hall," of course (because that would be too crass, too biographical) but "family circumstances, and in particular the stabilizing figure of Hall, do seem to have been on Shakespeare's mind at this time" (Bate 2008, p. 53).

So, obviously, is the relationship between fathers and daughters. In Shakespeare's earlier plays, the relationship is significant, but the dynamic is often one in which daughters free themselves (or are freed) from a father's control, whether that control is benign, incompetent, or malevolent. The comedies usually end with the daughters married (a happy escape according to many); the tragedies usually end with the daughters dead. In some plays, both: Cordelia springs to mind. In these late romances the dynamic has shifted slightly. Daughters no longer escape their fathers: instead the "emotional structure" (Lyne 2007, p. 81) of the play depends on a "comic transference of the daughter from father to husband, but under strict paternal control." Lyne's analysis suggests this transference is both comforting and admirable, but, putting aside the anatomy of patriarchy it exposes in which women are transferred, for good or bad, from father to husband, there is a dark underbelly to this new focus on daughters, one which may have discouraged critics from pursuing this particular biographical turn: the prevalence of incestuous overtones and undertones, most notably in *The Winter's Tale* and *The Tempest*. More of this later.

More palatable is an image of Stratford-born Shakespeare, at heart the family man, happiest in the country rather than the city, fascinated by nature, and its ability to cure. *Cymbeline* is the pleasing outcome of these interests, a play in which "Shakespeare's art of natural observation" is at its most acute. The playwright's turn to pastoral romance is above all a celebration of Stratford: of all his plays, *Cymbeline* and *The Winter's Tale* are the ones that have the most distinctive air of having been written back home in Stratford, a place redolent of "stability, community, garden, field and health" (Bate 2008, pp. 54–55). Shakespeare himself peddles this soft-focus view of country life. His rustics are usually more charming than his urban poor, *As You Like It*'s Corin being a case in point, positively dripping homespun wisdom and contentment with his lot:

> Sir, I am a true labourer. I earn that I eat, get that I wear; owe no man hate, envy no man's happiness; glad of other men's good, content with my harm; and the greatest of my pride is to see my ewes graze and my lambs suck.
>
> *(3.2.70–74)*

Two deaths intrude upon this idyllic view of Stratford and English country life. On 2 September 1608 William's mother, Mary Arden, died and was buried a week later. With both parents dead, new grandfather William was now head of the family. William's (much) younger brother, Edmund, died at only 27, and was buried in 1607 in what is now Southwark Cathedral. Edmund may have had a son, "born out of wedlock," who died earlier that year, because there is a record in St. Giles, Cripplegate on 12 August 1607 of "Edward Shakespeare, son of Edward Shakespeare, player, b(ase-born)." William may have paid for what would have been an expensive interment for Edmund. He may have taken Edmund to be his theatrical apprentice.

Once again, a series of possibilities coalesce into a probability in the hand of biographers: "It is highly probable that Ned Shakespeare lodged with Will and played with the Chamberlain's/King's Men at least until the completion of his apprenticeship, or even until his death" (Bate 2008, p. 49). An alternative, but equally speculative, understanding of William's relationship with his younger brother is derived not from the barely existent archive, but from the plays. The fratricide is a recurring figure in Shakespeare's drama, with rivalry between brothers invariably a source of friction if not danger, from Richard of Gloucester back in the early 1590s, through to *The Tempest*, 20 years later and via the most infamous of fratricides, Claudius in *Hamlet*. As Bevington puts it (2005, p. 51) succinctly: "Younger brothers in Shakespeare need careful watching."

Claudius is fully conscious of his biblical ancestor, Cain.

> It smells to heaven.
> It hath the primal eldest curse upon't.
> A brother's murder.
>
> *(3.3.36–38)*

Whether there is an agenda behind William Shakespeare's concern with younger brothers derived from personal experience rather than the Book of Genesis is another question. Bevington sees a pattern to the rivalries: "the older, banished brother is usually seen as bookish and impractical while the younger is more of a machiavel," as in *The Tempest* when wily politician Antonio plans to oust the intellectual Prospero, and murder him and his daughter by casting them to sea in a dangerous boat (Bevington 2005, p. 46). With a hop, skip, and a jump we now reach "Prospero as self-portrait" Shakespeare territory. Before heading there, let's return to *Pericles*, a play that may reveal a Shakespeare preoccupied with Stratford family life, but which also shows him returning to collaboration as a London playwright.

Things were happening for the King's Men. The Children of her Majesty's Revels were finally removed from Blackfriars and, at last in August 1609, Richard Burbage and his company got their theater, 12 years after his father, James, had started building. *Pericles* was published in 1609, having been registered the previous year, and so after the birth of Elizabeth, William's granddaughter. Shakespeare worked with George Wilkins, a playwright who, like Middleton, had recently begun to work for the Globe company, and who put together the first nine scenes. Wilkins peaked in the years immediately prior to contributing his bit to *Pericles*, but he found that writing did not pay, or at least his didn't. He went on become an inn-keeper (definitely) and pimp (almost certainly) in a thoroughly seedy area of London.

Whether Shakespeare and Wilkins collaborated from the outset, or the former took over after the latter had sketched out the plot and started on the play, or indeed whether Wilkins was the one to get hold of an unfinished script and completed it independently of Shakespeare, remains, predictably, unclear. The two writers did not need to be close because, as collaborations go, this was a relatively straightforward creative transaction. The story was uncomplicatedly episodic. One of the advantages of writing a romance was that the plot did not need to be particularly complex or coherent.

There would be no further Wilkins/Shakespeare works. *Pericles* may have been a one-off collaboration because Wilkins was (even by the standard of playwrights) an unsavory individual. He was in trouble with the law as early as 1602, and regularly in court from 1610 until the end of his life. In one case, he was accused of "abusinge one Randall Borkes and kikkinge a woman on the Belly which was then great with childe" (Prior 1972, p. 144), and this was not the only time he was arraigned for violence against women. He may also have been a recusant. *Pericles* and another of Wilkins's plays, T*he Travels of the Three English Brothers*, were in the repertory of Cholmeley's Players, a Yorkshire-based company of recusant players, who performed them on tour in the homes of Catholic families in the years immediately after the writing of *Pericles*.

Three dominant ways of understanding Shakespeare's professional career are visible in analyses of *Pericles*. The play is a response to significant events in William Shakespeare's family life during this period: his daughter's marriage, becoming a grandfather, the loss of his mother, but let's leave out the incest. Or, focusing on Shakespeare's life as a playwright, as a creator, *Pericles* is another rebellious challenge to dramatic orthodoxy, specifically Ben Jonson's "neoclassical dramaturgy." In the years ahead, Shakespeare will continue to flout the unities, depicting "miraculous events in fabulous settings and ornate, grandiloquent language," with his rival Jonson remaining wedded to the Ciceronian definition of comic realism as "the imitation of life, the mirror of custom, the image of truth," confining the action of his comedies within the limits of a single day and a fixed location (Riggs 2015, p. 194). The publication of the fourth edition of *Richard II* in 1608, complete with the controversial deposition scene advertised as a textual addition, complements this view of Shakespeare the risk-taker, but is less concerned with his formal experiments, more with his political daring, or least, more confident of his position or less concerned about the dangerous parallels between Queen Elizabeth and King Richard which had been made back in the 1590s.

The third understanding of William Shakespeare sees him as a pragmatic professional man. *Pericles* was a money-maker after a period in which the playwright's income would have suffered from the closure of the theaters between July 1608 and December 1609 due to plague. Shakespeare attempted to recover an outstanding debt or loan of six pounds through the Stratford-upon-Avon courts in a case that dragged on from August 1608 to June 1609. And he wrote, with Wilkins, the popular *Pericles*, a play which would please all his various audiences.

It's a complicated picture at this time, with various strands visible, but not cohering into a clear sense of where Shakespeare's energies are focused. A riskily political *Richard II* is printed, and there's a collaboration of some kind with the dodgy George Wilkins. A marriage, a birth, two deaths; plague continues, and extreme weather (the great frost of the winter of 1607–1608) makes daily life even more challenging than normal for all Jacobeans. *Timon*, *Pericles*, and even *Antony and Cleopatra* (if we accept Potter's argument as to its being an experiment in tragi-comedy) show a playwright still changing as a writer, exploring, sometimes stumbling.

The most interesting play from this period, to my mind at least, reveals a playwright engaging with contemporary events, specifically the riots, uprisings and social unrest in Northamptonshire, Leicestershire, and William's own Warwickshire known collectively as the Midlands Revolt.[2] Over 10 years earlier, the poor harvests of the mid-1590s had led to riots and thence to the orders against riots which were issued in 1594 and 1595. In 1608, these *Orders*, which permitted justices of the peace to check on grain-hoarders who could then be forced to bring their stock to market, or to sell their grain to the poor at an affordable price, were invoked once again, when the Midlands were particularly hard hit by scarcity of grain following the severe winter of 1606–1607. Adding to the problem was the enclosure of land by wealthy farmers, whereby land traditionally available for communal open-field farming was turned into hedged fields for the pasturing of sheep, which pushed even more people towards starvation.

Shakespeare's *Tragedy of Coriolanus* is set in Rome during the early days of the Republic, far in place and time from the English Midlands in the first decade of the seventeenth century. But time and space collapse when the First Citizen in ancient Rome asks the rioters whether they "are all resolved rather to die than to famish?" (1.1.3–4), echoing a petition from the desperate "Diggers of Warwickshire" which stated that they thought it better to manfully die than pine to death for lack of food. The sense of the past meshing with the present can only have been heightened by the tradition, in Shakespeare's time, of playing historical parts in modern dress. So, the "company of mutinous citizens" would have been dressed as Jacobean laborers and artisans – like some in the audience, in fact.

Shakespeare did not need to be in Stratford to know about the civil unrest in his home county and beyond. It is likely, nevertheless, that he was in the town on a number of occasions in this period: for his daughter, Susanna's, marriage to John Hall on 5 June 1607, when the unrest was at its height; and then in 1608, for his mother's funeral in early September; and then six weeks later, to stand as godfather to the son of his friend, Henry Walker, on 16 October.

It is uncontroversial to present Shakespeare as aware of the hungry rioters in his home region. It is far harder to find consensus as to the Stratford property owner's view of those rioters. Indeed, Emma Smith uses *Coriolanus* to ask "how far biography is, or is not, an admissible element of literary criticism" (2019, p. 274). She is seeking to understand Shakespeare's own position in relation to the "complaints of the rural poor" (ibid.). "One of the biographical facts we have about Shakespeare is his own speculation on barley prices, hoarding eighty bushels in his barns at New Place in Stratford" (ibid.). She also notes that he was involved in plans to enclose land. "Shakespeare seems to have been concerned to protect his own rights and income as a freeholder, not with the more collective concerns about enclosure as the forcible privatization of land previously held in common" (ibid.). That's as close as Smith will get, before turning to the difficulty (futility? crassness? both are implied) of pinning down anything in this "antagonistic play" (ibid., p. 275), or more generally, in any Shakespeare play. Drama's dialogic nature, as ever, resists any easy identification of the playwright's judgments.

Others view Shakespeare as an opportunist, simply picking up on something topical that will entice an audience to the theater. The riots provide him with "an effective dramatic hook with which to snag his audience's attention" (Bliss 2010, p. 26). The play's violent opening engages the audience on a personal, even visceral level, but the message remains conservative and cautionary. The patrician Menenius tells the angry plebeians that violence will not achieve political change:

> you may as well
> Strike at the heaven with your staves, as lift them
> Against the Roman state, whose course will on
> The way it takes, cracking ten thousand curbs
> Of more strong link asunder than can ever
> Appear in your impediment.
>
> *(1.1.62–67)*

This is a familiar representation of the futility of mob violence, and a familiar critique of those who set themselves as leaders of the mob. Cade has no agency in *Henry VI Part II*, operating merely as a pawn of the Duke of York: "I have seduced a headstrong Kentishman, / John Cade of Ashford" (3.1.355–356). Nevertheless, Cade learns fast, understanding he can manipulate the people who cry God Save the King one minute, and follow him the next: "Was ever feather so lightly blown to and fro / as this multitude?" (4.8.55–56). At the height of his career, Shakespeare sounds the same note. In *Julius Caesar*, Cinna the Poet is torn apart by the mob in a case of mistaken identity, and the crowd is consistently presented as fickle. The character of Coriolanus goes even further, insisting that the common people deserve their suffering.

For Bliss (2010, p. 25), Coriolanus is a cipher for the early seventeenth-century gentry "whose enclosures produced depopulation, unemployment, poverty, and, in years of bad harvests, extreme dearth." The next and more challenging step is to decide whether the play shows Coriolanus as misguided in his contempt for the plebeians. If so, then Shakespeare may be offering a critique of those heartless gentry.

For me, it is more plausible to understand Coriolanus as a man who views himself above all ties that bind, beyond simply a military or political leader's responsibilities towards those they lead. Coriolanus is a "thing of blood" (2.2.107) a loner: when he leaves Rome, Shakespeare changes his source to make sure he does it alone. He is a man who denies the bonds of family: "Wife, mother, child, I know not" (5.2.81). He is "a kind of nothing, titleless" (5.1.13). Coriolanus believes, he needs to believe, that a man is "author of himself / And knows no other kin" (5.3.36–37). But the play teaches him that he is no such thing. He is brought back into the fold, not so much by his monstrous mother (to whom Shakespeare gives some of the best, nastiest lines in the play: "Anger's my meat. I sup upon myself, / And so shall starve with feeding," 4.2.50–51), but by the silent pleading of his wife:

> I melt, and am not
> Of stronger earth than others.
> *(5.3.28–29)*

Coriolanus's hubris dissolves in his realization that the bonds of marriage are necessary and inescapable. This is not necessarily a celebration of love or desire. The play shows Coriolanus's attachment to battle and to men who battle as far more erotic than his relationship with his wife. The real excitement lies in "unbuckling helms, fisting each other's throat."

> O! Let me clip ye
> In arms as sound as when I wooed, in heart
> As merry as when our nuptial day was done
> And tapers burned to bedward.
> *(1.6.29–32)*

> Let me twine
> Mine arms about that body where against
> My grained ash an hundred times hath broke
> And scarred the moon with splinters.
> *(4.5.109–113)*

> I have nightly since
> Dreamt of encounters 'twixt thyself and me –
> We have been down together in my sleep,
> Unbuckling helms, fisting each other's throat –
> And waked half dead with nothing.
> *(4.5.125–129)*

All this rampant homoeroticism disgusts the Third Servingman ("Our general himself makes a mistress of him," 4.5.200), but quite what it might tell us about William Shakespeare's sexuality is another question.

The play raises another question implicit to much of Shakespeare's drama. In the early tragedy, *Romeo and Juliet* (1594–1595), Romeo is self-indulgently emotional, traumatized by his fear that he has killed Tybalt. He offers to stab himself. The Nurse snatches the dagger away, and then young Romeo is lectured by wise old Friar Lawrence:

> Hold thy desperate hand!
> Art thou a man? Thy form cries out thou art;
> Thy tears are womanish, thy wild acts denote
> The unreasonable fury of a beast.
> Unseemly woman in a seeming man,
> And ill-beseeming beast in seeming both,
> Thou has amazed me. By my holy order,
> I thought thy disposition better tempered.
> *(3.3.108–115)*

This question – "Art thou a man?" – is asked over and over again by Shakespeare's plays. Here the Friar appeals to the conventional idea that Romeo's disposition should be better "tempered," and many of Shakespeare's comedies show young men learning to be more balanced, more calm. But the admonishment that stings is that Romeo is being "womanish," becoming "Unseemly woman in a seeming man." To be womanish is to be weak and Shakespeare will often demonstrate what happens when a man relinquishes his dominance: the more-or-less monstrous masculine woman takes over.

Unlike Romeo, Hamlet does not need to be told about his potential or actual effeminacy: he knows and fears it himself. Earlier comedic (or occasionally tragic) lovers were not self-aware enough to be anxious about the problem. But from Hamlet through Troilus and to Coriolanus, Shakespeare creates men who equate weakness and emotion with dangerous femininity and its close cousin, infantilization.

> But I am weaker than a woman's tear,
> Tamer than sleep, fonder than ignorance,
> Less valiant than the virgin in the night,
> And skilless as unpractised infancy.
> *(Troilus and Cressida, 1.1.9–12)*

In this context, Coriolanus's capitulation to his wife is hardly a celebration of true family values. Instead it returns him to childhood. "Art thou a man?" No, Coriolanus is the "boy" he is deemed by Aufidius at the end of the play. More specifically, and more politically, it is the Roman Republic that makes men men, "infuses them with manly virtue, because the public realm is associated with Roman 'firmness' and the private realm with 'the melting spirits of women'" (Kahn 2011, p. 227).

It has to be said that there is absolutely nothing "melting" about the self-devouring Volumnia, Coriolanus's mother. There may have been good theater reasons for Shakespeare to create this profoundly challenging woman's part which would, of course, have been played by a boy actor. Shakespeare's writing of Volumnia suggests that there was an adolescent capable of becoming the powerful stage presences that are Lady Macbeth, Cleopatra, and Volumnia. But was there also a personal reason Shakespeare creates this most monstrous of mothers? Admittedly, other female characters are worse: we do not see Lady Macbeth, Regan, and Goneril being mothers, but their words about motherhood are violent and profoundly disturbing. Gertrude – at least according to her son – is a monstrous mother. Moreover, there is a striking absence of kindly mothers in Shakespeare or, more starkly, a striking absence of mothers. Emma Smith writes persuasively about this ("think Queen Lear ... Mrs. Prospero") in her analysis of *Much Ado About Nothing* (2019, p. 137):

> There are clues in the early texts of *Much Ado About Nothing* that Shakespeare originally conceived of a role for Hero's mother in the drama, and that he went so far as to give her a name, Innogen ... Innogen never speaks, however, and most scholars assume that during the course of writing the play her role atrophied and she was no longer relevant.

As Smith points out, "the effect of this excision is to isolate the two young women of the play. The failed wedding scene accentuates their vulnerability within an essentially patriarchal structure. What would Innogen have said to a husband who denounced their daughter on the say-so of a callow young soldier and a saturnine malcontent?" (2019, p. 137).

We will never know because this challenge is "precisely what Shakespeare did not want" (2019, pp. 137–138). So, the "incompletely erased Innogen" (p. 138) shows us a Shakespeare keen to sustain patriarchal business as usual, a Shakespeare capable of writing a play "profoundly uneasy about female sexuality" (ibid.). Whether the character's erasure shows us a Shakespeare who was cut off from, uninterested in, his *own* mother in the mid-1590s, or a Shakespeare who would become increasingly disturbed by grotesque mothers and their cruelty towards adult sons as the years went by, remains as ever the fascinating, but unanswerable, question.

No work epitomizes the problematics of biography more than "Shakespeare's Sonnets," finally printed in 1609, but some 20 years in the making. "Why now?"

is a good question with which to start. But even before that, there's another question. Did Shakespeare actually have anything to do with the work's publication? For many years, it was accepted that he was not involved. The fact that only about half of his plays were published in his lifetime, and the relative scrappiness of the printing of the *Sonnets* compared to *Venus* and *Lucrece* some 15 years earlier, are cited in corroboration. Shakespeare certainly did not *need* to be involved, because he lived in an era without any notion of intellectual property, one in which whichever person owned a manuscript also owned the rights.

In recent years, however, it has been argued that the publication of the *Sonnets* should be seen as a significant act on the part not only of Shakespeare but also of his theater company. The year 1609 saw the publication of the last two new Shakespeare plays, *Troilus* and *Pericles*, with both title pages mentioning performance at the Globe. A prose preface, added to some of the former's editions, even mentions (in an eloquent burst of praise of Shakespeare's "dexterity and power of wit," his "salt of wit") that its author has "brought forth Venus. Amongst all there is none more witty than this" (https://shakespeare.folger.edu/shakespeares-works/troilus-and-cressida/preface). In print at least, Shakespeare remains best known as a poet. That his name appears in large letters on the 1609 *Sonnets* suggests he has an "exploitable reputation" (Hammond 2012, p. 11).[3] Publishing a volume of poetry was a good way to maintain a professional profile at a time when the theaters were closed, and presumably the sonnets' author had time to put his verses in order. And to revise them. The sonnet (138, 13–14) which ends with the couplet:

> Therefore I lie with her and she with me,
> And in our faults by lies we flattered be

becomes over the years more subtle, sophisticated, complicated, real, and witty. Shakespeare, always a reviser, turns "a poem about lying about your age into an edgy work on mutually knowing deception" (Burrow 2007, p. 147).

If the publication was indeed a renewed quest for patronage, then the identity of "Master W.H.," to whom the volume is dedicated, becomes even more significant. Unfortunately, we do not even know if this was the printer's dedication or Shakespeare's, and whether it belongs to the literary politics of the 1590s (when most of the poems were written) or 1609, the volume's date of publication. As dedicatee, William Herbert, Earl of Pembroke, makes more sense in 1609 than the other strong contender, the Earl of Southampton, and also takes into account that the 1623 Folio would be dedicated to Pembroke, even though Southampton was still alive.[4] Perhaps the King's Men were looking to the Earl of Pembroke for support in their campaign to take up residency at the Blackfriars Theatre in 1609. William Herbert fits, up to a point, the character of the young man in the sonnets. He had refused to marry four thoroughly eligible women by 1601, and it has been argued (Shrank 2001, pp. 428–429) that his mother Mary commissioned Shakespeare to write 17 sonnets urging marriage upon young William, all in honor of his seventeenth birthday in 1597.

Whoever the intended patron, the *Sonnets* stand as a somewhat backward-looking endeavor. Twenty first-edition books of sonnets appeared during the 1590s, but after 1600 there was a marked slowdown. The delay in print publication may be the key, not to unlocking the biographical secrets of the sonnets, but to understanding why they are so well hidden. Fifteen, 20 years earlier, at the height of the sonnet vogue, the games being played with identities, the blurring of public and private, were part and parcel of the genre's writing and reception. By 1609, that world had gone. In their printed form, any context "would have been provided less by the knowingness of 'private friends' than by the form and ordering of the quarto" (Kerrigan 1986, p. 10). Does this mean, therefore, that the real-life identities of the characters don't matter in the *Sonnets'* new incarnation? Not entirely: "Shakespeare stands behind the first person of his sequence as Sidney had stood behind Astrophel – sometimes near the poetic 'I', sometimes farther off, but never without some degree of rhetorical projection." Indeed, Kerrigan, superb in so many ways on these poems, is strangely troubled by the presence of the first-person "Will," to the extent of setting him to one side: "If the bawdy quibbles on will are set aside as the fruits of an obsession, the poet's name never appears in his book" (1986, p. 21).

I am not sure that we can or should set aside the "bawdy quibbles on will." Sonnet sequences often loiter with intent at the margins of erotic (auto)biography. The volume was sold as *Shakespeare's Sonnets* (not *Astrophil and Stella* or *The Affectionate Shepherd*), so the reader is offered "Shakespeare" on a literary plate. Edmund Spenser's *Amoretti* includes praise of his beloved's sweet-smelling nipples ("like young-blossomed jasmins," Sonnet 64, l. 12). Philip Sidney's Astrophil demands that Stella "pity the tale/tail of me" (Sonnet 45, l. 14), demanding that Penelope Rich take notice of both his story and his penis. Yes, as anyone familiar with this most self-conscious and self-deconstructing of literary forms will know, "these are works of art: fictions, not confessional statements" – but sonnets foreground the connection between writer and text, fact and fiction (Hammond 2012, p. 3).

Smith (2012) offers one of the best critiques of reading Shakespeare's work as his autobiography, but the Sonnets test her reluctance to do so to its limit, primarily because of the genre's dynamic. Poets were *expected* to represent themselves. As Shakespeare teases: "I am that I am" (Sonnet 121, l. 9) – except when I am not. Now you see me, now you don't. Authorial revelation, and sophisticated – and at times puerile – eroticism, were the hallmarks of many an English sonnet sequence. Or in the case of Shakespeare's sonnets, a sophisticated homoeroticism, from the nods to Virgil's second eclogue to descriptions of the young man as "not acquainted" (Sonnet 20, l. 3), that is, without a quaint, or vagina.

Homoeroticism is, however, too narrow a description. The object of desire in Sonnet 20 has some thing "to my purpose nothing" (l. 12): that "thing" could be both penis and vagina, so all bets are off. In Sonnet 135, *Will* designates not only the poet's first name but also both male *and* female sexual organs. No wonder the poem has been called "defiantly anti-Platonic" (Trevor 2007, p. 227). But what to make of the character Will? The manic puns on the word (which encompass future intention, sexual desire, male and female genitalia, and Shakespeare's own name) are funny and painful at the same time. There are some deep Shakespearean ironies at work here. He is a poet who hopes in verse that his verse will give him (and the man he loves) posterity. The most obvious way to do that is to build his own name into the sequence. It would also make sense to name the male object of desire or love, something Shakespeare does not do. It is a perplexing move since the poet asserts that he is determined to achieve the immortality of his beloved through poetry: "My love shall in my verse ever live young" (Sonnet 19, l. 14) and "Your name from hence immortal life shall have" (Sonnet 81, l. 5).

For some reason, Shakespeare remains uninterested in naming (and shaming or celebrating) identifiable individuals. This may be his most subtle sleight of sonneteering hand. "My love" can mean, at least, two things: the object of affection and, crucially, the speaker's own love. It is Shakespeare the poet's love that will live for ever, his art that is immortalized – not necessarily the (nameless) beloved.[5] If it is the object of his affection, then the lack of name allows the man (and the woman) to become all objects of desire.

Or perhaps, who needs names when you are Shakespeare, the playwright who from time to time forgets what his characters are called? His characters have an extraordinary power over us despite their anonymity. This is particularly true of the woman in the *Sonnets*, known for centuries as "The Dark Lady," a title created out of almost nothing. The word "dark" is only used once, and it is unclear that it refers to the woman, and the word "lady" does not appear at all. The misogyny and racism lurking behind "The Dark Lady" are powerful threads in Shakespeare criticism, if not in Shakespeare's work, but the need to name comes from us, the reader, not from the poems.

With no name, the woman is simply, and literally, an object of his desire: Will's "flesh" "rising at thy name, doth point out thee" (Sonnet 151, l. 9). And that desire is despised.

> Th' expense of spirit in a waste of shame
> Is lust in action; and, till action, lust
> Is perjured, murd'rous, bloody, full of blame,
> Savage, extreme, rude, cruel, not to trust;
> Enjoyed no sooner but despised straight ...
> ...

All this the world well knows, yet none knows well
To shun the heaven that leads men to this hell.
(Sonnet 129, 1–5; 13–14)

By Sonnet 144, Will's two loves are demarcated as "a better angel" (l. 3) (the young man) and a "worser spirit" (a woman, "coloured ill," l. 4). Hell is her vagina, drawing in both Will and the young man. Desire for a woman is merely a sickness or disease, generating only self-deception:

For I have sworn thee fair, and thought thee bright,
Who art as black as hell, as dark as night.
(13–14)

If the story is not fiction, if these poems operate on any level as self-disclosure, if *The Sonnets of William Shakespeare* reveal their author, then it is not a man some people want to know. William Wordsworth may have written that "with this key / Shakespeare unlocked his heart" (*Scorn Not the Sonnet*, ll. 2–3) but he also denounced the poems – at least those to his female lover – as "abominably harsh, obscure, and worthless" (http://catdir.loc.gov/catdir/samples/prin031/2002074981.html). The necessary shifts are still being made. Bate (2008, pp. 234–235) identifies Davies as the rival poet of the sonnets and positions Shakespeare's return to the poems as a response to "a newly bisexualised court" (of James I) rather than the expression of "some urgent personal homosexual desire." This does not quite take into account that Shakespeare had written his most obviously male–male couple (Patroclus says, amongst many other explicit references to his being more than friends with Achilles, "your great love to me, restrains you thus. / Sweet, rouse yourself," 3.3.223–224) in *Troilus*, probably before the accession of James to the throne, so boy love was always on his mind.

Or, perhaps, it is argued, Shakespeare is not exploring his own *experience* of desire for a young man, or his disgust with a female lover. The *Sonnets* show us only Shakespeare's "private imagination." There was, perhaps, "something which engaged him deeply in the thought of an older man obsessed with a younger man, and the two of them forming a tense emotional triangle with an experienced woman" (Hammond 2012, p. 6). The *thought* of an older man? Others edge towards seeing the poems as a product of William's brief encounter with the Earl of Southampton in the 1590s. Real experiences with real people generated the poems, but the story itself is fiction. But even this does not quite make the poems safe for family viewing. Even if Shakespeare never experienced homosexual desire and misogynistic disgust, he is encouraging his readers to engage with those feelings, an engagement which makes the published *Sonnets* (whether circulated in the 1590s in manuscript or collected in print in 1609) akin to erotica. The reader becomes a privileged "voyeur" (Smith 2016, p. 44), who can "both experience the desires and see the deeds, all without any personal consequences" and what desires and deeds: Shakespeare offers the reader "a knowingness about sexuality that includes penis, anus, and vagina, varyingly intense degrees of desire, and delight in the words that express that plenitude" (ibid.).

Putting aside for a moment consideration of the *Sonnets* as erotic autobiography, if their publication in 1609 was a renewed quest for aristocratic patronage, Shakespeare was about as successful as he had been in the 1590s. That is, not very. And, unlike the runaway success of *Venus and Adonis* (and the reasonable success of *The Rape of Lucrece*), Shakespeare's *Sonnets* didn't even do well with the reading public.

It is yet another reminder that Shakespeare, although well-established as a playwright, was not the literary superstar he would become. Writing on the 1608 publication of the quarto *King Lear*, Peter Blayney observes that identification of Shakespeare as its author on the title page might have read differently to its first purchasers than it does to us. He suggests that although we might like to "imagine the delighted book-buying public flocking eagerly to the shops to buy the latest master-work from the pen of their favourite playwright," we would be wrong to do so: "most of Shakespeare's plays had a relatively undistinguished publishing history before 1623" (quoted in Shaughnessy 2018, p. 12). The reality is that the 1609 edition of the *Sonnets* was the only one to appear in Shakespeare's lifetime, and there was so little interest that an edition in 1640 could claim it was the first. The poems didn't even make it into the Folio of 1623, whereas Jonson's complete *Works* of 1616 contained his poetry and his drama. We like the "emotional turmoil and non-vanilla sex" (Orgel 2007, p. 140). There is no evidence that Shakespeare's contemporaries did. Indeed, it has been suggested that the collection's sheer diversity "baffled its early readers" (Kerrigan 1986, p. 8). The *Sonnets* of 1609 pretty much sank without trace. There was to be no repeat of the celebrity of the early 1590s, of "sweet" William Shakespeare. But then the playhouses reopened.

Chapter Eight

William Shakespeare was back writing plays, thanks to the reopening of the theaters in the spring of 1610 after their long closure. The usual scholarly uncertainties about dating, performance, and authorship remain. For example, *Cymbeline* was included in the Folio of 1623, suggesting that Shakespeare was its main author, but there is no clear evidence as to when the play was written or first performed. The year 1609 is suggested by some, and a first performance at the Globe in 1610. Scholars are more confident in asserting that William Shakespeare, playwright, had changed creative direction – not completely, but significantly – and there are some who wonder why. *Cymbeline* "has the appearance of being the outcome of some peculiar, and perhaps decisive, turning point in Shakespeare's private or professional life" (Nosworthy 1955, p. xi). The only problem is it has proved impossible to find what that turning point might have been.

For many over the years, Shakespeare is newly fascinated by redemption, his turn to tragi-comedy an explicitly Christian response to his years of writing pagan drama, a sign of his determination to achieve "complete regeneration," evidence of his "new proneness to contemplation," a state of mind akin to the religious (Nosworthy 1955, p. xliv). *Cymbeline*, according to this reading of the works and life, becomes the first, if halting, step towards this apotheosis. Nosworthy argues (1955, p. xxvii) that Shakespeare

> was no longer concerned with historical drama or with comedy of intrigue but with the golden inconsequences of romance, which is a thing *per se*, existing in undefined dimensions of space and time, and is devoted, to the exclusion of more mundane affairs, to the adventures of princes and princesses, to the finding of long-lost children, to wizards and witches, and hermits dwelling in desert places, to the righting of old wrongs, and to the life that is happy ever after.

The Life of the Author: William Shakespeare, First Edition. Anna Beer.
© 2021 John Wiley & Sons, Ltd. Published 2021 by John Wiley & Sons, Ltd.

That, at least, was the view until fairly recently when the cluster of plays (*Cymbeline*, *The Winter's Tale*, and *The Tempest*) were considered. Now critics are more likely to see an elderly male playwright strangely preoccupied with sexual panic, rather than a serene man offering fantasies of the "life that is happy ever after," a man writing plays filled with scenes of sexual jealousy, fear of female infidelity, and husbands' cruelty towards honest wives. It is as if Shakespeare is rerunning *Othello*, that queasy tragedy predicated on a domestic comedy plot. The romances he writes from *Pericles* onward creak under the weight of violence and death. The audience get happy endings but the cost is high. In *The Winter's Tale* Leontes's son Mammilius dies of grief, his baby daughter is exposed to die on his strict instructions, and his friend and counsellor, Antigonus, is eaten by a bear. It is only through the intervention of widow Paulina, that Leontes's honest wife, Hermione, survives.

Marriage still remains the only possible ending. This is nowhere more obvious, not to mention contrived, than in *The Winter's Tale*, the play in which Shakespeare (sole author it seems this time out) creates one of his most powerful, eloquent female characters. Paulina is the protagonist who resolves the crisis of the play. No supernatural powers are at work by the end, only Paulina's determination to ensure the survival of her queen and the reeducation of her king. Throughout she is the only person courageous enough to stand up to the tyranny of Leontes, to speak truth to power. The widow Paulina directs the final scene of reconciliation. The reward for this powerful, instrumental, brave woman is to be married off to the nonentity Camillo. The first scene of Shakespeare's last play (a collaboration – more of which later) anatomizes and legitimizes the taming of the "dreaded" Amazon Queen Hippolyta.

> Honored Hippolyta,
> Most dreaded Amazonian, that hast slain
> The scythe-tusked boar; that with thy arm, as strong
> As it is white, wast near to make the male
> To thy sex captive, but that this thy lord,
> Born to uphold creation in that honor
> First nature styled it in, shrunk thee into
> The bound thou wast o'erflowing, at once subduing
> Thy force and thy affection.
>
> (*Two Noble Kinsmen*, 1.1.78–85)

This is the social and political ideal for Shakespeare's era, for women to be "shrunk," to be "subdued." As James I explained: "I am the husband, and all the whole isle is my lawful wife; I am the head and it is my body" (Sommerville 1995, p. 136). There is no alternative. Paulina comes at the end of a long line of women characters – Kate, Isabella, Beatrice – who strive for, sometimes briefly obtain autonomy, but cannot sustain it to the curtain call (if there had been a curtain in Shakespeare's theaters). We attempt to give their power back to them – Kate is not tamed, she is simply acting a part; Beatrice tells Benedick to "Kill Claudio" (act 4, scene 1, p. 288); Isabella refuses the Duke; Paulina leads all the characters off stage – so we know who is in charge really. Did Shakespeare imagine and perhaps even suggest these interpretations? Is that his gift? It has certainly been his legacy. The hallmark of a complex work of art, one test of its "greatness," is whether it "cannot only endure but also benefit from any number of ... strong rereadings" (Garber 2004, p. 6). Those strong rereadings have come thick and fast over the centuries, from happy endings to *Lear* to postcolonial reworkings of *The Tempest*.

And so with the life as well. Religiously informed transcendence is out, and an old man dealing with "painful issues" is in, even for the most conservative of critics (Bevington 2005, p. 234): "sexual jealousy and compulsive sexual longing, disillusionment about political life, scepticism about providentiality and the existence of the gods, the difficulties of trying to achieve compatibility, temptation to commit crimes for the sake of self-advancement, and male fears of domination by controlling women" with anxieties about "lost male potency" just adding salt to the wounds.

Poststructuralist criticism reassures us that these "painful issues" need not derive from Shakespeare's own psyche. That these late romances do not move easily towards happy endings, towards marriages "based on romantic love, two people made one flesh for life in mutual sympathy and trust," can be viewed as a reflection of his world, rather than the man. Shakespeare's plays simply reveal the struggle to incorporate love and passion into marriage, expose a "precariousness in the early modern account" of the institution, because his society still understood desire as a form of passion located outside marriage (Belsey 1996). Marriage for love becomes proposed as the "remedy for desire" (ibid., p. 14), but it was an uncertain remedy: "incorporating desire within marriage is evidently like inviting a bandit in to defend law and order. It might work, but it's a risky strategy" (ibid., p. 18).

Alternatively, rather than simply reflecting the anxieties of his time, Shakespeare somehow moved past them – past these "fears of lost male potency and of diminishing options for self-fulfilment, and anxiety about the approach of death," this dark preoccupation with "ungrateful children, especially daughters" – and, remarkably, makes "a crucial recuperative move." Now, "daughters turn out to be the means to recovery of the endangered self. So do long-lost wives, although here the vision is more fleeting and is abandoned" (Bevington 2005, p. 234). No uneasy alliance between poststructuralism and cultural materialism here, but this still stops short, just, of mapping the darker concerns of these plays on to William's relationship with his daughters and wife, or his feelings about potency and mortality.

Fortunately, for those who wish keep their Shakespeare fragrant, if we are going to read from the plays to the man, then there is a more wholesome story to be told. The aged Shepherd and his son the rustic Clown in *The Winter's Tale* do not have prototypes. Therefore Shakespeare "created this surprisingly genial portrait of a father and son for a reason." And that reason is both benign and rare: "For once in Shakespeare, and perhaps once only, a father and a son become a source of unshadowed good feeling" (Tromley 2010, p. 265).[1] *The Winter's Tale* becomes a fairytale rewriting of the relationship between William and his own father.

When it comes to the representation of fathers and daughters in these later plays, it is not so much posterity that is at stake, but power, as Shakespeare explores the control, or lack of control, that a father can and should exert over his daughters. The sexual activities and choices of errant sons do appear as a theme in several plays but paternal control of daughters' (sexual) bodies is almost always central.

Jonathan Bate (1995, p. 11) highlights, unwittingly, the discrepancy. Considering the ways in which Shakespeare plays with dramatic expectations in his early tragedy, *Titus Andronicus*, he asks:

> What do you do when twenty-one of your sons have been killed in battle, you've killed the twenty-second in a fit of pique, your daughter has been raped and had her hands cut off and her tongue cut out, two further sons have been wrongly accused of murdering your son-in-law and the remaining one sentenced to exile, you've been told that the two who are condemned will be reprieved if you chop off your hand, and you do so, only to have the hand and the heads of the two sons sent back to you in scorn?

Bate's point is that the audience would expect a rant from Titus, but "human nature" (by which he means default-male human nature) does not obey dramatic decorum. Titus laughs, and makes a deeply macabre visual joke at/ to/with Lavinia: "Bear thou my hand, sweet wench, between thy teeth" (3.1.283).

As Bate (1995, p. 12) demonstrates, this is all very clear (Lavinia has become the *hand*maid of Revenge, "a role which will later involve her in dextrous work with a basin between her stumps") and Titus "certainly gets the last laugh against his enemies." But what is also clear is that Shakespeare's portrayal of the dynamics of fatherhood is gendered. Sons are killed, daughters are raped: both acts dishonor the father.

The controlling father appears throughout Shakespeare's work, and across the genres. From Leonato in *Much Ado* to Leontes in *The Winter's Tale*, from

Shylock in *The Merchant of Venice* to Brabantio in *Othello* or Polonius in *Hamlet*, Shakespeare's plots, both comic and tragic, pivot on a father's desire to discipline an errant daughter. That desire is rarely truly challenged, the daughters' acts of rebellion invariably contained, and their duty to their father reasserted as foundational. Egeus, Hermia's father, complains in *A Midsummer Night's Dream* that Lysander has "Turned her obedience, which is due to me, / To stubborn harshness" (1.1.37–38).

Therefore:

> I beg the ancient privilege of Athens;
> As she is mine, I may dispose of her;
> Which shall be either to this gentleman
> Or to her death, according to our law
> Immediately provided in that case.
>
> *(1.1.41–45)*

This prompts a lecture from the Duke Theseus to Hermia about her appropriate filial duty:

> Be advised, fair maid.
> To you your father should be as a god,
> One that composed your beauties; yea, and one
> To whom you are but as a form in wax
> By him imprinted, and within his power
> To leave the figure, or disfigure it.
>
> *(1.1.46–51)*

Like Romeo, Hermia is viewed as unformed. But as a woman, she knows that the only option for her is to exchange one "god" for another: replace father with husband, her new sovereign.

Leonato is equally punitive towards his daughter, Hero, in *Much Ado About Nothing*, from a similar period, the mid-1590s. His "response to Hero's distress is a disaster. Treating her as an appendage, he has little sense of Hero as a person, hence nothing of Beatrice's – or even the Friar's – grounds for thinking Hero innocent. Leonato depends on what he thinks he knows, that princes and counts are men of honour and women sexually unreliable" (Zitner 1993, p. 41).

The post-1609 romances are far more focused on the *reunion* of fathers and daughters, admittedly highly implausibly. The family unit is violated, loss occurs but there is recovery. Does this indicate a golden era for William Shakespeare, the father of adult daughters, grandfather of little Elizabeth, on his way to returning – at last – to his place as *pater familias* in Stratford?

There's a far more disturbing way of understanding the depiction of fathers and daughters in these plays (Smith 2019, pp. 296–298). It's "arguable that all these relationships bear the traces of incestuous paternal desire" (ibid., p. 296). From *Pericles*, which begins with an explicit scene of father–daughter incest at Antioch, through Prospero's aggressive response to "any threat to Miranda's chastity" in *The Tempest*, via a stepmother's jealousy of her husband's natural daughter in *Cymbeline*, incest is never far away. Shakespeare's very removal of the dynamic in his reworking of his source for *The Winter's Tale*, the way in which he structures the play "to suppress – or perhaps, as a more psychoanalytical vocabulary might put it, to sublimate – incestuous desire" (Smith 2019, p. 298) is revealing.

> If we read carefully, however, we might still read Leontes' first encounter with the adult Perdita as marked by this taboo. The young couple's entrance follows a discussion between Leontes and Paulina about Hermione's beauty, in which Paulina extracts from the king a promise that he will not remarry without her permission. When he sees Perdita, then, Leontes' mind is on his queen, but he is full of praise for the young bride's beauty and tells Florizel he is "sorry / Your choice is not so rich in worth as beauty" (5.1.212–13). When Florizel says that his father will grant Leontes anything, the king's hypothetical wish is not for the couple's marriage but for himself: "I'd beg your precious mistress" (222), which earns from Paulina the remonstrance, "Your eye hath too much youth in't" (224).
>
> There is no further discussion between father and daughter. It is almost as if the play stares into the face of Pandosto's incestuous desires from Greene's source story, and is too frightened to go further.
>
> *(ibid.)*

It is "not rocket science" (p. 297) to see incest in these plays, argues Smith. But even this superb, provocative literary analysis shuts its eyes to the equally obvious biographical turn hinted at, but not pursued, when the playwright is seen as suppressing or sublimating incestuous desire. No, it is "the play," not its author, which "stares into the face" of incestuous desires and is "frightened to go further" (ibid., p. 298).

It is far more comfortable to return to the consideration of Shakespeare's professional life. He continued to move between court and public theater worlds, because the two were inextricably linked. For example, *The Winter's Tale*, performed at the Globe in May 1611, borrowed a dance from a court entertainment earlier in the year. Robert Johnson, the court lutenist and composer, wrote music for three of Shakespeare's plays in the early 1610s. And Shakespeare remained a very successful "King's Man," understanding that the only political system he knew directly, monarchy, was theatrical and spectacular in its very nature. Elizabeth I had said back in 1586: "we princes are set upon stages in the sight and view of all the world." Her successor, James I, wrote that a "King is as one set on a scaffold, whose smallest actions and gestures all the people gazingly do behold." James (and his wife Anne), far more than Elizabeth, hired playwrights to write and produce masques to celebrate their power.

But not William Shakespeare. Some argue that this omission reveals something important about William Shakespeare's priorities as a writer and as a man. If he had been invited to write a masque he would have said no, however tempting the offer.

If he had

> cared about visibility, prestige or money, the rewards were great; the writer responsible for the masque earned more than eight times what a dramatist was typically paid for a single play. And on the creative side, in addition to the almost unlimited budget and the potential for special effects, the masque offered the very thing he had seemingly wished for in the opening Chorus to Henry the Fifth: "princes to act / And monarchs to behold the swelling scene" (1.0.3–4).

> That Shakespeare never accepted such a commission tells us as much about him as a writer as the plays he left behind. There was a price to be paid for writing masques, which were shamelessly sycophantic and propagandistic, compromises he didn't care to make. He must have also recognised that it was an elite and evanescent art form that didn't suit his interests or his talents. If this was a typical Jacobean masque, the evening's entertainment devolved into serious drinking and feasting after the closing dance. By then, I suspect, Shakespeare was already back at his lodgings, doing what he had been doing well into the night for over fifteen years: writing.

> *(Shapiro 2015, p. 5)*

This vision of Shakespeare, the man of integrity, content with the quiet life of writing, is slightly compromised by one of the few anecdotes about him from the early years of King James's reign, admittedly recorded some 30 years later. It has William carving his name into the paneling of the Tabard Inn in Southwark, along with the "roistering" Ben Jonson, Richard Burbage, and Laurence Fletcher. But it is specifically the court masques, louche events even by the standards of the day, that Shapiro sees Shakespeare avoiding.

But was he so aloof from the court and its masques? The evidence suggests much more cross-over, whether in characterization (Jonson thought that Caliban belonged in a masque), casting (Jonson, again, used some of Shakespeare's material in his *Masque of Oberon*), or performance venue: *Cymbeline* was performed at the Globe in May 1611, *The Tempest* – which contains a masque although admittedly a failed masque – at court in November 1611.

For all this, the question remains: why didn't he do the same thing for a masque? Just one court spectacular, to show the world he could. It is yet another provocative (and one would think) unanswerable question.

Perhaps he didn't *need* to write masques for, in 1611, William Shakespeare was doing well. Perhaps he didn't *want* to write masques for, in 1611, there were still things he wanted to do in the public theaters. Active as an actor and playwright for some 20 years, he remained drawn to the new, whether the emerging genre of tragi-comedy, or bringing the innovations in staging being introduced at court onto the stage of the Globe. He is also, as ever, responding to another playwright's work.

The Tempest is, for Shakespeare, unusually short, and unusually tidy, obeying the unities of time and place called for by traditional, classical dramatic theory. Yet, even when following the rules, Shakespeare demonstrates just how different he remains from his main creative rival of these years, Ben Jonson, master of, and champion of, the unities. Contrast Jonson's *The Alchemist* with Shakespeare's *The Tempest*. Both plays may observe the unities of time and place, but *The Alchemist* plays out *in* the Blackfriars district (that is, the very streets surrounding the theater). *The Tempest* is set on a magical island. Jonson's is an indoor, urban comedy (note all the knocking on doors), Shakespeare's takes place in nature. Jonson writes of shopkeepers and prostitutes; Shakespeare of princes and genderless spirits. Yes, Shakespeare "with a mere flick of his powerful wrist, shows that he can practise the unities, all right, in case anyone was in doubt" (Bevington 2005, pp. 219–220), but he retains his particular brand of drama. There's also a very Shakespearean sleight of hand at work. To achieve the correct performance and story time, a lengthy flashback scene is needed, one "that is very difficult to perform effectively because its main purpose is the undramatic one of telling, rather than showing" (Smith 2019, p. 293). Maybe Shakespeare wasn't quite as slick with the unities as all that.

As a King's Man (knowing the court) and as a veteran of the public theaters, Shakespeare must have known that commercial theater companies couldn't match the production values of court productions. What he could do is bring a bit of spectacle and magic to the South Bank.

It helped that there was a new space for his work, the Blackfriars theater: enclosed, candlelit, so different from the King's Men's longstanding open-air stage, the Globe. And, in 1611, it was the perfect venue for Shakespeare's new play, *The Tempest*. In the old dining hall of the Blackfriars monastery, Shakespeare capitalized on all the performance possibilities unavailable to the company at the Globe. He adapted to the smaller stage, the more intimate venue, writing fewer lines between a character entering and that character either speaking or moving within earshot of those already on stage. McMullan (2016) has done the maths, and it is in these details that we glimpse the sheer professionalism of Shakespeare, his ability to adapt to different venues. He creates numerous opportunities for spectacle, even using *"a quaint device"* (*The Tempest*, 3.3.52 [stage direction]) to make a banquet disappear, or having Juno descend from the roof above. Neither of these stunts were impossible at the Globe: they were at Blackfriars. The five-act structure was now codified, with music in the intervals – for logistical reasons rather than aesthetic. The beeswax candles needed trimming. But Shakespeare seizes the opportunity to make music, those "sounds and sweet airs that give delight and hurt not" (*The Tempest*, 3.2.136) essential to his new play: music leads Ferdinand to Miranda, each song is crucial to the play's action, not mere decoration. *The Tempest* is the first play we are sure Shakespeare wrote for an indoor theater. As McMullan (2016) writes "the brio with which Shakespeare exploits the potential of the space in *The Tempest* resonates down the centuries as each generation remakes the play for its own moment. There have been many extraordinary performances of *The Tempest* since 1611, but arguably none more so than that very first afternoon at the Blackfriars." Next stop was the court, where the King's Men played before James on "Hallowmas night" (1 November) 1611.

The Tempest was traditionally seen as Shakespeare's final play, the work of a supremely confident master of his art sending a message to future generations. "Prospero's farewell is not only Shakespeare's farewell to the stage, but his dying breath, signalled by his liberation of the life-spirit, Ariel" (Smith 2019, p. 308). Smith demolishes this brilliantly: there's "a small inconvenience in his interpretation, given that Shakespeare does not die for another five years, but let that pass."

The short, neat, and tidy *Tempest* would not be Shakespeare's last outing as a dramatist. In fact, 1613 would be a busy year for William Shakespeare. The year before, he was in court, asked to resolve a dispute regarding a dowry he had helped to negotiate eight years earlier. The only difficulty was that Shakespeare as witness professed complete ignorance of "what implements and necessaries of household stuff" (Nelson and Folger Shakespeare Library Staff 2020) were given. Eight years was a long time ago. The year 1613 provides a slightly more substantial archival harvest. In the spring of that year, Shakespeare bought property in London, together with William Johnson, John Jackson, and John Hemming. The Gatehouse, Blackfriars, cost £140. The deal involved "elaborate arrangements, calling for trustees and a mortgage [whose] practical effect would be to deprive Shakespeare's widow of her dower right to a third share for life in this part of the estate; for in a joint tenancy, Chancery would not recognize Anne's privilege unless her husband had survived the other trustees" (Schoenbaum 1987, p. 274).[2]

In the same year, Shakespeare collaborated with Richard Burbage on an impresa for the shield carried by the Earl of Rutland at the Accession Day tournament on 24 March, both men earning 44 shillings. William designed the shield, and Richard painted it.

There is little sign of a slowing-down, and this is true of playwriting too. Shakespeare collaborated with John Fletcher on *Henry VIII* and the now-lost *Cardenio*.[3] The play which does survive marks a return to English history – and recent history at that. Prospero's beautiful speech at the end of *The Tempest* – so often touted as Shakespeare's farewell to the stage – turns out to be just the first of a series of powerfully written passages considering the relationship between theater and life. The Prologue to *Henry VIII* explores the uncertain boundaries between history, comedy, and tragedy, and concludes with a dissection of what happens when you watch drama, and – perhaps even more significantly – a celebration of the sheer power of the dramatist.

> Be sad, as we would make ye. Think ye see
> The very persons of our noble story
> As they were living; think you see them great,
> And followed with the general throng and sweat
> Of thousand friends; then, in a moment, see
> How soon this mightiness meets misery:
> And if you can be merry then, I'll say
> A man may weep upon his wedding-day.
> *(Prologue, ll. 25–32)*

Even if these words on the power of theater to "make" us feel, make us "see" are not Shakespeare's, they should be.

Then, on 29 June 1613, fire struck the Globe playhouse during a performance of *Henry VIII*. Luckily, there were enough theater people on the scene to save the important things: props and books, plots and costumes. Even more remarkably, the playhouse was rebuilt within a year in modern style, with a new brick foundation, and with a tiled rather than thatched roof. But the fire marked the end of an era: Shakespeare would write no more plays for the Globe.

Fire in London was closely followed by problems in Stratford. In July of 1613, Shakespeare's daughter, Susanna (married for six years), sued John Lane for defamation through the church courts. Lane had claimed that Susanna had "the running of the reins" (that is, she has the sexually transmitted disease of gonorrhoea), caught from having sex with Ralph Smith, a married hatter and haberdasher, "at the house of John Palmer, a gentleman of Clopton" (Wells 2001b). Lane lost the case and was promptly excommunicated. He was in trouble again six years later, when he was charged with riotous behavior, drunkenness, and libeling the vicar and aldermen.

In 1613, Susanna was represented in her case against Lane by Robert Whatcott, who would later witness her father's will. This episode is (almost) the most salacious thing in the Shakespeare family records, rivaling the "thug" William moment in the Wayte documents of some 17 years earlier, in 1596. The church court proceedings act as a reminder of the lack of privacy in small town life, with rumors spreading through Stratford "as wildly as the fire that had destroyed the Globe a month earlier. It was difficult to keep anything a secret both in the Stratford of Shakespeare's time and among the close-knit theatrical circles of actors who worked together, like a brotherhood, for many years" (Edmondson and Wells 2015a, pp. 329–330).

The nature of these close-knit circles, of Stratford and London, makes it all the more astonishing that there are so few scurrilous anecdotes circulating about Shakespeare's sexual tastes or misdemeanors. John Milton would not be so lucky a generation later, attacked and ridiculed for his alleged predilection for men and his effeminacy, from being derided as the "Lady of Christ's" (College Cambridge) to the kind of man who sells his buttocks for a few pence in Rome. William Shakespeare, in contrast, remains astonishingly anonymous.

He had one more play – or at least half a play – in him, however: *The Two Noble Kinsmen* written for the Blackfriars playhouse. In collaboration again with John Fletcher, Shakespeare produced a play which "offers contradictory indications about the direction it intends to take" (Potter 2015, p. 2). It didn't get into the Folio of 1623, perhaps because Fletcher didn't consider it to be finished or was planning to revise it for a court production. The ending is particularly strange. The young knight Palamon is on the way to being executed when news comes that his friend and rival, Arcite, has fallen off his horse. This conveniently leaves only one male suitor for Emilia, who is handed over to Palamon (and from whom we hear nothing more). Theseus ends it all with some banal platitudes and a refusal to make sense of anything that has happened. Few are comfortable suggesting that the Bard would ever have rushed to finish a scene.

> Oh, you heavenly charmers,
> What things you make of us! For what we lack
> We laugh, for what we have are sorry, still
> Are children in some kind. Let us be thankful
> For that which is, and with you leave dispute
> That are above our question. Let's go off
> And bear us like the time.
>
> *(5.4.131–137)*

It seems he'll say anything to get off the stage. Meanwhile, the Epilogue which follows "is rather startling in its attempts to make the audience follow Theseus' advice and cheer up" (Potter 2015, p. 5).

None of this is very surprising. Numerous other plays from this period have similarly abrupt shifts of tone. Collaboration, particularly if it wasn't going well, might lead to inconsistencies. Even sole-authored works, such as those of Webster (*The Duchess of Malfi*, which was being rehearsed at around this time) can be disconcerting to watch precisely because they lurch between laughter and horror. Tragicomedy by its very nature ran the risk of being disjointed, implausible, imbalanced. Potter (2015, p. 2) explains the theory: Guarini stressed in his *Compendio della Poesia Tragicomica* (1602) that the genre's "object was not to alternate tragic and comic scenes but to create a genuinely mixed genre with a unified mood and atmosphere, lacking both the horrific elements of classical tragedy and the grotesque elements of classical comedy." The genre theory at work here – explaining the mix – was not always clear to Shakespeare's contemporaries. *Cymbeline*, with a plot taken from legendary British history coupled with an episode from Boccaccio's *Decameron*, a heady blend of chronicle with fantasy with comedy, is titled *The Tragedie of Cymbeline* in the Folio.

In succeeding centuries, other factors came into play as the success or failure of these late plays were considered. With some of the plays after 1609, we are dealing with authors, rather than an author, and dealing in assumptions about the collaborative process, and about who wrote what. There is still a tendency to attribute particular, less successful, passages to Shakespeare's collaborator. Moreover, if we see Shakespeare as a good guy, then the parceling out of scenes becomes even more biased. See for example the analysis of the brothel scenes in *Pericles* which are "much more violent and sexually brutal than anything similar in the rest of Shakespeare" and, whilst the "pornographic prurience" of the threats to Marina's virtue "must have greatly titillated those Elizabethan [sic] audiences who enjoyed this play so much," these scenes are owed "to Wilkins, directly or indirectly, and through them we look into a grimmer world which Shakespeare rarely chose to enter" (Drabble 2015, p. 339). Many would disagree, pointing to Shakespeare's willingness to depict at least threats of rape.

The Two Noble Kinsmen has more than its fair share of echoes of previous works by Shakespeare. In her madness, the Jailer's Daughter sings (as did Ophelia in *Hamlet*) and she sings the song "Willow, Willow" (as did Desdemona in *Othello*). Fletcher and Shakespeare foreground an intimate friendship between men, which is then disrupted by a woman. Shakespeare had begun here. *The Two Gentlemen of Verona*, written over 20 years earlier, around the time that a preteen John Fletcher was heading to Oxford University, offers a similarly idealized, passionate male–male friendship. The opening scene between the two gentlemen, Valentine and Proteus, can sound almost like pillow-talk. When Proteus seeks to "force" Sylvia, Valentine intervenes and the bromance is over. However, back in the early 1590s, young-ish William Shakespeare provided the quickest ever apology and reconciliation between two men. One has just attempted to rape the other's girlfriend, but blink – and they're back together again. Twenty years on, it takes a lot more to repair the childhood friendship between Polixenes and Leontes (more time, more deaths, more suffering), but Shakespeare achieves the reconciliation in his *Winter's Tale*.

Now in *Two Noble Kinsmen* Shakespeare, with Fletcher, will visit the bond between men one last time.

Palamon:	Is there record of any two that loved
	Better than we do, Arcite?
Arcite:	Sure there cannot.
Palamon:	I do not think it possible our friendship
	Should ever leave us.
Arcite:	Till our deaths it cannot.

(2.2.112–115)

At which point, Emilia enters to disrupt the loving moment. Palamon is imprisoned, Arcite banished and the two men seem separated for ever. Yet, by the middle of the play the boys are back together, rekindling their friendship with talk of their (hetero)sexual exploits. Things only go wrong when they start talking about Emilia.

There is a very curious dynamic at work in these scenes. On one level there is a powerful homoerotic charge (the two men are dressing each other in armor), accompanied by a dance of courtesy. On another level, they want to kill each other. By act 5, the passionate friendship is still center stage: "it is not clear when the men embrace or whether they do so once or twice" says the play's editor (Potter 2015, p. 288), but the fact is they absolutely do embrace.

Again and again, Shakespeare has celebrated and explored friendship between men, from the charged, half-suppressed eroticism of the sonnets ("But if the while I think on thee, dear friend, / All losses are restored and sorrows end," Sonnet 30, ll. 13–14) through the relationship between Antonio and Sebastian, which moves a prosaic older man to verse: "I do adore thee so / That danger shall seem sport, and I will go" (2.1.43–44). Without the erotic charge, Shakespeare finds it easier to mock these friendships. Beatrice is spot-on concerning Benedick's shallow friendships, and Claudio's fickleness, when it comes to men: "Who is his companion now? He hath every month a new sworn brother" (*Much Ado*, 1.1.68–69). Shakespeare can offer brutal anatomies of toxic political friendships, from *Timon* and *Julius Caesar*, through to *Henry VIII*, but he will not mock the soldiers who love their fellow warriors. These men, Hal and Hotspur, Coriolanus and Aufidius, may fight to the death, but they are true to each other in ways that men and women rarely are in Shakespeare's fictional worlds. Hal will bid a touching, respectful goodbye to Hotspur ("Fare thee well, great heart," *Henry IV Part I*, 5.4.86) – in sharp contrast to Falstaff's grotesque stabbing of his corpse.

These passionate friendships are disrupted by death or displaced by erotic attachment and/or marriage to a woman. What is intriguing about *Two Noble Kinsmen* is that Shakespeare and Fletcher include an intense attachment between two, admittedly very young, women. Here is Emilia describing her intimacy with a childhood friend. The opening lines of this passionate speech carefully position the girls' love as inferior to that of men, but as the speech continues (and continues) the intensity of their connection becomes overwhelming.

> You talk of Pirithous' and Theseus' love.
> Theirs has more ground, is more maturely seasoned,
> More buckled with strong judgement, and their needs
> The one of th'other may be said to water
> Their intertangled roots of love – but I
> And she I sigh and spoke of were things innocent,
> Loved for we did and like the elements
> That know not what nor why, yet do effect
> Rare issues by their operance; our souls
> Did so to one another. What she liked
> Was then of me approved; what not, condemned –
> No more arraignment. The flower that I would pluck
> And put between my breasts (then but beginning
> To swell about the blossom), oh, she would long
> Till she had such another, and commit it
> To the like innocent cradle, where phoenix-like
> They died in perfume. On my head no toy
> But was her pattern; her affections – pretty,
> Though happily her careless wear – I followed
> For my most serious decking; had mine ear
> Stol'n some new air or at adventure hummed one
> From musical coinage, why, it was a note
> Whereon her spirits would sojourn – rather, dwell on,
> And sing it in her slumbers.
>
> *(1.3.55–78)*

This love between two adolescent girls is disrupted by death, but Emilia draws a moral from her "rehearsal" of their friendship and "true love."

> This rehearsal,
> Which fury-innocent wots well, comes in
> Like old importment's bastard, has this end:
> That the true love 'tween maid and maid may be
> More than in sex dividual.
>
> *(1.3.78–82)*

The third line of this quotation is difficult to make sense of, and therefore often emended, but it contains the word "bastard." Here we have one final twist to the portrayal of sons born in "lusty stealth" (*King Lear*, 1.2.11) that pre-occupied Shakespeare, if not Fletcher, through the 1590s and 1600s. There "seems some connection, not clearly worked out, between innocent (in the sense of baby) and bastard" partially obscured by the fury (rapidity and breath-lessness) with which Emilia evidently speaks (Potter 2015, p. 172). If Emilia is describing herself or her love as "innocent of fury," she is contrasting it with the aggressive heterosexual desire experienced by Palamon and Arcite. "The phrase is an oxymoron, because furies are normally sent to punish the guilty and are guilty themselves." Put simply, Emilia reclaims same-sex love for innocence.

It's a stretch, but only as far as most interpretations are a stretch. I admit I like the idea that in this final collaborative play the cynicism and violence of characters such as Thersites and Edmund, however dynamic and thrilling, is countered by Emilia's discreet (if confused and confusing) reclaiming of same-sex desire as "true love." This is a redefinition of terms as significant as "why bastard? Wherefore base?" (*King Lear*, 1.2.6). Whether it is Shakespeare's stretch is a completely different matter.

As with same-sex love, so with death. Shakespeare, the comic playwright, had been doing this kind of thing for decades: "Almost all Shakespeare's comedies confront death, the bold antagonist of laughter and happy endings" (Kerrigan 1982, p. 13). Going right back to his earliest days, *The Comedy of Errors* begins with the sentencing to death of Egeon (Shakespeare's addition to his source) in the very first scene, and he is only saved in the very last. Deaths are not always averted: the princess's father dies in *Love's Labour's Lost*, com-plicating the mood of this most sparkling of comedies, and in *The Winter's Tale* Mammilius and Antigonus die.

Emma Smith writes persuasively about these deaths, and the almost shocking dramatic lurch from tragedy to comedy which they precede. The deaths of Mammilius and Antigonus, the expected death of Perdita, none of these consti-tute endpoints:

> In refusing to fade to black on the sorrowful and bereft tragic figure, the play forces us to consider what comes next. What really happens when you've screwed up royally, and lost everything because of your bloody-mindedness? What is it like when, rather than dying majesti-cally (like Othello, for example, "upon a kiss"), you are condemned to wake up every day and remember again what you have done? Shakespeare's tragedies are bleak, to be sure, but their apocalyptic con-clusions actually spare us the real unbearable mundanity of grief, guilt and the consequences of our actions.
>
> *(Smith 2019, pp. 290–291)*

The Two Noble Kinsmen explores grief in a less subtle way, but still *thanatos* imposes itself upon *eros*. The three queens enter, their demands for their husbands' funeral rites interrupting the marriage festivities:

> give us the bones
> Of our dead kings that we may chapel them;
> And of thy boundless goodness take some note
> That for our crowned heads we have no roof,
> Save this which is the lion's and the bear's
> And vault to every thing.
>
> *(1.1.49–54)*

This intrusion leads one editor to ask why Shakespeare "might have had reason to think of mortality" in 1613 (Potter 2015, p. 15). Various reasons are suggested. Two involve actual deaths. In February 1613, William lost the last of his three younger brothers. In November 1612, Henry, Prince of Wales, died after a short illness.

Shakespeare's focus is, strikingly, as much on love as death in this final play, which leads some to posit one last intense, self-destructive (and well-hidden) relationship, of the kind anatomized in Palamon's description of the destructive force of Venus. Or perhaps he is writing out his own ambivalent feelings towards the Earl of Southampton: William becomes the Jailer's Daughter, suffering the pangs of love (and madness) for the unobtainable Palamon. All, as ever, remains speculation – and contested.

In terms of theater craft, there is more consensus. The play reveals Shakespeare to be, still, a collaborative, imitative, eclectic writer: *The Two Noble Kinsmen* is "a Jacobean dramatization of a medieval English tale based on an Italian romance version of a Latin epic about one of the oldest and most tragic Greek legends; it has two authors and two heroes" (Potter 2015, p. 1). And it reveals that he is still master of the use of theater space, in this case the indoor stage at the Blackfriars. Above all, the play reveals its authors' complete command of the sexual politics of theater itself. The Prologue presents a virgin play to the crowd: she is worth "two hours' travel" (worth the ride).

In sharp contrast to that other Shakespearean farewell (Prospero's philosophical riff on dreams), this is a hard-headed summary of the professional playwright's task: theater is both prostitution and marriage. Sex and drama are transactions. In *The Two Noble Kinsmen*, the Epilogue really is a farewell – to the "gentlemen" who have loved the play, the actors, and the playwrights: "us."

> We have our end; and ye shall have ere long,
> I dare say, many a better, to prolong
> Your old loves to us. We, and all our might,
> Rest at your service. Gentlemen, goodnight!
> *Flourish. Exit.*
>
> *(Epilogue, ll. 15–18)*

It may have taken a few more months truly to make an end, but Shakespeare's work was done. He left on his own terms, the one dramatist of his generation never to be imprisoned, never even in trouble, for his work. He had adapted to all the many changes in playing practice, written and rewritten truly great works for all the different venues where drama was made. Over his long career he was prolific: perhaps 40 plays if we include the lost *Cardenio* and *Love's Labour's Won*. Yet, whether alone or in collaboration, Shakespeare no doubt wrote more than that. Did he even consign some of his work to the bin? I have the feeling he would hang on to every word and wait for the right moment to bring it out again. But that is my bias as a biographer, to see and to admire the man as an professional, pragmatic playwright who understood what worked, and where, and how.

The triumphant litany of achievement begs the question: why on earth did Shakespeare retire when things were going so well? One explanation is age: William was approaching 50, an old man, at least by the standards of his time. Then again, he'd felt old for a long time, if we take seriously the words of "Will," a speaker preoccupied with his advanced age (at least in relation to the young man he loves) created by Shakespeare when he was not yet 30. And he'd been writing powerfully about old age and weakness for well over a decade. In *As You Like It*, Jaques has his famous lines about "the last scene of all," "second childishness and mere oblivion" (2.7.165), just before we see an old man carried in on the back of a young one. A few years on, and Shakepeare creates his searing, almost unbearable depiction of King Lear's descent into madness (would we now call it dementia?) and death.

The only defense against Death, the enemy of men, is to "breed." Or so Shakespeare, writing in the early 1590s, when his son Hamnet still lived, has his "Will" argue in the sonnets to a beautiful young man:

> nothing 'gainst Time's scythe can make defence,
> Save breed, to brave him when he takes thee hence.

(Sonnet 12, ll. 13–14)

By breeding, a man creates himself again: "your sweet semblance to some other give" (Sonnet 13, l. 4):

> Dear my love, you know,
> You had a father; let your son say so.

(Sonnet 13, ll. 13–14)

Breeding is here not just a matter of producing offspring, it is the begetting of sons. Concomitantly, the function of sex with women is primarily to produce (legitimate) sons: the "acute and self-conscious sense expressed by Shakespeare's culture of the necessity to harness sexual energy in the service of the reproduction of society, in ways both literal and ideological" (Chedgzoy 2015) put immense pressure on men to reproduce themselves in sons.

This understanding of inheritance and posterity is still very much alive in *Two Noble Kinsmen*, some 25 years on from the sonnets. Imprisoned, Palamon and Arcite gain courage and inspiration from their patrilineage: "Remember what your fathers were and conquer!" (2.2.36). Manhood is conflated with fatherhood, posterity with having a son.

When he retires to Stratford-upon-Avon, the old man William Shakespeare is the father of only daughters. The younger is already married (Susanna to Dr Hall). The older, Judith, at 31 "matronly" according to Dutton (1989, p. 157), on the point of marriage.[4] Only a month after the wedding, which took place in February 1616, Judith's new husband, Thomas Quiney, was in the ecclesiastical court confessing to fornication with a woman who had recently died in childbirth. The woman was Margaret Wheeler, who, with her child, had been buried on 15 March. Quiney was sentenced to perform public penance "clothed in a sheet" for three Sundays in Stratford church (Bearman 2020a). The sentence was commuted to acknowledgment of his crime wearing his own attire before the minister of Bishopton (close to Stratford) and his offering to pay 5 shillings to the poor of the parish.

These disturbing revelations about Quiney appear to have prompted his father-in-law to change his will. William had already drawn a will up, and now in March he got it signed and executed. He dictated so many changes that the entire first page of the will needed to be rewritten. Significantly, the words "son-in-law" were changed to "daughter Judith." This suggests that the revelation of Quiney's "incontinence" led father William to attempt to safeguard daughter Judith's interests. But the will is interesting in other ways. It is "unusual" because Shakespeare attempts to "guide his estate into the far future. He grants land in tail male, to forestall a division of property in future between daughters and wives, and the main legatee Susanna Hall is left nearly everything" (Honan 1998, p. 395). For some, this shows a father's favoritism, based on Susanna's intelligence: she "could sign her name to legal documents, and was lauded as witty beyond her sex; she was her father's favourite – so we gather from his will. Her sister Judith presumably had less wit than her sister, for she never learned to sign her name" (Schoenbaum 1991, p. 13). The will's provisions also reveal a man grappling with the implications of being without a son.

The will has been of most interest, however, not for what it shows about William the father, but William the husband.[5] What does his bequest of his "second-best bed" to his wife Anne tell us about their marriage? The legal situation is complicated and contested, and centers on understandings of dower law – what widows could and did receive in Shakespeare's time. It has recently been argued that the bequest has been interpreted as hostile when it is no such thing. Shakespeare would have known that, thanks to dower law, he could not "cut off" his widow by bequeathing her the bed even should he have wished to. This was because a church marriage – as had occurred back in 1582 – automatically engaged dower. No husband could "do anything to defeat or to lessen the survivor's entitlement" to dower, "no matter how much he ... might wish to."[6] Moreover, a bed was "not the defining symptom of any early modern relationship," therefore if "the best bed was no guarantee of affection, the second-best bed was no sign of antipathy" (Orlin 2016, pp. 50–52).

Against this, others insist the bequest was designed to cut out his wife: "by acknowledging Anne's existence with a named, specific item, he is able to deny her dower right to one-third of his estate" (Honan 1998, p. 305). Worse still, whilst acknowledging that William has made provision for his daughter and son-in-law to look after Anne on a day-to-day basis, he nevertheless "seems to wish to deny Anne *control* of any portion of his heritable estate" (ibid.).

William Shakespeare was putting his affairs in order in the early months of 1616, and offering a glimpse of his relationship with his wife and daughters (although the nature of those relationships remains contested). But to make a will was not necessarily a sign that he was in fear of death. Such sparse anecdotal evidence that survives suggests that his final illness was not, in fact, expected. Much, much later the vicar of Stratford recorded that Shakespeare, Michael Drayton, and Ben Jonson had "a merry meeting, and it seems drank too hard, for Shakespeare died of a fever there contracted" (Honan 1998, p. 311). This was perhaps typhoid fever, with its "incessant headache, lassitude, and sleeplessness, then terrible thirst and discomfort" (ibid., p. 313) accompanied by a shriveling of the features as seen in the death mask in Holy Trinity Church, where the nose is small and sharp, the upper lip elongated (ibid.).

Yet again, we don't know. In Shakespeare's and Fletcher's *Henry VIII*, Queen Katherine may have desired nothing more than an "honest chronicler" after her death, but William Shakespeare for all his celebrity as a playwright in London, for all that he had served two monarchs, remained the son of a glover in Stratford, who had done rather well. He had no chronicler, save for the church scribe who recorded his burial on 25 April 1616 (Bearman 2020b).

[1]616
April
3 Thomas Dixson
5 Marg[a]ret daughter of John James
9 Two twins of Rich Burman
15 Will Parie gentleman
16 A Infant of Thomas Woodward
17 Will Hartt Hatter X

21 Elizabeth daughter of Will Bramich
23 An[n]e Cocks Widow
24 Richard Pynder
25 Will Shakespeare gentleman X

Seven years later, the remarkable First Folio is published, yours for one pound. For all the problems with reading from text to life, or life to text, it remains the closest thing we have to an honest chronicle of its author.

Notes

Prologue

1 Lois Potter (2019) explores, powerfully and honestly, her experience of writing a literary life, analyzing the paths taken or not taken by biographers: "Very few people have actually wanted to write a biography of Shakespeare, and I was not one of them. The reasons are obvious. We know too much about the works and too little about the life" (p. 391). Further, she offers some telling insights into the academic publishing industry.

2 Worse still, what evidence there is does not always constitute a clear guide. At some point after buying a copy of Thomas Speght's 1598 edition of Chaucer's *Works*, Gabriel Harvey made some annotations, among which is a note that "The younger sort takes much delight in Shakespeares Venus, & Adonis: but his Lucrece, & his tragedie of Hamlet, prince of Denmarke, haue it in them, to please the wiser sort" (BL Add. MS 42518, fol. 394^v). It is hard to know when Harvey made this note and to which version of the play he is referring. One of his annotations implies a very early date: he lists some "florishing metricians," including not only Shakespeare but Spenser, who died on 16 January 1599, and Thomas Watson, who died in 1592. Since Harvey must have bought the book in 1598 or later, either he did not know Watson was dead or his use of "florishing" did not imply "living." The note refers to literary works which "the Earle of Essex commendes" but, since Essex was executed on 25 February 1601, it must have been written earlier. However, it also refers to "Owens new Epigrams" and, since these were not published until 1607, we seem to re-enter the world of the impossible (Thompson and Taylor 2006).

Chapter One

1 Shapiro (2005b, p. 9) writes persuasively about the ways in which the traditional "cradle-to-grave" form of biography over-elevates the significance of childhood. He challenges "the unspoken assumption that what makes people who they are now also made people who they were back then." Shapiro is "not so sure," and neither am I. Shapiro's compelling response to this doubt has been to focus on particular years in Shakespeare's adult life: so far, 1599 and 1606. My less dazzling approach is to show what we (think we) know about William Shakespeare's lived experience, and to offer (necessarily cautious) thoughts about the connection, direct and indirect, between that lived experience and the remarkable works of literature he created.

2 Playing companies put on plays that worked for the locality in which they were touring (*Harry of Cornwall* in the west of England or *Arden of Faversham* in Kent). The Earl of Worcester's Men had four runs in Stratford-upon-Avon within seven years in the late 1570s and early 1580s.

3 An Act for the Punishment of Vagabonds, and for Relief of the Poor and Impotent (Vagabond Act), 14 Elizabeth I, c. 5, 1572 Parliamentary Archives, HL/PO/PU/1/1572/14Eliz1n5.

4 Holger Schott Syme (2012) provides fascinating details about distances and rates of progress, horses, and baggage, whilst Dutton (2018, p. 47) gives the precise tour locations for one company.

5 William's mother's family, the Ardens, were traditional Catholics, outwardly conforming to the Church of England, yet continuing to hold pre-Reformation thought patterns asserts Wood (2015).

6 An entry in the bishop of Worcester's Register recorded the grant of a marriage license to "wm Shaxpere et Anna whateley" (Bishop of Worcester's Register, Worcestershire Record Office). The next day there's a marriage licence bond, for the marriage of "willm Shagspere … and Anne hathwey" under the special condition of a single asking of the banns. The couple needed a special dispensation to do so, not necessarily because of the pregnancy itself (which could be concealed in its early stages, although given the fact that at least one in four brides were pregnant on their wedding day, concealment may not have been necessary), but because the ban on weddings during Advent would have meant a long delay.

7 Gilbert and Joan Shakespeare were born when William was four and five, respectively. Richard arrived when William was 10, then Edmund, a final son for John and Mary, was born in 1580, when William was 16. The evidence for William's care for his little brother Edmund is sparse.

8   James Shapiro (2005a) also brings the streets of London alive for readers, evoking a fluid, shadowy world of business deals, dangerous and legitimate liaisons, but above all of theater.

9   Bart van Es (2013, p. 6) like everyone else, including me, does not know about the "lost years" but thinks the "strongest likelihood is that Shakespeare found work in some minor capacity connected with the law courts." Van Es is seeking a plausible path to Shakespeare the playwright since "the legal world was by far the biggest supplier of playwriting talent and many authors who lacked a university education (for example, Thomas Kyd and John Webster) started out in this way".

10   The evidence rests on a bequest to "William Shakeshafte" (either an actor or musician) and the fact that "one of the Stratford schoolmasters in 1579–81, John Cottam, was the brother of a Jesuit priest and he came from that same part of Lancashire, suggesting possible lines of communication" (Dutton 2018, p. 51).

11   Those vested in the theory that Shakespeare spent the lost years in Lancashire argue he took care to represent the Stanley and Clifford families favorably in his plays, most notably in *Richard III*. Ferdinando, Lord Strange, was the son of Margaret Clifford.

12   Shakespeare's own Stratford-upon-Avon council had moved to ban players from using their Guild Hall for performances and then to stop all performances, although whether they were driven to this on account of the damage done by the Queen's players in 1587, costing 16 pence "for mending," or by religious ideology is unclear.

13   For the finances, see Dutton (2018, p. 48).

Chapter Two

1   One curriculum vitae (Potter 2012) for Shakespeare from 1589 runs: an unspecified touring company (1587–1589); Strange's Men (1589–1593); Pembroke's Men (1593–1594). Of the seven actors listed in Strange's Men, six would go on to become founder-members with Shakespeare of the Lord Chamberlain's Men in 1594/1595. Coincidence? Dutton (2018, p. 63) doesn't think so. But however plausible this trajectory might be there is no evidence to prove it true. Another argument goes that Shakespeare was with the Queen's Men before 1594, since no fewer than six of his plays have similar plots to those performed by that company. Then again, in an era of borrowing and imitation, Shakespeare could quite easily have seen or read these plays.

2   The play made 76 shillings and 8 pence for Henslowe. This sum represented his income for allowing the actors to use his theater. Dutton (2018, p. 64) has the finances. Marlowe's *Jew of Malta* did better in the run overall, but the *Henry* play comes second.

3   Marjorie Garber, rather gloriously, imagines this exchange as a game in which Marlowe's oeuvre is gradually counted out by Shakespeare's stronger hand. Finally, with desperation, Marlowe lays down *Tamburlaine the Great Parts I and II*. Shakespeare, "with an apologetic smile," presents his cards: "'Henry IV, Part I', he says deliberately, 'Henry IV Part II, and Henry V'" (Garber 1979, pp. 3–9).

4   See Dutton (2018, pp. 260 ff.) for more on acting techniques and the era's fascination with meta-theatricality.

5   The placenames, Wincot and Burtonheath (Barton on the Heath), make Christopher Sly a Warwickshire man. The character, for Bate (2008, p. 44), operates therefore almost as a "parody" of Shakespeare's "own country bumpkin origins".

6   Honan (2005, p. 192) shows that mockery and parody featured in some of the many, many responses to Marlowe's work. A play, once in print, was "a larder for anybody's use".

7   Taylor (2016, p. 149) goes even further, suggesting that Shakespeare recognized that *Lucrece* was simply not very good. It was this self-assessment of his ability as a poet led him to refocus on playwriting.

8   Syme (2012, p. 269) has shown that there is no documentary evidence to prove Shakespeare was a *founding* member of the troupe in the spring of 1594.

9   The duopoly (if it existed at all) may well have been engineered by the Privy Council, and more specifically, by Lord Chamberlain Hunsdon and his son-in-law Lord Admiral Howard, to ensure the supply of the queen's plays every Christmas.

10 For information about the practicalities of theater (from boy actors to the economics of play performance) see Potter (2012, pp. 139–143).

11 Biographers would love to find a document, any document, showing a direct connection between Will Shakespeare and Kit Marlowe. They have to be content with one direct quotation of Marlowe's *Hero and Leander* - "Whoever loved that loved not at first sight?" – which stands as a "warm, close tribute of a kind" Shakespeare "paid to no other contemporary," or so argues Honan (2005, p. 191), and the phrase "great reckoning" in *As You Like It* which may be an allusion to the fact that Marlowe, it was reported, was killed over the reckoning of a bill.

Chapter Three

1 The British Library website, which should know better, repeats the completely unsubstantiated story that Shakespeare himself acted the role of John of Gaunt in *Richard II*. We either seem to want our Shakespeare to be a patriotic elder statesman, even if he only acts the part or we want him to be a rebel of some kind: "this is the kind of 'natural' writer Shakespeare was himself, an instinctive, allusive, unpredictable, 'wild' free-thinker as well as a scrupulous craftsman" (Mabey 2005, RSC programme).

2 All that is certain is that the play was known by 1598, when Francis Meres in his *Palladis Tamia* puts it in his list of Shakespeare's works.

3 The strongest contender is the marriage of Lord Chamberlain Hunsdon's granddaughter on 19 February 1596. The date for the wedding was chosen after proper astrological consideration to occur when the new moon was due to appear in conjunction with Venus. The marriage negotiations had not run smooth which, for those who link *Midsummer's Night's Dream* to the occasion, explains the play's preoccupation with erotic conflict.

4 The writer of a late 1595 letter to Robert Cecil attempts to entice him to visit in the evening by saying that King Richard II "will present himself to your view." This could have been a painting, or a play by someone other than Shakespeare, but it was more likely a specially commissioned evening performance of one of the Chamberlain's Men's newest plays argues Gurr (2003, pp. 1–3).

5 Smith (2013, p. 193) argues that Lopez's Jewishness was not the most significant element in his prosecution and was in fact "strategically suppressed in the official publication of the trial proceedings." It is Lopez's Catholicism that is important at the time "since Judaism, unlike Catholicism, was not a political threat in 1594," with the result being that many of the works of the time identify Lopez as a dangerous papist rather than as a Jew. Smith's claim that at the time of *The Merchant of Venice* no extant printed source had identified Lopez as Jewish is something of a stretch. Francis Bacon, who took part in the trial, wrote that Lopez was "suspected" to be "secretly a Jew" though he conformed to "the rites of the Christian religion" (Shapiro 1996, pp. 72–73).

6 Two further anonymous history plays, *Thomas of Woodstock* (another play about Richard II) and *Edmund Ironside*, both found in the same British Library manuscript, have also been attributed to Shakespeare, but most scholars believe they are not his work.

7 Some see Hamnet in any boy who dies young (Arthur in *King John*, young Macduff in *Macbeth*, Mamillius in *The Winter's Tale*), William in any father who grieves, guiltily, for dead sons: Macduff, Northumberland in *Henry IV Part II*, Leontes in *The Winter's Tale*, and Alonso in *The Tempest*.

8 "gold, on a bend sable [black], a spear of the first, the point steeled argent [silver]" (it is altered from "argent" to "proper," or natural-colored, in the first draft, and described as argent in the second draft) (see https:// shakespearedocumented.folger.edu/resource/document/ grant-arms-john-shakespeare-draft-1).

9 The Curtain, built in 1577, was the second London playhouse. Standing north of the London Wall, it had a similar structure but was slightly smaller than the nearby Theatre.

Chapter Four

1 At around this time, Shakespeare was trying to make good an "especially humiliating reversal for the family [which] involved the loss of a house and tract of land near Stratford." The house and land had been part of Mary Arden's dowry, but John Shakespeare had mortgaged them when he needed funds. William's parents had already made two attempts to reclaim the property or get a cash payment, but third time was not lucky, and the Shakespeares withdrew their claim. "For husband, wife, and eldest son, the loss may have felt like a permanent stigma" (Tromly 2010, p. 247).

2 It appears to be a myth that the play was written at Queen Elizabeth's direction, who "was so eager to see it Acted, that she commanded it to be finished in fourteen days" (or so said the advertisement to *The Comical Gallant: or the Amours of Sir John Falstaffe*, published in 1702). The story got even better in Rowe's life of Shakespeare. The queen loved Falstaff so much she commanded Shakespeare "to continue it for one Play more, and to shew him in Love." Despite its late arrival at the Shakespeare Biography Ball, the usually skeptical Schoenbaum (1987, p. 51), likes the story, thinking the queen's royal command might well have been motivated by Shakespeare's failure to deliver on his promise, made in the Epilogue to *Henry IV Part II* to bring Falstaff back onto the stage in a future play.

3 This is yet another footnote about dating, if only to hammer home the impossibility (and possibly the futility) of the task. *Merry Wives* has been dated to late 1596 on the basis of Falstaff's reference to "a region in Guiana" (*Merry Wives of Windsor*, 1.3.66). Shakespeare was, it is said, referring to Sir Walter Ralegh's (failed) expedition in search of the gold of El Dorado in 1595, which was written up by Ralegh and circulated in manuscript then

print, in 1596, in his (failed) attempted to drum up support for a further exploration of the Guiana region. *Merry Wives* has also been dated to 1597 because of a reference to the Garter Feast of that year. Most scholars err towards an even later date, pointing to the 1599 offstage death of Falstaff in *Henry V*. A character as good as the fat man could not die, so was brought back to life in a comedy. Others point to what might be a sly reference to the rebuilding of the Theatre and the feelings of the Chamberlain's Men at having their playhouse "rendered inaccessible because it was trapped on a piece of land that belonged to someone else" (Stern 2004, p. 13). In this reading, Shakespeare channels the company's emotional outrage into the character of Ford, who is furious at the loss of his property (his wife rather than a theater): "A fair house, built on another man's ground, so that I have lost my edifice, by mistaking the place, where I erected it" (*Merry Wives of Windsor*, 2.2.205–207).

4 Shakespeare may have noticed Meres's praise. MacDonald (2005, pp. 187–188) argues that Shakespeare wrote or revised a couple of his "rival poet" sonnets and composed the famous Sonnet 55 ("Not marble nor the gilded monuments / Of princes, shall outlive this powerful rhyme," ll. 1–2) in response to Meres's treatise.

5 According to Hammond (2012), sonnets 1 to 60 were written mainly in first half of the 1590s but revised or added to after 1600, perhaps as late as 1608–1609; numbers 61 to 103 were written mainly in first half of the 1590s; numbers 104–126 were written around or shortly after 1600; and the final set in the eventual printed edition (127–154) were written back in the first half of the 1590s.

6 There's evidence that Shakespeare and Barnfield "kept a close eye on each other" (Hadfield 2015, p. 202), at least in the sense of the former keeping an eye on the latter's work. Shakespeare's infamous Sonnet 20 is, in part at least, a reworking of Barnfield's Sonnet 10, which describes Ganymede, the poet's object of desire, with a body created by Venus and therefore made for love, but a mind inclined to chastity: "He loves to be beloved, but not to love" (l. 14). Shakespeare has the young man created by Nature to be a woman, with feminine features, but – regrettably – male genitals which preclude his (sexual) "use".

7 Masten (2016) offers fascinating readings of the speaker's exhortation to the young man to "make sweet some vial," each playing "around the rhetoric of vile sodomy," the "multiplicity" of the "vile vial," the "improper vessel," the anus. That Shakespeare is sexually explicit is not surprising. Ben Jonson for one owned three complete (that is, unexpurgated) editions of the Latin poet Martial whose epigram 2.28 lists all the sorts of penetrative sexual activity a man named Sextillus abstains from, and then ends by saying "two possibilities

remain." In the margin, Ben Jonson, ever the scholar, writes "Fellator cunniling".

8 "Given the already considerable feats of memorization, information processing and verbal and gestural action and co-ordination that he is required to undertake, limiting the sources of his cues is one way of managing cognitive load" (McMillin 2004). Simon Palfrey and Tiffany Stern (2007) and Evelyn Tribble (2011) follow McMillin's lead, exploring from different angles the implications of the fact that in the early modern theater (and, indeed, up until the nineteenth century), actors were provided not with the full text of the play, but with their own parts and (one-, two-, or three-word) cues only: see Shaughnessy (2018) for a summary.

9 "This boy first tells the women, 'for the love you bear to men, to like as much of this play as please you' (Epilogue 10–11). He then charges the men 'for the love you bear to women – as I perceive by your simpering none of you hates them – that between you and the women the play may please' (Epilogue 12–14). The 'play' in this second instance is a bawdy double entendre. The play they have just seen can serve as stimulant and foreplay to the sex-play to follow, confirming contemporary suspicions that plays were essentially pornographic" (McCoy 2015, p. 79).

10 A "sharp, and permanent, drop in Henslowe's takings at the nearby Rose Theatre after June 1599 suggests the presence of a rival on Bankside" (Daniell 1998, p. 16).

11 In her analysis of Shakespeare's sources, Lois Potter (2012, p. 340) notes that Guarini's *Il Pastor Fido* (which contains a crucial defense of the genre of tragi-comedy) was only available in Italian. Therefore, Shakespeare "probably worked his way through it in Italian during one of the many periods of plague closure." Neill (2006, p. 20) also argues that Shakespeare almost certainly read the Cinthio stories in the original Italian.

12 The references "bear no trace of personal animosity on Jonson's part. Nevertheless, his initiative did prompt a response from his newly-designated rival" (Riggs 2015, p. 189). Riggs, as was seen earlier, sees that "response" in the form of the character of Jaques in *As You Like It*, a play which "endorses a poetics of irony, indirection and paradox".

Chapter Five

1 "All hail, all faithful souls, whose bodies do here and everywhere rest in the dust" (*Salvete vos omnes fideles animae, quarum corpora hic et ubique requiescat in pulvere*).

2   The play might have been performed a year before Manningham saw it at the
Middle Temple. On 6 January 1601, the Feast of the Epiphany, the Lord
Chamberlain's Men performed a play at Whitehall for Queen Elizabeth and
Virginio Orsini, Duke of Bracciano. No expense was spared: the play "shall be
best furnished with rich apparel, have great variety and change of music and
dances, and of a subject that may be most pleasing to her Majesty" (Elam
2008, p. 93). It is possible that the play chosen was *Twelfth Night*. Not only is
the title fitting (it was the twelfth night of the Christmas celebrations), but the
character Orsino appears to honor the visiting Duke. The Orsini connection is
explored in Elam (2008, pp. 93–94).

3   "A woman falls in love with another woman in disguise as a man who is her/
himself in love with a man. It all turns out hetero in the end, but the thrust of
the play is on desire rather than on the identity imposed at the conclusion"
(Menon 2016, p. 37).

Chapter Six

1   To make things even more fraught for those who want to work out what
Shakespeare "really wrote," there are 5000 variations between the quarto and
the Folio, the two surviving texts of *Troilus*.

2   Public Record Office, Privy Seal Office, Warrants for the Privy Seal, P.S.O.
2/22; Chancery, Warrants for the Great Seal, C. 82/1690.

3   The play "turns what might seem like disadvantages into assets; its sheer
ferocity, its intense concentration on the destructiveness of economic relations
and its virulent critique of human ingratitude have won it a valued place
among present-day performers and playgoers" (Dawson and Minton 2008, p. 1).

4   Middleton (probably) wrote *A Yorkshire Tragedy* in 1605, and (almost
definitely) wrote *The Revenger's Tragedy* the following year for the King's Men.
As for Shakespeare's reading of Plutarch, the story of Timon and the
relationship of Antony and Octavius Caesar (which also gets a mention in
Macbeth) appear in Plutarch's life of Anthony, so it is possible that
Shakespeare was thinking about *Antony and Cleopatra* while writing *Macbeth*
and *Timon*.

5   We know that *King Lear* was performed at court in December 1606, but some
date the play to the previous year, due to the allusions to the eclipses of
September and October 1605.

6   The Gunpowder Plot might even provide a clue to the dating of *Timon*. In
3.3.33–34, Timon's servant speaks of "those that under hot ardent zeal would
set whole realms on fire." This could also simply be a reference in general
terms to religious extremists.

7 See for example Kyd's extremely popular *Soliman and Perseda*. The work is described by its Chorus as a "tragedy," but "in its coincidences, its love-token, its geographical dimensions, and its keen interest in chivalry, the play is significantly engaged with the romance tradition" (Publicover 2017, pp. 96–97).

8 In the source, North's translation of Plutarch, Domitius as he is called, is a very minor figure who is "sick of an ague" when he deserts to Caesar and is subsequently sent "all his caryage, trayne, and men" by Antony. Although he attempts to communicate to Antony that he repents of his open treason, he dies almost immediately after his repentance (North 1579, p. 298).

Chapter Seven

1 Shapiro (2015, p. 357) adopts a similarly confident tone when describing the three years *after* the *annus mirabilis* of 1606: they were "relatively quiet ones for Shakespeare – *Pericles*, *Coriolanus* and *All's Well*".

2 No one is sure of the date of composition. The allusion to "coal of fire upon ice" might tie the play to the great frost of the winter of 1607–1608. Or perhaps Jonson adds a "mocking echo" of *Coriolanus* to his play, *Epicene*, which would place Shakespeare's work later, moving it to February 1610 when the theaters probably reopened after long closures because of plague (Bliss 2010, pp. 50–51). In content and approach, *Coriolanus* has clear affinities with *Timon*, another play which is equally difficult to date. Both works focus on ingratitude, but "where Timon and Alcibiades parallel and reflect on each other's experience, *Coriolanus* integrates much of the range of the experience into a single character but one now emotionally engaged with friends and family in a way that Timon is not. What it means to be husband of Virgilia or son to Volumnia or, even, father to young Caius is crucial to the play's study of the ways in which Coriolanus constructs his own isolation. It seems fair to read this as a progress from *Timon* rather than to find *Timon* as a later isolating of aspects of *Coriolanus*. But, as with so many narratives of a writer's progress, the sequence can also be argued in reverse" (Bliss 2010, p. 72).

3 "The order in which they appeared in 1609 probably does not reflect the order in which they were composed, but it is quite likely that it is the order which Shakespeare determined, rather than an order created by a copyist or printer" (Hammond 2012, p. 9).

4 It all gets a bit strained – most of the theories do. Master has to be seen as a (somewhat disrespectful) hangover from the 1590s, since Pembroke received his title in 1601.

5 Kerrigan (1986, pp. 54–55) writes superbly about the two understandings of love: "As the object of love, he becomes love's end, the point where love declares itself as love. Indeed, love and the youth are so conjoined that there are many poems in which an interpretative effort is needed to determine whether the beloved or the poet's affection for him is comprised in the word 'love', and a number of places at which the two cannot be distinguished." One example comes in Sonnet 80 (l. 14): "The worst was this: my love was my decay".

Chapter Eight

1 Tromly (2010, p. 267) argues that this "man of fourscore three" (4.4.453) has "no fear of impotence and usurpation. Nor need he. Without insisting on their resemblance, or perhaps even noticing it, the father and his now middle-aged son are as one. In their final appearance at the end of 5.2, father and son enjoy a common satisfaction at having been elevated to the rank of gentleman. The Shepherd even changes his mode of address to his son, shifting from "boy" (which he uses nine times in 3.3 alone) to the more respectful 'son' in his final lines of the play".

2 See Nelson (2018b) for more information.

3 *Henry VIII* is not listed as a collaboration in the 1623 Folio, but most authorship studies suggest that the play contains passages written by John Fletcher. There is a record of a payment to the King's Men for a court performance of *Cardenno* [sic] in May 1613 and a Stationers' Register entry in 1653 of *The History of Cardenio* by "Mr. Fletcher and Shakespeare".

4 Having failed to obtain the special license required for marriage during Lent, Thomas and Judith were summoned to appear before the consistory court in Worcester Cathedral. He did not appear and was excommunicated. It remains unclear what happened to Judith. The offense was probably a technicality, since Stratford clergymen solemnized three marriages in February of that year (Wells 2001a, p. 489).

5 The will shows that Shakespeare, by 1616, is well and truly a Stratford man. Twenty-one out of 25 people mentioned in the document belong to his Warwickshire world. London is, in contrast, very poorly represented (Brock 2015, p. 226).

6 A lot rests on whether "dower" did still obtain in Stratford in this era. Orlin (2016) is sure it did. Others, including Jonathan Bate (2008, p. 192) and Katherine Duncan-Jones (2001, p. 275), contest that view.

References

Adelman, J. (1992). *Suffocating Mothers: Fantasies of Maternal Origin in Shakespeare's Plays*. New York: Routledge.

Arnold, O. (2018). Problem comedies: *Troilus and Cressida, Measure for Measure, and All's Well That Ends Well*. In: *The Oxford Handbook of Shakespearean Comedy* (ed. H. Hirschfeld) 537–554. Oxford: Oxford University Press.

Barker, S. and Hinds, H. eds (2002). *The Routledge Anthology of Renaissance Drama*. Taylor & Francis.

Barnfield, R. (1595). *Cynthia VVith Certaine Sonnets, and the Legend of Cassandra*. Printed for Humfrey Lownes, and are to bee sold at the vvest doore of Paules.

Bate, J. ed. (1995). *Titus Andronicus*. The Arden Shakespeare Third Series. London/New York: Routledge.

Bate, J. (1997). *The Genius of Shakespeare*. Oxford: Oxford University Press.

Bate, J. (2008). *Soul of the Age: The Life, Mind, and World of William Shakespeare*. London: Penguin.

Bearman, R. (2020a). A record of a hearing in the Stratford-upon-Avon Peculiar Court following a charge brought against Thomas Quiney of incontinence with Margaret Wheeler. *Shakespeare Documented* (website). https://shakespearedocumented. folger.edu/resource/document/record-hearing-stratford-upon-avon-peculiar-court-following-charge-brought-against

Bearman, R. (2020b). Parish register entry recording William Shakespeare's burial. *Shakespeare Documented* (website). https://shakespearedocumented. folger.edu/resource/document/parish-register-entry-recording-william-shakespeares-burial

Bednarz, J. (2018). Encountering the Elizabethan stage. In: *The Oxford Handbook of Shakespearean Comedy* (ed. H. Hirschfeld) 21–35. Oxford: Oxford University Press.

Bell, I. (2010). Rethinking Shakespeare's Dark Lady. In: *A Companion to Shakespeare's Sonnets* (ed. M. Schoenfeldt) 293–313. Oxford: Wiley Blackwell.

Belleforest, F. de. (n.d.). The history of Hamlet. *Internet Shakespeare Editions* (website). https://internetshakespeare.uvic.ca/doc/Belleforest_M/complete/index.html

The Life of the Author: William Shakespeare, First Edition. Anna Beer.
© 2021 John Wiley & Sons, Ltd. Published 2021 by John Wiley & Sons, Ltd.

Belsey, C. (1985). Disrupting sexual difference: Meaning and gender in the comedies. In: *Alternative Shakespeares* (ed. J. Drakakis) 169–193. London: Methuen.

Belsey, C. (1996). The serpent in the garden: Shakespeare, marriage and material culture. *The Seventeenth Century* 11(1): 1–20.

Belsey, C. (2007). The rape of Lucrece. In: *The Cambridge Companion to Shakespeare's Poetry* (ed. P. Cheney) 90–107. Cambridge: Cambridge University Press.

Bevington, D. M. (2005). *The Seven Ages of Human Experience*. Malden: Blackwell.

Bevington, D. M. (2010). *Shakespeare and Biography*. Oxford: Oxford University Press.

Bevington, D. M. (n.d.). *Hamlet: Internet Shakespeare*. https://internetshakespeare. uvic.ca/doc/Lr_TextIntro/section/The+two+versions+of+King+Lear/?view=print

Billington, M. ed. (1990). *Directors' Approaches to "Twelfth Night."* Nick Hern Books.

Blakemore-Evans, G. ed. (2003). *Romeo and Juliet*. New Cambridge Shakespeare Series. Cambridge University Press.

Bliss, L. ed. (2010). *Coriolanus*. New Cambridge Shakespeare Series. Cambridge University Press.

Braunmuller, A. R. ed. (1998). *The Life and Death of King John*. Oxford: Oxford University Press.

Breitenberg, M. (1996). *Anxious Masculinity in Early Modern England*. Cambridge/ New York: Cambridge University Press.

Brennan, M. G. (2004). English contact with Europe. In: *Shakespeare and Renaissance Europe* (eds A. Hadfield and P. Hammond) 53–97. London: Bloomsbury.

Brigden, S. (2000). *New Worlds, Lost Worlds: The Rule of the Tudors 1485–1603*. London: Allen Lane.

Briggs, J. (1997). *This Stage-Play World: English Literature and Its Background, 1580–1625*. Oxford: Oxford University Press.

Brock, S. (2015). Last things: Shakespeare's neighbours and beneficiaries. In: *The Shakespeare Circle: An Alternative Biography* (eds P. Edmondson and S. Wells) 201–230. Cambridge: Cambridge University Press.

Brooks, H. ed. (2007). *A Midsummer Night's Dream*. The Arden Shakespeare Second Series. London: Bloomsbury.

Bruster, D. (1992). *Drama and the Market in the Age of Shakespeare*. Cambridge: Cambridge University Press.

Burrow, C. (2002). *The Complete Sonnets and Poems*. The Oxford Shakespeare. Oxford: Oxford University Press.

Burrow, C. (2007). Editing the Sonnets. In: *A Companion to Shakespeare's Sonnets* (ed. M. Schoenfeldt) 145–162. Oxford: Wiley Blackwell.

Callaghan, D. (2000). *Shakespeare without Women*. London/New York: Routledge.

Carleton, G. (1627). *A Thankfull Remembrance of Gods Mercy. In an Historicall Collection of the Great and Mercifull Deliverances of the Church and State of England, Since the Gospell Began Here to Flourish, from the Beginning of Queene Elizabeth*. London.

Chamberlain, J. (1939). *The Letters of John Chamberlain*. The American Philosophical Society.

Chambers, E. K. (1923). *The Elizabethan Stage*. 4 vols. Clarendon Press.

Chambers, E. K. (1930). *William Shakespeare: A Study of Facts and Problems*. 2 vols. Clarendon Press.

Charney, M. (2009). *Wrinkled Deep in Time: Aging in Shakespeare*. New York: Columbia University Press.

Chedgzoy, K. (2000). *William Shakespeare's "Measure for Measure"*. London: Northcote House Publishers.

Chedgzoy, K. (2001). Sexuality. In: *The Oxford Companion to Shakespeare*, 1st Edition (eds D. Dobson and S. Wells). https://www.oxfordreference.com/view/10.1093/acref/9780198117353.001.0001/acref-9780198117353

Daniel, S. (1601). *The Vvorks of Samuel Daniel Newly Augmented*. Printed by Valentine Simmes and W. White for Simon Waterson.

Daniell, D. ed. (1998). *Julius Caesar*. The Arden Shakespeare Third Series. London: Bloomsbury.

Dash, M. (2011). William Shakespeare, gangster. *Smithsonian Magazine*, 7 November. https://www.smithsonianmag.com/history/william-shakespeare-gangster-129238903

Dawson, A. and Minton, G. E. eds (2008). *Timon of Athens*. The Arden Shakespeare Third Series. London: Bloomsbury.

Dekker, T. (1602). *Satiromastix or the Untrussing of the Humorous Poet*. London: Edward White.

Dionne, C. (2007). Playing it accordingly. In: *All's Well, That Ends Well: New Critical Essays* (ed. G. Waller) 169–183. London/New York: Routledge.

Dollimore, J. and Sinfield, A. (1992). History and ideology, masculinity and miscegenation: The instance of *Henry V*. In: *Cultural Materialism and the Politics of Dissent Reading* (ed. A. Sinfield) 109–142. Berkeley: University of California Press.

Drabble, M. (2015). Afterword. In: *The Shakespeare Circle: An Alternative Biography* (eds P. Edmondson and S. Wells) 335–339. Cambridge: Cambridge University Press.

Duncan-Jones, K. (2001). *Ungentle Shakespeare: Scenes from His Life*. London: Bloomsbury.

Dutton, R. (1989). *William Shakespeare: A Literary Life*. Basingstoke: Macmillan Press.

Dutton, R. (2010). *Shake-speares sonnets*, Shakespeare's sonnets, and Shakespearean biography. In: *A Companion to Shakespeare's Sonnets* (ed. M. Schoenfeldt) 121–136. Oxford: Wiley Blackwell.

Dutton, R. (2016). *Shakespeare, Court Dramatist*. Oxford: Oxford University Press.

Dutton, R. (2018). *Shakespeare's Theatre: A History*. Oxford: Wiley Blackwell.

Edmondson, P. and Wells, S. (2015a). Closing remarks. In: *The Shakespeare Circle: An Alternative Biography* (eds P. Edmondson and S. Wells) 329–334. Cambridge: Cambridge University Press.

Edmondson, P. and Wells, S. (2015b). General introduction. In: *The Shakespeare Circle: An Alternative Biography* (eds P. Edmondson and S. Wells) 1–12. Cambridge: Cambridge University Press.

Edwards, P. ed. (2003). *Hamlet, Prince of Denmark*. New Cambridge Shakespeare. Cambridge: Cambridge University Press.

Elam, K. ed. (2008). *Twelfth Night and or What You Will*. The Arden Shakespeare Third Series. London: Bloomsbury.

Eliot, T. S. (1997). *The Sacred Wood: Essays on Poetry and Criticism*. London: Faber.

Erickson, P. (1992). *Rewriting Shakespeare, Rewriting Ourselves*. Berkeley: University of California Press.

Erne, L. (2013). *Shakespeare as Literary Dramatist*. 2nd Edition. Cambridge: Cambridge University Press.

Fallow, D. (2015). His father John Shakespeare. In: *The Shakespeare Circle: An Alternative Biography* (eds P. Edmondson and S. Wells) 26–39. Cambridge: Cambridge University Press.

Ficino, M. and Jayne, S. (1985). *Commentary on Plato's Symposium on Love*. 2nd Revised Edition. Spring Publications.

Gajda, A. (2012). *The Earl of Essex and Late Elizabethan Culture*. Oxford: Oxford University Press.

Garber, M. (1979). Marlovian vision/Shakespearean revision. *Research Opportunities in Renaissance Drama* 22: 1–13.

Garber, M. (2004). *Shakespeare After All*. New York: Pantheon Books.

Gosson, S. (1582). *Playes Confuted in Fiue Actions Prouing That They Are Not to be Suffred in a Christian Common Weale, by the Waye Both the Cauils of Thomas Lodge, and the Play of Playes, Written in Their Defence, and Other Obiections of Players Frendes, Are Truely Set Downe and Directlye Aunsweared. by steph. gosson, stud. oxon.* Imprinted for Thomas Gosson dwelling in Pater noster row at the signe of the Sunne.

Greenblatt, S. (2000). Introduction. In: *The Norton Shakespeare* (eds S. Greenblatt, W. Cohen, S. Gossett, J. E. Howard, K. Eisaman Maus, and G. McMullan). New York: W. W. Norton.

Greenblatt, S. (2001). *Hamlet in Purgatory*. Princeton: Princeton University Press.

Greenblatt, S. (2004). *Will in the World: How Shakespeare Became Shakespeare*. London: Jonathan Cape.

Gurr, A. ed. (2003). *King Richard II*. The New Cambridge Shakespeare. Cambridge: Cambridge University Press.

Haber, J. (2018). Comedy and eros: Sexualities on Shakespeare's stage. In: *The Oxford Handbook of Shakespearean Comedy* (ed. H. Hirschfeld) 281–297. Oxford: Oxford University Press.

Hadfield, A. (2004). Shakespeare and Renaissance Europe. In: *Shakespeare and Renaissance Europe* (eds A. Hadfield and P. Hammond) 1–21. London: The Arden Shakespeare.

Hadfield, A. (2015). Richard Barnfield, John Weever, William Basse and other encomiasts. In: *The Shakespeare Circle: An Alternative Biography* (eds P. Edmondson and S. Wells) 199–212. Cambridge: Cambridge University Press.

Hadfield, A. (2019). Shakespeare: Biography and belief. In: *The Cambridge Companion to Shakespeare and Religion* (ed. H. Hamlin) 18–33. Cambridge: Cambridge University Press.

Hammer, P. (2008). Shakespeare's *Richard II*, the Play of 7 February 1601, and the Essex Rising. *Shakespeare Quarterly* 59(1): 1–35.

Hammond, P. ed. (2012). *Shakespeare's Sonnets: An Original Spelling Text*. Oxford: Oxford University Press.

Hayward, J. (1599). *The First Parte of the Life and Raigne of King Henry the Fourth, Extending to the End of the First Yeere of His Raigne*. London: John Woolfe.

Henslowe, P. and Foakes, R. (2002). *Henslowe's Diary*. 2nd Edition. Cambridge University Press.

Heywood, T. (1612). *An Apology for Actors Containing Three Briefe Treatises. 1 Their Antiquity. 2 Their Ancient Dignity. 3 The True Vse of Their Quality. Written by Thomas Heywood*. Printed by Nicholas Okes.

Honan, P. (1998). *Shakespeare: A Life*. Oxford: Oxford University Press.

Honan, P. (2005). *Christopher Marlowe: Poet and Spy*. Oxford: Oxford University Press.

Howard, J. E. (1988). Crossdressing, the theatre, and gender struggle in early modern England. *Shakespeare Quarterly* 39(4): 418–440.

Howard, J. E. (1994). *The Stage and Social Struggle in Early Modern England*. London/New York: Routledge.

Howard, J. E. and Rackin, P. (1997). *Engendering a Nation: A Feminist Account of Shakespeare's English Histories*. London: Routledge.

Jacquez, M. (2017). Richard II, third edition. *Shakespeare Documented* (website). https://shakespearedocumented.folger.edu/exhibition/document/richard-ii-third-edition

Jewel, J. (n.d.). An homily against disobedience and willful rebellion (1571). *Internet Shakespeare Editions* (website). https://internetshakespeare.uvic.ca/doc/Homilies_2-21_M/section/The%20First%20Part

Jones, G. (2000). *The Healing*. London: The Serpent's Tail.

Jonson, B. (1927). *The Tale of a Tub. The Case is Altered. Every Man in His Humour. Every Man Out of His Humour*. Edited by C. H. Herford and P. Simpson. Oxford University Press.

Kahn, C. (2011). Shakespeare's classical tragedies. In: *The Cambridge Companion to Shakespearean Tragedy* (ed. C. McEachern) 218–239. Cambridge: Cambridge University Press.

Kerrigan, J. ed. (1982). *Love's Labour's Lost*. The New Penguin Shakespeare. Harmondsworth: Penguin Books.

Kerrigan, J. ed. (1986). *"The Sonnets" and "A Lover's Complaint."* The New Penguin Shakespeare. Harmondsworth: Penguin Books.

Kerrigan, J. (2016). *Shakespeare's Binding Language*. Oxford: Oxford University Press.

Kerrigan, J. (2018). *Shakespeare's Originality*. Oxford: Oxford University Press.

Klein, B. (2016). Antony and Cleopatra. In: *The Oxford Handbook of Shakespearean Tragedy* (eds M. Neil and D. Schalkwyk) 452–467. Oxford: Oxford University Press.

Levi, P. (1988). *The Life and Times of William Shakespeare*. London: Macmillan.

Lyne, R. (2007). *Shakespeare's Late Work*. Oxford: Oxford University Press.

Mabey, R. (2005). To the woods! Nature in *A Midsummer-Night's Dream* (RSC programme).

MacDonald, J. P. (2005). Francis Meres and the cultural contexts of Shakespeare's rival poet's sonnets. *RES* 56: 224–246.

MacFaul, T. (2012). *Problem Fathers in Shakespeare*. Cambridge: Cambridge University Press.

MacKinnon, L. (2015). His daughter Susanna Hall. In: *The Shakespeare Circle: An Alternative Biography* (eds P. Edmondson and S. Wells) 71–85. Cambridge University Press.

Maguire, L. and Smith, E. (2012). *30 Great Myths about Shakespeare*. Oxford: Wiley Blackwell.

Marcus, L. S. (1988). *Puzzling Shakespeare: Local Reading and Its Discontents*. Berkeley: University of California Press.

Marlowe, C. (1989). *Doctor Faustus*. Edited by R. Gill and R. King. A & C Black/W. W. Norton.

Marlowe, C. (1997). *Edward II*. Edited by M. Wiggins and R. Lindsey. Methuen Drama.

Masten, J. (2016). *Queer Philologies: Sex, Language and Affect in Shakespeare's Time*. Pennsylvania: University of Pennsylvania Press.

McCoy, R. C. (2015). *Faith in Shakespeare*. New York: Oxford University Press.

McMillin, S. (2004). The sharer and his boy: Rehearsing Shakespeare's women. In: *From Script to Stage in Early Modern England* (eds P. Holland and S. Orgel) 231–245. Basingstoke: Palgrave Macmillan.

McMullan, G. (2016). The first night of *The Tempest*. *British Library* (website). https://www.bl.uk/shakespeare/articles/the-first-night-of-the-tempest

Menon, M. (2016). HexaSexuality. In: *Shakespeare in Our Time* (eds D. Callaghan and S. Gossett) 35–39. London: Bloomsbury.

Montaigne, M. (1632). *The Essayes or, Morall, Politike, and Militarie Discourses of Lord Michael de Montaigne, Knight of the Noble Order of Saint Michael, and One of the Gentlemen in Ordinary of the French Kings Chamber*. Printed by M. Flesher, for Rich: Royston, in Ivie-lane next the exchequer office. http://www.gutenberg.org/cache/epub/5637/pg5637.html

Moulton, I. F. (2017). As you like it or what you will: Shakespeare's sonnets and Beccadelli's *Hermaphroditus*. In: *Queer Shakespeare: Desire and Sexuality* (ed. G. V. Stanivukovik) 87–106. London: Bloomsbury.

Mullaney, S. (1988). *In the Place of the Stage*. Chicago: University of Chicago Press.

Nashe, T. (1842). *Pierce Penniless, His Supplication to the Devil*. Edited by J. P. Collier. The Shakespeare Society.

Nashe, T. (1904–1910). *Works*. Edited by R. B. McKerrow. 5 vols. A. H. Bullen.

Neill, M. ed. (2006). *Othello, The Moor of Venice*. The Oxford Shakespeare. Oxford: Oxford University Press.

Nelson, A. H. (2015). His literary patrons. In: *The Shakespeare Circle: An Alternative Biography* (eds P. Edmondson and S. Wells) 275–288. Cambridge: Cambridge University Press.

Nelson, A. H. (2017). Examination of Augustine Phillips. *Shakespeare Documented* (website). https://shakespearedocumented.folger.edu/exhibition/document/examination-augustine-phillips

Nelson, A. H. (2018a). Account of the Master of the Great Wardrobe, recording the issue of red cloth to Shakespeare and his fellows for the entry of King James I into London. *Shakespeare Documented* (website). https://shakespearedocumented. folger.edu/resource/document/account-master-great-wardrobe-recording-issue-red-cloth-shakespeare-and-his

Nelson, A. H. (2018b). The Langley writ: Court of King's Bench writ of attachment against William Shakespeare, Michaelmas, 1596. *Shakespeare Documented* (website). https://shakespearedocumented.folger.edu/resource/document/ langley-writ-court-kings-bench-writ-attachment-against-william-shakespeare

Nelson, A. H. (2018c). Shakespeare purchases the Blackfriars Gatehouse: Enrollment of a bargain and sale conveying property from Henry Walker to Shakespeare. *Shakespeare Documented* (website). https://shakespearedocumented.folger.edu/ exhibition/document/shakespeare-purchases-blackfriars-gatehouse-enrollment-bargain-and-sale

Nelson, A. H. and Folger Shakespeare Library Staff. (2020). Interrogatories and depositions in Belott v Mountjoy, on behalf of Stephen Belott [including that made by William Shakespeare]. *Shakespeare Documented* (website). https:// shakespearedocumented.folger.edu/resource/document/bellott-v-mountjoy-first-set-depositions-bellotts-behalf-including-shakespeares

North, Sir Thomas. (1579). *Plutarch's Lives, Englished by Sir Thomas North in Ten Volumes*. London.

Northbrooke, J. (1577). *A Treatise against Dicing, Dancing, Plays, and Interludes. With Other Idle Pastimes*.

Nosworthy, J. M. ed. (1955). *Cymbeline*. The Arden Shakespeare Second Series. London: Cengage Learning.

Orgel, S. (1997). *Impersonations: The Performance of Gender in Shakespeare's England*. Cambridge: Cambridge University Press.

Orgel, S. (2007). Mr who is he? In: *A Companion to Shakespeare's Sonnets* (ed. M. Schoenfeldt) 121–136. Oxford: Wiley Blackwell.

Orlin, L. C. (2016). Shakespeare's marriage. In: *The Oxford Handbook of Shakespeare and Embodiment: Gender, Sexuality, and Race* (ed. V. Traub) 38–56. Oxford: Oxford University Press.

Palfrey, S. and Stern, T. (2007). *Shakespeare in Parts*. Oxford: Oxford University Press.

Patterson, A. (1999). Back by popular demand: Two versions of *Henry V*. In: *Shakespeare: The Critical Complex* (eds S. Orgel and S. Keilen) 313–346. London: Garland.

Pequigney, J. (1992). The two Antonios and same sex love in *Twelfth Night* and *The Merchant of Venice*. *English Literary Renaissance* 22(2): 201–221.

Platter, T. (1937). *Thomas Platter's Travels in England 1599*. Translated by Clare Williams. Jonathan Cape.

Potter, L. (2012). *The Life of William Shakespeare: A Critical Biography*. Oxford: Wiley Blackwell.

Potter, L. ed. (2015). *The Two Noble Kinsmen*. The Arden Shakespeare Third Series. London: Bloomsbury.

Potter, L. (2019). Writing Shakespeare's life. In: *A Companion to Literary Biography* (ed. R. Bradford) 391–404. Oxford: Wiley Blackwell.

Prior, R. (1972). The life of George Wilkins. *Shakespeare Survey* 25: 137–152.

Publicover, L. (2017). *Dramatic Geography: Romance, Intertheatricality, and Cultural Encounter in Early Modern Mediterranean Drama*. Oxford: Oxford University Press.

Richardson, C. (2015). His siblings. In: *The Shakespeare Circle: An Alternative Biography* (eds P. Edmondson and S. Wells) 40–48. Cambridge: Cambridge University Press.

Riggs, D. (2015). Ben Jonson. In: *The Shakespeare Circle: An Alternative Biography* (eds P. Edmondson and S. Wells) 186–198. Cambridge: Cambridge University Press.

Rose, M. (1988). *The Expanse of Spirit: Love and Sexuality in English Renaissance Drama*. Ithaca: Cornell University Press.

Rowse, A. L. (1973). *Shakespeare the Man*. London: Macmillan.

Rutter, C. C. (1999). *Documents of the Rose Playhouse*. Manchester: Manchester University Press.

Sanchez, M. (2017). Antisocial procreation in *Measure for Measure*. In: *Queer Shakespeare: Desire and Sexuality* (ed. G. Stanivukovic) 263–294. London: Bloomsbury Arden Shakespeare. Bloomsbury. https://doi.org/10.5040/978147 4295222.ch-013.

Scheil, K. (2015). His wife Anne Shakespeare and the Hathaways. In: *The Shakespeare Circle: An Alternative Biography* (eds P. Edmondson and S. Wells) 57–70. Cambridge: Cambridge University Press.

Schoenbaum, S. (1987). *William Shakespeare: A Compact Documentary Life*. Oxford: Oxford University Press.

Schoenbaum, S. (1991). *Shakespeare's Lives*. Oxford: Clarendon Press.

Shakespeare, W. (1987). *Othello (Plays in Performance)*. Edited by J. Hankey. Bristol Classical Press.

Shapiro, J. (1996). *Shakespeare and the Jews*. New York: Columbia University Press.

Shapiro, J. (2005a). *1599: A Year in the Life of William Shakespeare*. London: Faber and Faber.

Shapiro, J. (2005b). Toward a new biography of Shakespeare. In: *Shakespeare Survey 58* (ed. P. Holland) 9–14. Cambridge: Cambridge University Press.

Shapiro, J. (2015). *1606: William Shakespeare and the Year of Lear*. London: Faber and Faber.

Shaughnessy, R. (2018). *As You Like It: Shakespeare in Performance*. Manchester: Manchester University Press.

Shrank, C. (2001). Pembroke, William Herbert, 3rd Earl of. In: *The Oxford Companion to Shakespeare*, 1st Edition (eds D. Dobson and S. Wells). Oxford: Oxford University Press. https://www.oxfordreference.com/view/10.1093/acref/ 9780198117353.001.0001/acref-9780198117353

Sidney, P. (1962). *The Poems of Sir Philip Sidney*. Edited by W. A. Ringler. Oxford University Press.

Siemon, J. R. ed. (2009). *King Richard III*. The Arden Shakespeare Third Series. London: Bloomsbury.

Smith, B. R. (2016). Sexuality: Deeds, desire, delight. In: *Shakespeare in Our Time: A Shakespeare Association of America Collection* (eds D. Callaghan and S. Gossett) 23–30. London/New York: Bloomsbury.

Smith, E. (2012). *The Cambridge Shakespeare Guide*. Cambridge: Cambridge University Press.

Smith, E. (2013). Was Shylock Jewish? *Shakespeare Quarterly* 64(2): 188–219.

Smith, E. (2019). *This Is Shakespeare*. London: Pelican.

Snyder, S. ed. (1993). *All's Well That Ends Well*. Oxford: Oxford University Press.

Sommerville, J. ed. (1995). Speech to Parliament of 19 March 1604. In his *King James VI and I: Political Writings* 132–146. Cambridge Texts in the History of Political Thought. Cambridge University Press.

Stanivukovic, G. ed. (2017). *Queer Shakespeare: Desire and Sexuality*. London/New York: Bloomsbury.

Stern, T. (2004). *Making Shakespeare: From Stage to Page*. London/New York: Routledge.

Stern, T. (2010). Epilogues, prayers after plays, and Shakespeare's *2 Henry IV*. *Theatre Notebook* 64(3): 122–129.

Stewart, A. (2016). The undocumented lives of William Shakespeare. In: *The Oxford Handbook of Shakespeare and Embodiment: Gender, Sexuality and Race* (ed. V. Traub) 57–73. Oxford: Oxford University Press.

Stone, A. (2003). Shakespeare and Syphilis. *Clinical Medicine* 3(1): 90.

Syme, H. S. (2012). Three's company: Alternative histories of London's theatres in the 1590s. *Shakespeare Survey* 65(1): 269–289.

Taylor, G. (2016). Collaboration 2016. In: *Shakespeare in Our Time: A Shakespeare Association of America Collection* (eds D. Callaghan and S. Gossett) 141–148. London/New York: Bloomsbury.

Taylor, G., Jowett, J., Bourus, T., and Egan, G. eds (2016). *The New Oxford Shakespeare: The Complete Works. Modern Critical Edition*. Oxford: Oxford University Press.

Taylor, G. and Loughnane, R. (2017). The canon and chronology of Shakespeare's works. In: *The New Oxford Shakespeare: Authorship Companion* (eds G. Taylor and G. Egan) 417–602. Oxford: Oxford University Press.

Thomas, V. (1987). *The Moral Universe of Shakespeare's Problem Plays*. Croom Helm.

Thompson, A. and Taylor, N. eds (2006). *Hamlet: The Texts of 1603 and 1623*. The Arden Shakespeare Third Series. London: Bloomsbury.

Traub, V. ed. (2016). *The Oxford Handbook of Shakespeare and Embodiment: Gender, Sexuality, and Race*. Oxford University Press.

Trevor, D. (2007). Shakespeare's love objects. In: *A Companion to Shakespeare's Sonnets* (ed. M. Schoenfeldt) 224–241. Oxford: Wiley Blackwell.

Tribble, E. B. (2011). *Cognition in the Globe: Attention and Memory in Shakespeare's Theatre*. Basingstoke: Palgrave Macmillan.

Tromly, F. B. (2010). *Fathers and Sons in Shakespeare: The Debt Never Promised*. Toronto: University of Toronto Press.

Van Es, B. (2013). *Shakespeare in Company*. Oxford: Oxford University Press.

Van Es, B. (2016). His fellow actors Will Kemp, Robert Armin, and other members of the Lord Chamberlain's Men and the King's Men. In: *The Shakespeare Circle: An Alternative Biography* (eds P. Edmondson and S. Wells) 261–274. Cambridge: Cambridge University Press.

Vendler, H. (1999). *The Art of Shakespeare's Sonnets*. Cambridge: Belknap Press.

Wells, S. (2001a). Shakespeare, Judith (1585–1662). In: *The Oxford Companion to Shakespeare*, 1st Edition (eds D. Dobson and S. Wells). Oxford: Oxford University Press. https://www.oxfordreference.com/view/10.1093/acref/9780198117353.001.0001/acref-9780198117353

Wells, S. (2001b). Shakespeare, Susanna (Hall). In: *The Oxford Companion to Shakespeare*, 1st Edition (eds D. Dobson and S. Wells). Oxford: Oxford University Press.

Wells, G. (2015). His son-in-law John Hall. In: *The Shakespeare Circle: An Alternative Biography* (eds P. Edmondson and S. Wells) 71–85. Cambridge: Cambridge University Press.

Wickham, G., Berry, H., and Ingram, W. eds (2020). *English Professional Theatre, 1530–1660*. Cambridge University Press.

Wilders, J. ed. (1995). *Antony and Cleopatra*. The Arden Shakespeare Third Series. London: Routledge.

Wolfe, H. (2016). Shakespeare coat of arms discovery. *Folger Shakespeare Library* (website). https://www.folger.edu/shakespeare-coat-of-arms-discovery#:~:text=Folger%20Curator%20Finds%20New%20Evidence,status%20as%20a%20gentleman%2Dwriter

Wolfe, H. (2020a). Blackfriars playhouse: James Burbage purchases property in Blackfriars. *Shakespeare Documented* (website). https://shakespearedocumented.folger.edu/resource/document/blackfriars-playhouse-james-burbage-purchases-property-blackfriars

Wolfe, H. (2020b). John Manningham's diary: Earliest mention of *Twelfth Night* and a Shakespeare anecdote. *Shakespeare Documented* (website). https://shakespearedocumented.folger.edu/resource/document/john-manninghams-diary-earliest-mention-twelfth-night-and-shakespeare-anecdote

Wood, M. (2015). His mother Mary Shakespeare. In: *The Shakespeare Circle: An Alternative Biography* (eds P. Edmondson and S. Wells) 13–25. Cambridge: Cambridge University Press.

Zitner, S. P. ed. (1993). *Much Ado about Nothing*. Oxford: Oxford University Press.

Index

Works by Shakespeare appear under title; works by others under author's name. WS is William Shakespeare.

The Life of the Author: William Shakespeare, First Edition. Anna Beer.
© 2021 John Wiley & Sons, Ltd. Published 2021 by John Wiley & Sons, Ltd.